Reconstructing
Eden

A Comprehensive Plan for The Post-war Political
and Economic Development of Iraq

Thomas E. White

Robert C. Kelly

John M. Cape

Denise Youngblood Coleman

© CountryWatch, Inc. August 2003

Published by:
CountryWatch, Inc.
Two Riverway, Suite 1770
Houston, Texas 77056
800 879-3885 ext. 149 or 713 425-6549 (to order a book)
800 879-3885 or 713 355-6500 (for all other company products)
713 355-2008 (fax)

Additional books may be ordered on the CountryWatch website at:
http://www.countrywatch.com or by email at sales@countrywatch.com .

Cover Designed by: Brad Folis, Eden Communications, Houston, Texas.

Library of Congress Cataloging-in-Publication Data

Reconstructing Eden : a comprehensive plan for the post-war political and economic development of Iraq / Thomas E. White ... [et al.].-- 1st ed.
      p. cm.
Includes bibliographical references and index.
   ISBN 1-59097-051-9 (alk. paper)
   1. Iraq--Economic policy. 2. Economic development--Political aspects--Iraq. 3. War--Economic aspects--Iraq. 4. Iraq--History. I. White, Thomas E., 1945- II. Title.
   HC415.4.R43 2003
   338.9567--dc22

                                                        2003016508

This book is dedicated to the Coalition Forces, the Iraqi people, the relief and humanitarian aid workers and to others who have toiled and fought in pursuit of Iraq's liberation from tyranny.

Acknowledgements

We would like to acknowledge a few people whose assistance helped us put Reconstructing Eden together. In particular, we would like to thank Robert Baldwin for his constant and insightful economic observations; Saachi Roye for his technical contributions; and Mary Ann Azevedo for her timely copy-editing. Special thanks also to Vicki Sanditen, Helen Kelly, and John Suddarth who provided valuable book editing feedback and suggestions. Last, but not least, we would like to thank our spouses, Susan, Helen, Carol and Ryan for their personal support.

In all things, success depends upon previous preparation, and without such preparation there is sure to be failure .

Confucius

Table of Contents

Tables

Figures

Preface

Legend has it that the Garden of Eden, the biblical paradise, was located in Iraq somewhere near the confluence of the Tigris and Euphrates Rivers. Thousands of years ago, in this cradle of civilization, a thriving political culture and lush agricultural economy underpinned the early Sumer Empire. Several millennia later however, the ancient promise of political and economic greatness in Iraq lies shattered.

Following nearly two decades of failed military adventurism, the Iraqi government of Saddam Hussein was ousted in April of 2003 by a coalition of forces led by the United States. The once great Iraqi agricultural economy now imports most of its food requirements. The country's immense oil wealth, squandered for nearly a quarter century by the Saddam Hussein government and once a harbinger of new economic strength for Iraq, dribbles out a small fraction of its ultimate potential.

The Iraq conflict clearly demonstrated, as did the war in Afghanistan to oust the Taliban, that the United States currently possesses unmatched military superiority. Many observers argue that the unchallenged American military technological superiority may foreshadow the dawning of a new American Empire, an empire in which military force is the currency of international relations rather than more traditional diplomatic approaches.

There is, however, trouble in the formerly legendary paradise. What is becoming evident in the early stages of the Iraqi post-war era is that the United States advantage on the battlefield does not necessarily extend to nation building. While much of the story is yet to unfold, the apparent chaotic situation after the end of combat operations in Iraq, with daily images of looting and lawlessness being broadcast worldwide, threatens to turn what was a major military victory into a potential humanitarian, political and economic disaster.

It is quite clear in the immediate aftermath of hostilities that the plan for winning the peace is totally inadequate. Clearly the view that the war to "liberate" Iraq would instantly produce a pro-United States citizenry ready for economic and political rebirth ignored the harsh realities on the ground.

Part of the problem is perception as opposed to reality. The aftermath of every war includes transitional security issues. In the case of a regime change, there is an obvious requirement to impose some martial law to prevent chaos in the ensuing power vacuum. In Iraq, however, with the worldwide media focus on the country there is an urgent need on the part of American officials now in power to outline a clear and comprehensive plan for the post-war reconstruction of the country.

What is the reconstruction strategy for Iraq? What is the security development plan? What is the political development plan? What is the economic development plan? What does "all of this" mean for the average Iraqi citizen? These are the things that both the Iraqi people and the global community are demanding. These are the things that have yet to be clearly articulated to the people in Iraq and to the international community.

Many Iraqi citizens, soldiers in the coalition force serving in Iraq, and the American public are openly frustrated by the Bush Administration's refusal to provide concrete timetables for accomplishing specific milestones toward the development of the new Iraq. Specific questions are answered with generalities like "as long as it takes" and "it is unknowable." This has led many observers to conclude the Administration has no detailed post-war plan.

In Reconstructing Eden, we propose such a plan for the post-war reconstruction of Iraq. The intent of our plan is to provide a coordinated answer to the aforementioned questions and to provide a strategic vision to post-war activities for the new government in Iraq. While our intent here is not to quantify the cost to the United States in providing security assistance in the post-war era, our plan does provide for a specific set of actions and timetables in terms of rearming Iraq and re-deploying U.S. forces. These particular considerations will ultimately determine the cost of the War in 2003 to the United States.

In Chapter I, we provide a detailed background review of the political, cultural and economic history of Iraq and the events leading up to the War of 2003. The brutal and autocratic Hussein regime retarded political development in Iraq for over two decades. The combination of three major wars in the past 25 years and the economic sanctions against Iraq levied by the United Nations have devastated the Iraqi economy. Our review in Chapter I puts these events in perspective.

In Chapter II, we cover the history of the War of 2003 and the near term issues relating to the transition to self-rule. The review includes a discussion of the events leading up to the war, including the global debate on the search for weapons of mass destruction in Iraq, the new American national security strategy of preemption, the failure of diplomacy, the conduct of the war, the ultimate military conquest and finally the initial implementation of a transition administration and the changes in that administration demanded by significantly different conditions on the ground than those assumed in pre-war planning.

In Chapter III, we look at the resource base of the Iraqi economy. The Iraqi economy has been beset by mismanagement, sanctions, and corruption over the past 25 years. In order for Iraq to prosper, these conditions need to be reversed and a new economic order must be established. The obvious economic priorities are to rapidly improve the standard of living of the Iraqi people within the context of a stable, market-based economy. Central to this goal will be the rapid development of the petroleum sector in Iraq. The review looks at the structure of the Iraqi economy based on an economic input-output model developed by the authors. The review also covers the performance of each major segment of the Iraqi economy over the recent past including the petroleum, service, and agricultural sectors as well as manufacturing, electric power, and transportation.

In Chapter IV, we outline our vision of a strategic reconstruction plan for Iraq. The components of the plan include security, political, and economic development plans, and a plan to communicate to the Iraqi people and the international community why these actions will enable Iraq to emerge from a national nightmare and become a model for political and economic development in the Middle East.

The *security development plan* outlines the concrete steps that need to be taken in the post-war transition period to ensure that stable preconditions for political and economic development exist. The plan consists of three major elements: First, to defeat and bring to justice to Saddam Hussein and to all remnants of the Hussein government. Second, to establish law and order immediately underwritten by the overwhelming presence of

United States and coalition ground forces; Third, to build a new Iraqi defense and police infrastructure to enable the United States and Coalition Forces to withdraw and establish normal, long-term multi-lateral security arrangements just as the United States enjoys with many other Gulf States.

The *political development plan* outlines concrete steps and a timetable for putting together a new government in Iraq. The plan discusses overriding principles of the political development process including some inherent assumptions on the nature of the new government, the process and timetable for a constitutional convention, and the nature and structure of the federal and provincial governments. The political precursors advocated here are consistent with the cultural and political history of the Iraqi people discussed in the first chapter. The political development plan also addresses the critical question of rearmament in Iraq and its impact on politics, security, and the federal budget.

The *economic development plan* outlines the principles under which the reconstruction of Iraq can most efficiently be accomplished in the context of a stable and efficient market oriented economy. For obvious reasons, the primary focus of the economic development plan will be on the petroleum sector. The ability of Iraq to resume oil production is critical and instrumental to not only the economic but political success of reconstruction. We examine important issues in other economic sectors as well.

The *communications plan* outlines the methods to be employed to get the key elements of the reconstruction plan communicated to key stakeholders: the people of Iraq, the international community, and to the coalition troops actually serving on the ground in Iraq. We outline the key elements to stress and the communications outlets that must be exploited to ensure plan distribution.

In Chapter V, we conclude with a discussion of the key transitional issues, the impact of the demands of post-war nation building on the usefulness of the preemption strategy, the outlook for political and economic development in Iraq, and future risks and opportunities for the Iraqi people.

The widespread support in the United States of the attack on Iraq and the removal of the government of Saddam Hussein is eroding and will become a major political issue, certainly in the next Federal election, if American efforts at nation building fail.

Simply put, given the cost in lives and treasury to date, the United States, for its credibility to its own citizens and to the world at large, must be successful in rebuilding Iraq.

Time is of the essence in moving forward in Iraq. We urgently need to articulate a plan, and the downstream benefits of that plan, to the people of Iraq. Further, we need to show the Iraqi people and the global community that, through our reconstruction efforts in Iraq, the actions of the United States and its allies truly have a noble purpose.

Houston, Texas,
August 2003

I. Introduction

Military Power and Nation Building

Military Power and Preemption

The war in Iraq in 2003 (War of 2003), as well as the war in Afghanistan in the fall of 2001, is illustrative of the superior military power of the United States. Precision-guided munitions and other exemplars of advanced military technologies, in conjunction with remarkably well-trained coalition ground forces in Iraq easily overwhelmed Iraq's defense forces. Not only did the wars in Afghanistan and Iraq demonstrate the position of the United States as the world's only remaining superpower, they are also the first times that the United States exercised military power within the context of a new national security strategy of preemption.

The preemption strategy holds that the cost to the global community of an attack by terrorist groups -- using weapons of mass destruction -- is so great, that it is in the global national interest to undertake preemptive strikes against terrorists and the states that support them.[1]

The military supremacy demonstrated by the United States, most ostensibly by the war in Iraq, used in this fashion, is regarded by many as a harbinger of hitherto unknown American hegemony. It is also regarded as a portent of a new American empire. Regardless of these perspectives, the National Security Strategy outlined by the Bush administration, calls for pro-active engagement with the rest of the world.[2] Such engagement, however, may well include increased military action undertaken as part of the emerging concept of preemption.

Simply put, the combination of the greatly increased threat of international terrorism and an aggressive new National Security Strategy have combined to significantly lower the threshold for the use of American military force.

Whether or not this new approach is regarded as either threatening or necessary, the new security strategy of preemption also results in possibly deleterious effects. That is to say, preemption creates regime change, which, itself, results in a power vacuum. That power vacuum must be filled with effective

---

[1] The White House (2002a).

[2] See The White House (2002a) for full text of National Security Strategy.

nation building. This is the challenge that defines the post-war scenario in Iraq.

On May 1, 2003, the month-old war against the Saddam Hussein regime in Iraq was effectively declared over.[3] Earlier, on April 21, 2003, retired General Jay Garner arrived in Iraq to begin the difficult task of reconstructing the economic and political institutions of Iraq. In early May 2003, L. Paul Bremer III, a well-known counter-terrorism expert and former United States Ambassador to the Netherlands, replaced Garner. Bremer's replacement of Garner was widely regarded by the international community as a measure aimed at conveying the view that the American emphasis in Iraq had shifted from military objectives to those of the diplomatic variety. Bremer's experience as a diplomat was intended to build on this perception.

Since the war, however, there have been signs that the military supremacy of the United States is not matched by prowess in nation building. Clearly, the story of Iraq is a dynamic one and the ultimate evaluation of American efforts in rebuilding Iraq will be made in the future. As such, the aforementioned assertion is made with some degree of trepidation. Nevertheless, the early assessments of the efforts in Iraq have not been particularly favorable. The security situation in Iraq remains precarious. It has

---

[3] The White House (2003).

become increasingly apparent that the planning for a stable post-war Iraq was inadequate.

There are always transitional security challenges following armed conflict and changes in power. Post-war Iraq, however, has experienced a disturbing spate of violent protests. Attacks against Coalition Forces have become commonplace, and acts of sabotage and vandalism against Iraq's energy infrastructure have occurred. Violent altercations between Iraqi factions have also ensued. These scenarios initially were described as either "pockets of resistance by Ba'ath Party loyalists" or the extremist actions of militants and terrorists. In mid-July 2003, the American military commander in Iraq, General John Abizaid, noted that these attacks signaled the beginning of a guerilla war against the coalition.[4]

Reports on the streets of Baghdad shortly after the war also registered the dismay and disillusionment of Iraqis who did not favor the American outlook for a new Iraq. Included in this list of Iraqis were disgruntled former soldiers from the now-disbanded Iraqi army. Even Iraqi exiles – an interest group that had originally celebrated regime change in Iraq – have expressed frustration at the slow pace of political development and the lack of progress on the creation of an indigenous transitional authority.

---

[4] Associated Press (2003a).

The other post-September 11 war orchestrated by a United States-led coalition has had a similar result. In Afghanistan, the Taliban was quickly ousted, and Osama bin Laden and his cadre were quickly routed. Media reports shifted their attention from the military victories, the mechanics of fighter jets and daisy cutters, and historic analysis of other military conflicts in the South Asian country, to stories of liberation. Afghan women were freed from their burqu'as and schools for girls were re-opened. The conference determining a transitional form of government was charted under the Bonn Agreement, and the world became acquainted with the new Afghan leader, Hamid Karzai.

Since then, media attention has not focused with the same rapt attention on Karzai's plea for increased monetary and military support for Afghanistan as it undergoes a resurgence of warlordism. There has been very little attention placed on the fact that artificial caps placed on troop strength in Afghanistan has led to a tenuous security situation. Likewise, the failure of the United States to include economic development support for Afghanistan in its budget went largely under the radar.

Against this backdrop, the quiet reversion of Talibanism, and the return of the Taliban itself, has also occurred largely outside public consciousness because of the focus on Iraq. As such, almost two years after the war, the record of nation building in Afghanistan has been dismal.

A repeat performance of military supremacy, followed by anemic attempts at nation building in Iraq, will be viewed with disdain in the wider world. Indeed, a report sponsored by the Council on Foreign Relations and the Asia Society charged that Afghanistan was at risk of sliding into anarchy[5]. The report warned that the situation did not only augur negatively for Afghanistan itself, but also for the global war against terrorism. That is to say, a lack of commitment to sustained development and nation building can deleteriously result in political discontent. Political discontent may provide a breeding ground for foot soldiers for terrorist organizations. The ultimate outcome of political discontent may be violent conflict and even a return to terrorism.

The Nation Building Imperative

While the situation in Afghanistan is to be distinguished from Iraq in many ways, there are political, economic and security imperatives that must be fully addressed or the nation building endeavors in these two geopolitical hotspots will not be successful. In an interview with the United Kingdom-based *Observer*, David Lockwood, the deputy director of the Asia and Pacific Region for the United Nations Development Programme (UNDP), said: "It (Afghanistan's reconstruction) is the biggest

---

[5] Wisner (2003).

post-conflict reconstruction project in the world since the Marshall Plan in Europe."[6] Clearly, Lockwood's observation in 2001 was made prior to the War of 2003; reconstruction efforts in Iraq can easily be expected to exceed the scope of Afghanistan's situation. Regardless, the key point to be considered is the mammoth task of nation building. Yet the efforts thus far in Iraq, and as already seen in Afghanistan, hardly correspond with the imperatives.[7]

Even the financial commitments to reconstruction efforts, as compared with military spending, indicate this chasm. Whereas the military spending of the war was variously estimated at around $60 billion, the amount of money projected for reconstruction has not been projected with any degree of clarity. As of April 2003, the White House had requested only $2.4 billion for humanitarian aid and reconstruction in Iraq. In this regard, *Reuters* on April 11, 2003, published a story entitled "U.S. Officials Play Down Iraq Reconstruction Costs"[8]. The article alleged that the Bush Administration underestimated both the cost of rebuilding Iraq and the requirements associated with rebuilding Iraq.

---

[6] Brown (2001).

[7] Wright (2003). The Afghan foreign minister, Abdullah Abdullah, posed questions about the United States' efforts in Afghanistan and offered a warning about United States credibility in these regards.

[8] Entous (2003).

Specifically, the article claimed that the White House was unable to provide an estimate of the costs associated with reconstruction. White House spokespersons, however, were adamant that international aid and oil revenues would mitigate potential costs to taxpayers. More significant was the assertion that there was no need for expensive reconstruction efforts since there had been relatively little damage to the country's infrastructure and its oil fields. Indeed, the working assumption appeared to be that if Iraq's infrastructure survived the war intact, it would be ready for use following the conclusion of military activities. Left completely ignored, was the possibility that looting, vandalism, and possible guerilla war activities against the coalition might damage the country's infrastructure. In this regard, the minimal number of ground forces in Iraq assigned to police activities was unable to prevent the massive looting and destruction that ensued following the fall of Baghdad.

The article also cited a claim by United States Secretary of Defense, Donald Rumsfeld, who said that because of the precision of the bombing campaign, there was simply little rebuilding to do. Likewise, White House budget director, Mitch Daniels, observed that because of technological advancements, the aggregate costs of military activities, such as bombing targets, had decreased since the Vietnam War, even though the actual costs of weaponry had increased. In fact, the costs of both the war in Afghanistan and the War of 2003 have proven to be quite high.

On July 9, 2003, in testimony before the United States Senate on the aftermath of the war in Iraq, Secretary of Defense Rumsfeld stunned the Senate Armed Services Committee when he predicted an indefinite stay by American troops to thwart subversion of the nation building efforts. The current run rate of costs to support the deployment is $3.9 billion per month.[9]

In the end, however, the actual amount of money spent on Iraq will not be the determining factor in the success of reconstruction and nation building. The cost of the actual Marshall Plan in the post-World War II period was, in fact, a small percentage of European GDP. Ultimately, conscious prioritization, experienced management and administration, thoughtful planning, and wise use of resources, are the paramount considerations.

Yet, the massive difference in the amount of money spent on the war effort itself, including post-war security efforts and the money budgeted for reconstruction costs, is quite startling. Moreover, the sorts of statements articulated by Daniels and Rumsfeld, as recorded in the *Reuters article*, are illustrative of the prevailing perception that the United States' reconstruction program is oriented toward the physical renovation of Iraq, and does not extend into the wider sphere of comprehensive and effective nation building. It goes without saying that the reality may well differ from this public perception.

---

[9] Firestone (2003).

Regardless, Iraq offers a unique opportunity for nation building because of the wealth of its energy resources, and its human and intellectual capital. Iraq is oil-rich and has a relatively well-educated populace. As such, its promise far exceeds that of a post-war Afghanistan. The challenge is not simply to harness the economic potential of Iraq, but to incorporate the political and societal dynamics in transitioning to a new Iraq.

Legal Structure and Development

Economist and international development specialist, Hernando de Soto, has postulated the view that distorted development and underdevelopment is a result of the political, economic and societal infrastructure, rather than the adequacy of resources.

In his seminal work, *The Mystery of Capital: Why Capitalism Triumphs in the West and Fails Everywhere Else*, de Soto argues that the core problem facing countries in the developing world is that they have not fully established the unseen network of laws that transforms assets into capital.[10]

In essence, the system of jurisprudence in the West, which determines how money is generated and saved, how stocks and bonds are traded, how property is appraised and owned, *et al,* does not exist in many developing countries. Although the

---

[10] de Soto (2000) .

fulcrum of de Soto's claim is legalistic in nature, his stance is more correctly understood as a cultural and political matter. That is to say, the political machinery and cultural undertones of a given country are the elements that texture the juridical instruments used in asset management and wealth generation. Stated differently, the establishment of a legal system both creates and maximizes these two economic effects. In the case of Iraq, therefore, the wider systemic network of the country must be recognized and accepted as legitimate before a developmental program can progress.

The Importance of a Smooth Transition

Joseph Stiglitz, the former head of the World Bank, asserts the view in *Globalization and Its Discontents* that ubiquitous remedies have been offered to deal with the economic and financial crises facing various countries of the world.[11] The generic "one size fits all" approach, couched in ideological adherence to classic market philosophies, has often ended in failure across a developing world that is in dire need of aid and assistance.

For Stiglitz, sequenced transitions into market economies, along with strong institutional frameworks and legal structures, within the specific historical and cultural contexts of countries themselves, should be pursued. He criticizes reflexive

---

[11] Stiglitz (2002).

privatization, automatic deregulation, and austerity measures in structural adjustment programs, for failing to attend to these localized considerations. By way of example, Stiglitz points to the steady economic success of post-communist Poland in comparison to the economic crisis of post-communist Russia. In the case of Russia, there was no transition program out of communism; there were no processes or mechanisms in place to shift Russia's entire political and economic structures from one system into another. Likewise, for Iraq, the pace of transformation, the wider context in which such transformation takes place, and the existence of a comprehensive development program that considers Iraq's unique situation, are key elements of successful reconstruction.

Democracy and Wealth Creation in Iraq

The notion of a free and democratic society in a post-war Iraq has also been frequently cited as an objective. Freedom and democracy, however, are not aspects of political being that emerge spontaneously, although they certainly have organic aspects of growth.

In this regard, Cambridge economist Amartya Sen has offered the view that civil freedom and political liberty occurs in conjunction with human and economic development. In *Development as Freedom*, Sen posits a question about the real purpose of wealth.[12] Sen then responds by offering the viewpoint that poverty results in a lack of freedom, while wealth offers a pathway to liberty.

Since Iraq's oil resources tender the promise of great wealth for the country's citizenry, Sen's corollary is that the ideal conditions of economic development simultaneously create the conditions of political and social freedom or what Sen terms, "substantive freedom." Sen ideally conceives of a society in which social, political, and economic institutions maximize the value of the human condition, so that human development, economic solvency, and political freedom are part of the same dynamic.

Iraq, like many developing countries, is home to a large number of youth. According to the October 1987 census, approximately 57 percent of the population was under the age of twenty.[13] Some observers have suggested that impatient youth in countries with similar demographic trends will more adamantly demand freedom and economic progress than older generations. Whether or not the aforementioned suggestion is true, there certainly seems to be a connection between democracy and human development. Returning to the writings of Sen, although his

---

[12] Sen (2000).

[13] A 1987 Iraqi census shows that 57 percent of the population was under the age of twenty. Library of Congress (n.d.). According to another study, the population of Iraq under the age of twenty was estimated at 52.5 percent for 2003; U.S. Census Bureau (2003).

perspective can be located in the domain of liberal philosophy, the practical aspect of his paradigm is that countries with strong democratic instruments, high rates of literacy, and impressive GDPs, often enjoy low infant mortality rates as well. Following Sen's theory, a program of wealth generation and development will be required in constructing Iraq as a model of democracy in the Middle East.

Building Constitutional Consensus

The true liberation of Iraq will not be achieved until the country is a sovereign entity with self-government and autonomy. With that objective in mind, Iraq must go through a process of building constitutional consensus in a collective forum. That collective forum will, ideally, be reflective of Iraq's cultural diversity and religious pluralism. Harvard philosopher John Rawls builds upon classic notions of the "social contract" and expounds upon the idea of a well-ordered society, with a strong institutional framework. Such a nation is held together not by shared moral beliefs, but by political understandings of justice.[14] In *Political Liberalism*, Rawls describes the procedures in which constitutional consensus can be established, based on principles of political rights and liberties, and within the context of democratic processes. Rawls also understands that political development and political institutions should be reflective of the diversity of society.

---

[14] Rawls (1995).

Iraq is yet to face its own moment of self-determination. The first efforts toward developing a Governing Council for Iraq took place in July 2003. The council functions as a predecessor to a new sovereign and democratic government. The council will have the authority to appoint and/or remove cabinet ministers, draft the budget and create a new constitution. Still, it exists under the aegis of the Coalition Provisional Authority (CPA). For that reason, some observers have referred to the structure and system as being similar to that of a constitutional monarchy, in which the crown ratifies legislation and certifies policies that are developed. Despite such criticism, several members of the council vocalized their intent to wield their new powers without pressure from the United States and the United Kingdom.

Those from Western democracies should remember that the freedoms and rights that exist in such nation states today have evolved over decades and in some cases over hundreds of years. In the United States, for example, initially voting rights belonged only to white male landowners and women only received the right to vote 80 years ago. Modern democratic traditions in Japan and West Germany were established over a ten-year occupation period, and these nations were more developed at the outset than is Iraq. Indeed, the Japanese constitution included provisions for women's rights beyond those articulated in the United States constitution. Other inclusions, such as the maintenance of the Emperor's throne and monarchy show how traditional and cultural domains of power and influence were preserved. Both those responsible for nation building in Iraq and their "would-be" critics must be both determined and patient.

Much of the attention placed on the new Governing Council has been on its very formation, its composition, and on the question of whether or not it would be a puppet of the coalition authority. Far less emphasis has been given to the need for strong government. Rawls' hypothetical case of building constitutional consensus and his system of political engineering offer a case study of how the forms and functions of the legislative process, as well as the system of jurisprudence, can create a civil society in which good government can flourish. Following this line of thinking, Iraq's Governing Council must be the fulcrum for good government in the future.

Pragmatic Nation Building

Against this backdrop of thinkers, nation building in Iraq is considered. The ideas and concepts briefly outlined are not programs to be adopted. Furthermore, the purpose here is not to debate if democracy and free markets are appropriate frameworks for application in Iraq, but instead, democratic procedures and a free market economy are pre-supposed. Stated differently, the post-war plan for Iraq entails procedures and institutions commensurate with notions of 20th century democratic republics. The perspectives delineated are presented only to bring to mind the risks and benefits involved in the nation building enterprise.

Thus, the objective of coalition authorities is to present a practical program for Iraq's reconstruction and nation building. If the task ahead in Iraq is to include democratization and the concomitant emergence of a free market economy, then the processes and measures involved in achieving these ends extend well beyond the domain of structural renovation and oil production. Indeed, if the United States and its coalition partners are serious about democratizing and developing Iraq, then they should anticipate an extended stay in Iraq. Ultimately, the establishment of legitimacy will measure successful nation building in Iraq.

Certainly, the military success and the occupation and control of Iraq by Coalition Forces, indicate that the United States has achieved some degree of authority in Iraq. Legitimacy, however, is a more nuanced condition and is to be distinguished from authority. It could be derived from the post-Hussein legacy of oppression and abuse, or it could be derived from future United Nations resolutions, which endorse prior military action after the fact. Legitimacy can also be garnered via effective nation building.

When General Douglas MacArthur first arrived in Japan following the end of World War II to lead the United States' occupation of that country, he was confronted with popular furor and derision. When he left Japan six years later, however, many

Japanese people watched him leave with heavy hearts and tears. Some observers have said that the test of effective and comprehensive nation building in Iraq may well be evaluated using the MacArthur standard.

In fact, the situation in Iraq's case is quite distinct from Japan in the post-World War II period. The Potsdam Declaration ending World War II and assuming Japan's eventual surrender included the order for General MacArthur to democratize Japan. The article stipulates the following, "The Japanese government shall remove all obstacles to the revival and strengthening of democratic tendencies among the Japanese people."[15] Thus the acceptance of the Potsdam Declaration signaled not only the ultimate and unquestioned defeat of Japan, but also its acceptance of a new course, with a new future.

Understanding the complex challenges that came with the imposition of democracy, MacArthur made the strategic decision to retain Emperor Hirohito on the throne. Economic and political reforms were directed by MacArthur, however, they were delivered via the Japanese throne. Indeed, a new Japanese constitution, new legislation, land reformation programs, and economic liberalization, were all accomplished in this manner. Despite these positive developments, MacArthur's position in

---

[15] Okazaki (2003). Outlines the reasons for successful occupation and democratization of Japan, as well as the pitfalls and blights that marred the process.

Japan was, in effect, an indirect occupation of sorts. The presence of United States bases in Japan during the Cold War served to consolidate this indirect occupation. Nevertheless, the trade imbalances in the Cold War period and unrestricted access to American markets that favored Japan's economy, resulted in remarkable economic development, and garnered something of a latent legitimacy.[16]

Members of the Bush Administration have said that invading Coalition Forces would be met with flowers thrown by Iraqis grateful for their liberation. Gratitude, however, has a short shelf life in the political sphere. Within the context of Maslow's hierarchy of needs, freedom is a philosophical state appreciated only after basic needs of security, shelter, and nourishment are met. As was the case in Japan, the success of nation building, and the effectiveness of economic development in particular, will confer the greatest possibility of legitimacy to the coalition presence in Iraq.

The People of Iraq

Population Dynamics

The general trajectory of Iraqi population dynamics in modern times can be largely characterized by urbanization, with a steady

---

[16] Johnson (2002).

movement of people from the rural (especially southern) region to the urban (especially central) region.[17]

The basic trends of the 1980s were rooted in the particularly exploitive character of agricultural practices used on the land itself and the people who farmed the land. Declining productivity of the land, stemming from the failure to develop drainage along the irrigation facilities and the living conditions of the producers, resulted in both the depopulation of rural areas and declining productivity in the agricultural sector.[18]

After World War II, this urbanization trend was accelerated, and during the war of the 1980s, migration from heavily bombed areas of the south, such as Al Basrah, resulted in the influx of people into Baghdad. The government, however, tried to deal with the demographic issues by resettling refugees in less populated parts of the country.[19]

Ethnic Groups

Today, the majority of Iraq's more than 25 million people -- approximately 77 percent of the total population -- are Arabs. Arabs are the predominant ethnic group of the Middle East and are believed to have originated in the area of present-day Saudi

---

[17] CountryWatch (2003a).

[18] *Ibid.*

[19] *Ibid.*

Arabia and Yemen. Centuries of intermarriage and migration along caravan routes have resulted in the fact that Arabs cannot be particularly regarded as a pure ethnic group. There is, however, a shared Arab culture in the Middle East, which can be identified in the Arabs of Iraq.[20]

Kurds make up a substantial minority, numbering up to 20 percent of the Iraqi population. Kurds also live in Turkey, Syria and Iran. Once mainly nomadic or semi-nomadic, Kurdish society was characterized by a combination of urban centers, villages, and pastoral tribes dating back to the time of the Ottoman Empire. Historical sources indicate that from the eighteenth century onward, Kurds in Iraq were mainly peasants engaged in agriculture and arboriculture. By the nineteenth century, about 20 percent of Iraqi Kurds lived in historic Kurdish cities such as Kirkuk, Sulaymaniyah, and Irbil. The gradual migration to the cities, particularly of the young intelligentsia, helped nurture Kurdish nationalism. Historically, the Kurds have lived under foreign governance for centuries, and in recent years, there have been attempts to create a sovereign Kurdistan.[21]

---

[20] *Ibid.*

[21] *Ibid.*

The rest of the Iraqi population includes ethnic communities of Turkmen, Lurs, Armenians and Assyrians. Small pockets of Iranians also live along the Iraq-Iran border.[22]

Religions

Islam is the major religion practiced by about 97 percent of the total population. Iraqi Muslims are divided amongst Shi'a and Sunni practitioners; Shi'a Muslims make up the majority Muslim sect in Iraq. There is also a small Christian minority within the Iraqi population. The Christian churches in the Middle East tend to be patriarchal and hierarchical, often operating with a great deal of independence. Of the Christian population, there is a small surviving Gnostic sect called the Mandeans, who also live in southern Iraq between Baghdad and Al Basrah. This sect is sometimes referred to as the Christians of St. John, although some origins of the religion are thought to pre-date Christianity. There are also Yazidis in the north of Iraq around Mosul. Although close to the Kurdish culture in social structure, this religion is not well accepted by followers of Shi'a and Sunni Islam. Yazidism integrates aspects of Zoroastrianism, Manicheism, Judaism, Christianity and Islam. Reports also suggest that there is a tiny minority of Jews in Baghdad.[23]

---

[22] *Ibid.*

[23] *Ibid.*

Languages

Arabic is the official language of Iraq, although Kurdish is officially recognized in Kurdish regions. While Arabic is derived from the Afro-Asiatic family of languages, Kurdish is sourced in the Indo-European family of languages. Azerbaijani, Armenian, Assyrian, Farsi, Turkish, and Turkman languages are also spoken. In addition, ethnologists have recorded the use of languages from the other Neo-Aramaic or Neo-Syriac linguistic groups belonging to the Afro-Asiatic family of languages. Indo-European languages such as Behdini, Domani and Luri have also been reported.[24]

Throughout the Arab world, the Arabic language exists in three forms: (1) Classical Arabic of the Koran; (2) the literary language developed from the classical version, which is referred to as Modern Standard Arabic, and which has virtually the same structure wherever used; and (3) the spoken language, which, in Iraq is an Iraqi Arabic dialect. Educated Arabs tend to be bilingual in both Modern Standard Arabic and in their own dialect of spoken Arabic. Even uneducated Arabic speakers, however, can usually understand the meaning of something said in Modern Standard Arabic, although they may be unable to speak the language itself. Classical Arabic, apart from Koranic texts, is predominantly the domain of scholars.[25]

---

[24] *Ibid.*

[25] *Ibid.*

Cultural Conflicts

The major cultural conflicts in Iraq today are said to center on ethnicity and religion. These contemporary cultural conflicts, and their historical roots, have political ramifications and must be considered in the creation of a new Iraqi government.

In recent decades, international attention has been paid to the differences between Iraq's Arab majority and its Kurdish minority that predominates in the north of Iraq. Kurds have become increasingly adamant about expressing the distinctiveness of their Kurdish identity, and the need for their own self-government. The politics of this issue remain a matter of debate. In a post-war Iraq, Kurds hope for an autonomous Kurdistan under a federal Iraqi system. They have promised not to pursue absolute independence that, if achieved, would rupture Iraq's territorial integrity. Instead, the leaders of the Kurds have communicated that they would accept strong measures of self-government within the nation of Iraq. Neighboring Turkey has worried that greater Kurdish autonomy would be a threat and as such, the Kurdish issue has evolved into being a contentious regional matter. Maintaining relative Kurdish autonomy will be an imperative of any new Iraqi government.[26]

In the realm of religion, the major divide lies between Shi'a, who predominate in southern Iraq, and Sunni Muslims, who largely

---

[26] *Ibid.*

inhabit the central Iraq, and the capital city of Baghdad in particular. Although Shi'a Muslims constitute the clear majority in Iraq, the country has been politically controlled by Sunnis, albeit within the context of a secular political system. Sunni political dominance stretches back to the genesis of the Iraqi state. During times of rule by foreign powers (as noted below), Shi'as often distanced themselves from the political process, essentially leaving the Sunni minority to fill key positions in the political infrastructure. It is not accidental that Sunnis dominate in Iraq's capital city and the center of political power. Sunnis also benefited from the education system and advanced themselves in the military. While their educated status helped in assuring some degree of success, it was really their ascendancy within the military that assured Sunnis of their hold on power.

While the division of political power between the two sects can be traced back to the beginning of the Iraqi state, the schism between Shi'a and Sunni Muslims goes back to the death of the Islamic prophet Mohammed, and his desire for his nephew and son-in-law, Ali, to carry on the Muslim tradition. This result did not occur as planned and over decades, followers of Ali, and his son Hassan, became the predecessors to Shi'a Islam. The central division between the two Muslim sects lies in the Shi'a view that the Caliphate was illegitimate because it did not follow the desires of Mohammed for Ali to lead Muslims. Shi'a Islam, over time, has become associated with alienation and thus many non-Arab Muslims follow this sect. Martyrdom and self-flagellation are unique components of Shi'a practice. For their part, Sunnis contend that Shi'a Islam does not follow Koranic principles, as well as associated theological and juridical schools. Indeed, they regard Shi'as as innovators of Islam to a degree. Sunni Islam is fundamentally predicated on the Hadiths (collective sayings and principles of Mohammed) and as such, Sunnis claim to be the correct adherents of Islam. In practice, the ritual differences between the two sects, such as the importance of the Hadj (pilgrimage to Mecca) have developed over time.[27]

Despite this evidence of the Shi'a / Sunni divide, the fact remains that national loyalty has sometimes tied these two sects together. In certain cases, national interests have also aligned the two Islamic sects with the Kurds to the north as well.

Following the conventional narrative, the British helped to liberate Iraq from Ottoman despotism in the 1920s. Iraq was then placed under a League of Nations mandate and administered by the British. Shi'as, Sunnis and Kurds soon revolted in defiance of quasi-colonial control by the British, which followed the liberation from the Ottoman Turks. All three groups were then subjected to British bombing campaigns aimed at subduing their dissent. Although the military effort successfully quashed the rebellion and saved the Hashemite throne, which had been installed by the British, a nationalist coup d'etat in the late 1950s

---

[27] *Ibid.*

brought leftists to power. Subsequent coup d'etats by Ba'athists followed in the next decade and set the tone for a modern, secular Iraq.

History shows that the British stoked nationalist sentiment in the early part of the century when the focus was upon defeating the Ottoman Turks. At that time, Iraqi nationalism was exploited to benefit British objectives. In this way, historians often note that the manipulation of nationalism, in conjunction with strong military control, actually pre-dates the rule of Saddam Hussein and can also be attributed to the British.

Also noteworthy is the fact that Iraq's Shi'as are Arabs and not from other ethnic groups; thus, regardless of sectarian differences, there has been a shared Shi'a and Sunni antipathy by the Arabs in Iraq of the Iranian Persians to the east for many centuries. The Ba'athist Iraqi government skillfully exploited this age-old enmity in its propaganda, publicizing the war of the 1980s with Iran as part of the ancient struggle between the Arab and Persian empires. The war compelled Saddam Hussein's Ba'ath party to further integrate Shi'a into Iraqi society for practical purposes. The war also placed inordinate demands on the regime for manpower, which could only be met by levying the Shi'a community. Although this process of integration was neither perfect nor fully manifested, it does suggest that the so-called Shi'a / Sunni divide in Iraq is far more nuanced than is commonly recognized and the tension of that divide has often been mitigated by national interests.[28]

Perhaps the most overlooked conflict in Iraqi society is between the religious factions of society (regardless of sect) and the secular Ba'athists. Under the Hussein regime, religious values were present, but always subordinated to the interests of the regime. As Iraq emerges from that regime, there have been reports of Iraqis denouncing the replacement of Hussein's government with one constituted by Western powers. They have asserted that Iraq is a Muslim country. This sort of declaration was largely silenced during the rule of Saddam Hussein; however, it is increasingly being registered today. Indeed, in early discussions of a post-war Iraq, tribal elders, Iraqi exiles, and other interest groups, have expressed differing visions of their future government, and some of these views do not accept the notion that Iraq should be a secular nation state.[29]

The post-war developmental and nation building plan for Iraq will have to consider this complicated set of factors and considerations in creating a fully representative government. It is apparent that while Saddam Hussein was able to quiet Shi'a discontent within the context of a political dictatorship, such submissiveness cannot be expected in an emerging democracy.

---

[28] *Ibid.*

[29] *Ibid.*

Shi'as have made it clear that they will have a voice in the new and democratic Iraq. Indeed, their presence within the newly established Governing Council proportionately reflects the fact that they are the majority segment of the population. Likewise, Kurds, Sunnis, and even exiled groups have also been represented on the council.

Human Development

In the realm of human development, the literacy rate for the total population is about 60 percent with the rate for males at 70 percent and 50 percent rate for females. The population of Iraq has generally been well educated and with a reasonably high literacy rate in comparison with other countries in the region. Iraq has a developed public school infrastructure. Typically, there are six years of primary (elementary) education, followed by three years of intermediate secondary, and then, three years of intermediate preparatory education.[30]

Iraq's academic infrastructure is quite sophisticated, with a developed scientific community, 44 teacher training schools and institutes, three colleges and technical institutes, and eight universities, the oldest of which was established in 1957. Each of these institutions has been government-owned and operated. Iraq is also home to a number of cultural centers, such as historic museums. In the late 1970s, the numbers of students in technical

---

[30] *Ibid.*

fields rose by 300 percent, while the number of female students rose by 45 percent.

Since the war with Iran in the 1980s, however, the quality of Iraq's educational system was drastically affected. Notably, primary school enrollment, which was an impressive 100 percent in 1980, had decreased by 15 percent by 1988. The Gulf War and its after-effects further decreased access to education and the quality of education that was provided. By the late 1990s, school enrollment had declined to only 53 percent. One of the key nation building tasks will be to re-establish a strong educational system in Iraq that restores the quality of education to pre-1980s levels.[31]

In terms of health and welfare, the infant mortality rate in Iraq is 55.16 deaths per 1,000 live births, according to 2003 estimates. Life expectancy at birth for the total population is 67.8 years of age, specifically 66.7 years of age for males, and 69 years of age for females, as expressed in 2003 estimates. According to various sources, population growth was estimated at close to 3 percent for 2003, and the fertility rate at 4.5 children per woman for 2003. Also, as noted earlier, Iraq is also home to a highly youthful population. These human development factors suggest that successful nation building, economic development and

---

[31] *Ibid.*

opportunities for youth, would be clearly beneficial to Iraq's young population.[32]

These opportunities notwithstanding, it must be noted that there has been great suffering as a consequence of United Nations sanctions on Iraq. In this regard, the United Nations said that Iraq had "experienced a shift from relative affluence to massive poverty".[33] In addition to the significant fall in GDP as a consequence of declining oil production, there was a massive increase in the price of essential commodities. By 1995, prices of basic goods increased 850 times the 1990 levels. The number of children on the streets of Iraq's cities had increased as Iraqi families became increasingly reliant on child labor to secure household incomes.[34]

Since the Gulf War of 1991, one of the areas where international embargoes have had the strongest and most deleterious effect is on the health services. As a consequence of sanctions, medication and medical equipment became increasingly difficult to obtain and almost impossible to fund.[35] Consequently, infant mortality rates increased to such an extent that they were among the

---

[32] *Ibid.*

[33] United Nations (1999).

[34] UNICEF (2003), see Grassi (2003) and see also Williams and Meehan (2003).

[35] World Health Organization (1997).

highest in the world.[36] A report by the New England Journal of Medicine also revealed these disturbing increases in childhood mortality.[37]

The destruction of the Iraqi infrastructure in the 1991 Gulf War also had significant effects on public health. Food supplies were drastically decreased, and a survey showed that over a quarter of all Iraqi children under the age of five years suffered from chronic malnutrition as a result of these conditions.[38] Most notable was the claim that several hundred thousands of Iraqi children had died as a consequence of malnutrition. About 70 percent of Iraqi women were shown to be suffering from anemia[39].

In addition, sanitary conditions deteriorated. Water quality was compromised so that it was unusable in 50 percent of urban areas and over 30 percent of rural areas, while raw sewage flowed through streets and even in some homes.[40] Consequently, the capacity to stop the spreading of diseases was significantly compromised. As well, in 2000, UNICEF reported that infant mortality had risen by 160 percent since 1991.[41]

---

[36] United Nations (1999).

[37] Acherio (1992), pp. 931-936.

[38] United Nations (1999).

[39] *Ibid.*

[40] *Ibid.*

[41] United Nations (2000).

Improving the basic human conditions of the Iraqi people will be another principal objective in the process of nation building; however, the legacy of human rights abuse is yet another challenge to be faced.

Under the Hussein regime, Iraqis suffered a catalogue of human rights abuses. Indeed, the Iraqi government under Saddam Hussein suppressed a wide range of groups. The regime typically used discrimination in public life, at work, and at school to control and organize society at its whim. The regime also arrested and detained countless Iraqis, some of whom remain incommunicado. In addition, the regime tortured Iraqis suspected of crimes, staged trials for those under arrest, and sentenced prisoners to extended imprisonment -- usually under terrible conditions. Execution -- using horrendous methodology -- was also customary.

Most of the people persecuted in Iraq were opponents of the ruling regime, since free speech in Iraq under Saddam Hussein was severely curtailed. The legal system of Iraq under the Hussein regime did not comply with international jurisprudence, and the judges and other legal practitioners were often military officers and civil servants without adequate training in matters of law. Human rights conditions in Kurdish areas were generally better than those elsewhere in Iraq because of the lack of control over Kurdish areas by Saddam Hussein's regime.

A new Iraq freed of Saddam Hussein cannot be allowed to fall into another state of tyranny. Ideally, the new Governing Council, which will chart the course for Iraq's political future, will be charged with developing a constitution in which the freedom and rights of individuals would be protected by law.

A Brief History of Iraq

Geographic Factors Influencing Historical Evolution

Iraqi history displays a continuity shaped by adaptation to the ebb and flow of the Tigris and Euphrates Rivers. Allowed to flow unchecked, the rivers wrought destruction in terrible floods that inundated whole towns. When irrigation dikes controlled the rivers and other waterworks, the land became extremely fertile.[42]

The Tigris and the Euphrates Rivers' potential to be destructive or productive, has resulted in two distinct legacies found throughout Iraqi history. On the one hand, Mesopotamia's enormous water resources and lush river valleys allowed for the plentiful food and economic production. Surplus food production, joint irrigation and flood control efforts, in turn, facilitated the growth of a powerful and expanding state. In this way, an impressive

---

[42] Library of Congress (n.d.). As noted by the Library of Congress, information contained in the *Country Studies On-Line* is not copyrighted and thus is available for free and unrestricted use, with attribution, as is the case in its usage here.

evolution of culture and civilization began at Sumer, later in Babylon and Assyria, and was preserved by rulers such as Hammurabi (1792-1750 B.C.E.), Cyrus (550-530 B.C.E.), Darius (520-485 B.C.E.), Alexander the Great (336-323 B.C.E.), and the Abbasids (750-1258 C.E.).[43]

On the other hand, Mesopotamia could also be an extremely threatening environment, driving its peoples to seek security from the forces of nature. Throughout Iraqi history, various groups have formed autonomous, self-contained social units; and these efforts to build security-providing structures have exerted a powerful impact on Iraqi culture. Examples include: allegiance to ancient religious deities at Ur and Eridu; membership in the Shi'at Ali (or Party of Ali, the small group of followers that supported Ali ibn Abu Talib as the rightful leader of the Islamic community in the seventh century); residence in the "asnaf" (guilds) or the "mahallat" (city quarters) of Baghdad under the Ottoman Turks; and membership in one of a multitude of tribes.[44]

Two factors that inhibited political centralization were the absence of stone, and Iraq's geographic location as the eastern flank of the Arab world. For much of Iraqi history, the lack of stone hindered the building of roads. As a result, many parts of the country have remained beyond government control. Also,

---

[43] *Ibid.*

[44] *Ibid.*

Iraq attracted waves of ethnically diverse people, partly due to the fact it borders non-Arab Turkey and Iran and partly as a result of the great agricultural potential of its river valley. Although this influx of people enriched Iraqi culture, it has disrupted the country's internal balance and has led to deep-seated schisms.[45]

The Ancient Civilizations

Iraq became a sovereign, independent state in 1932, and has been a republic since the 1958 coup d'etat that ended the reign of King Faisal II. Although the modern state, the Republic of Iraq, is quite young, the history of the land and its people dates back more than 5,000 years. Here, in ancient Mesopotamia (the land between the Tigris and Euphrates Rivers), the first civilization, Sumer, appeared in the Near East. Sumer is distinguished historically by two of its major cultural contributions. First, Sumer was the birthplace of some of the earliest forms of written communication – both pictographic modalities and later, cuneiform. Second, one of the first civilizations in the world to record works of literature was Sumer, as exemplified by the great epic of Gilgamesh.

The earliest period of Sumerian history is believed to have been from 3360 B.C.E. to 2400 B.C.E. It is characterized by changes in the political structure from religious to political authority. The second phase of Sumerian history was from 2400 B.C.E. to 2200 B.C.E., when Sargon I, King of the Semitic city of Akkad,

---

[45] *Ibid.*

conquered Sumer. Control by the Akkadians lasted only 200 years and marked the reemergence of Sumer under the king of Ur. This third phase was characterized by a synthesis of Sumerian and Akkadian cultures, which prevailed after the waning of Sumerian civilization.[46]

The ascendancy of the Amorites followed and is distinguished by the establishment of Babylon as the capital. During the time of the sixth Amorite ruler, King Hammurabi (1792-1750 B.C.E.), Babylonian rule extended across a vast area covering most of the Tigris-Euphrates river valley, the Persian Gulf and Assyria. In order to rule over such a large area, Hammurabi created an elaborate administrative structure, which included the famous legal system known as "The Code of Hammurabi".[47]

The Assyrians gained power and influence in the region as early as 1200 B.C.E., however, they moved westward only in the ninth century B.C.E. By 859 B.C.E., they reached the Mediterranean, where they occupied Phoenician cities, and later, Babylon fell to Assyrian rule.[48]

The Chaldeans followed Assyrian power in 612 B.C.E. The famed King Nebuchadnezzar (605-562 B.C.E.) conquered surrounding areas, including the kingdom of Judah. The

---

[46] Washington State University (n.d. - a).

[47] Washington State University (n.d. - b).

[48] Washington State University (n.d. - c).

Chaldeans hoped to recreate Babylon's past glory and as such, it was during the Chaldean period that the Hanging Gardens of Babylon -- one of the Seven Wonders of the Ancient World -- were created.[49]

Achaemenid Iran was gaining power at that time and in 539 B.C.E., Babylon fell to Cyrus the Great (550-530 B.C.E.). Babylon was then included in the Iranian empire under Cyrus the Great. Iranian rule continued for more than 200 years. During this time, there was a significant influx of Achaemenid Iranians into Mesopotamia, thus complicating the region's ethnically diverse population. The flow of Iranians into Iraq at that time began a notable demographic trend that would continue intermittently throughout much of Iraqi history. Another cultural change that took place under Iranian rule was the disappearance of the Mesopotamian languages and the widespread use of Aramaic.[50]

By the fourth century B.C.E., most of Babylon did not look favorably on rule by the Achaemenids. Alexander the Great of Macedon was thus hailed as a great liberator when he arrived in 331 B.C.E. His respect for Babylonia culture was also well-received. Originally, Alexander hoped to establish one of the seats of his empire in Babylon, and he intended to build a pathway from the Euphrates to the Persian Gulf. These plans

---

[49] Washington State University (n.d. - d).

[50] Library of Congress (n.d.).

were never realized during the time of Greek rule, although Alexander notably died in Babylon following an expedition to the Indian sub-continent. Greek occupation was marked by the construction of many cities, extensive regional trade, as well as the Hellenization of the region's art, culture and philosophy.[51]

The Parthians (or Arsacids) from Central Asia, having previously conquered Iran, held growing influence over trade extending from Asia to the Greco-Roman world by 126 B.C.E. The Parthians ruled until 227 C.E. when another wave of Iranians, the Sassanids, conquered the region. Sassanid occupation lasted until 636 C.E. and appeared to have little direct effect on the region. Some historians have even suggested that they neglected basic irrigation of Mesopotamia's land, thus contributing to its loss of fertility.[52]

Islam and Arabization

By the time the Sassanid Empire fell to Muslim warriors from Arabia, Mesopotamia was in decline.[53] The Muslim conquest of Mesopotamia, in the seventh century, was made easier because the subjects of the Sassanid Empire believed they had nothing to lose by cooperating with the conquering warriors. The Muslim warriors were themselves restrained by religious law, which

---

[51] *Ibid.*

[52] *Ibid.*

[53] *Ibid.*

prohibited attacks against those who had not actually engaged in warfare. They also were compelled to settle the new land under the aegis of Islamic law.[54]

Al Basrah was the first port established under Arab Muslim rule.[55] Other developments that occurred under Arab Muslim rule was the establishment of the "divan" (diwan in Arabic) administrative system, which essentially centralized political administration, including the process of taxation. Arabic replaced Persian, which had become the language of use under Iranian rule. As well, Arabs and the indigenous population intermarried, thus contributing to the predominance of Arab ethnicity in modern Iraq. The most significant result of these cultural shifts was the conversion of people to Islam. In this way, Iraq was both Arabized and Islamicized over the ensuing years.

Around 750 C.E., Baghdad was established under the Abbasid Dynasty, also called the "blessed dynasty." Baghdad developed into being a Middle Eastern power, a venue for trade linking Asia and the Mediterranean, and the center of great scientific, literary and philosophical creativity. By 800 C.E., within the region, Baghdad was second only to Constantinople in size and influence.[56]

---

[54] *Ibid.*

[55] *Ibid.*

[56] *Ibid.*

Divisions between the Shi'a and Sunni sects of Islam contributed to rising tensions. Islam, which had functioned as a unifying force, became divisive. The Abbasids were eventually weakened by this internal strife, leading to their collapse. Power and control fell to various groups including the Buwayhids from Iran (945 C.E. – 1055 C.E. and the Turkic Seljuks (1055 C.E. to 1194 C.E.).[57]

The Seljucks were themselves ousted by the Mongols, under Genghis Khan, in the 12th century. Baghdad fell in 1248 C.E., however, Iraq remained largely neglected and ignored by its Mongol rulers. Political and economic strife, as well as social and cultural disintegration, occurred in the wake of the Mongol conquest. Baghdad and Al Basrah lost their prominence. Most significant was the neglect of Iraq's agricultural lands and irrigation system. The consequences of this neglect would be long-standing as Iraq moved into a period of decline.[58]

The Ottoman Empire

Iraq then became the site of conflict between various Iranian civilizations to the east and the Turks to the northwest. Tribal warfare was rampant during this period. In 1405 C.E., Iraq fell under the control of Turkish tribes from Anatolia. A century later, Iraq came under Iranian Safavid control. By the early 16th

---

[57] *Ibid.*

[58] *Ibid.*

century, Iraq was conquered by the Ottoman Turks and became part of the Ottoman Empire. Ottoman rule improved the Iraqi economy, most particularly with regard to its agricultural lands.[59]

Throughout Iraqi history, the conflict between political fragmentation and centralization was reflected in the struggles among tribes and cities for the food-producing flatlands of the river valleys. When a central power neglected to keep the waterworks in repair, land fell into disuse, and tribes attacked settled peoples for precious and scarce agricultural commodities. For nearly 600 years, between the collapse of the Abbasid Empire in the 13th century and the waning years of the Ottoman era in the late 19th century, government authority was tenuous, and tribal Iraq was, in effect, autonomous.[60]

Beginning in the middle of the 19th century, the "tanzimat" reforms (an administrative and legal reorganization of the Ottoman Empire), the emergence of private property, and the tying of Iraq to the world capitalist market severely altered Iraq's social structure. Tribal sheikhs had traditionally provided both spiritual leadership and tribal security. Land reform and increasing links with the West transformed many sheikhs into profit-seeking landlords, whose tribesmen became impoverished sharecroppers. Moreover, as Western economic penetration

---

[59] *Ibid.*
[60] CountryWatch (2003a) and see also Library of Congress (n.d.).

increased, machine-made British textiles displaced the products of Iraq's once-prosperous craftsmen.[61]

20th Century Iraq

At the beginning of the 20th century, Iraq's disconnected, and often antagonistic, ethnic, religious and tribal social groups professed little or no allegiance to the central government. As a result, the all-consuming concern of contemporary Iraqi history has been the forging of a nation-state out of this diverse and conflict-ridden social structure, in addition to the concurrent transformation of parochial loyalties, both tribal and ethnic, into a national identity.[62]

During the 20th century, as the power of tribal Iraq waned, Baghdad benefited from the rise of a centralized governmental apparatus, a burgeoning bureaucracy, increased educational opportunities, and the growth of the oil industry. The transformation of the urban-tribal balance resulted in a massive rural-to-urban migration. The disruption of parochial loyalties, and the rise of new class relations based on economics, fueled frequent tribal rebellions and urban uprisings during much of the 20th century.[63]

---

[61] *Ibid.*

[62] *Ibid.*

[63] *Ibid.*

In particular, Iraq's social fabric was in the throes of a destabilizing transition in the first half of the 20th century. At the same time, because of its foreign roots, the Iraqi political system suffered from a severe legitimacy crisis. Then, caught in the crosshairs of World War I, Iraq was invaded by the British, who had discovered that Turkey would enter the conflict on the side of the Germans. Using growing nationalistic sentiment among Iraqis to their advantage, the British were able to take control of Iraq from the Turks. By March of 1917 the British had captured Baghdad.

A few years later, beginning with its League of Nations mandate in 1920, the British government had laid out the institutional framework for Iraqi government and politics.

British Rule

Britain imposed a Hashemite monarchy, defined the territorial limits of Iraq with little regard for natural frontiers or traditional tribal and ethnic settlements and influenced the writing of a constitution and the structure of parliament consistent with this approach. In this regard, Faisal was crowned as Iraq's first king. Like all Hashemites, King Faisal claimed to be a direct descendent of the Muslim prophet Mohammed. In 1932, Iraq officially became an independent state, however, British influence continued to affect the Iraqi political scene. The British supported narrowly based groups, such as the tribal sheikhs, over the growing, urban-based nationalist movement, and resorted to military force when British interests were threatened, as in the 1941 Rashid Ali coup.[64]

As such, between 1918 and 1958, British policy in Iraq had far-reaching effects. The majority of Iraqis were excluded from the political process, and the process itself failed to develop procedures for resolving internal conflicts other than rule by decree and the frequent use of repressive measures. Also, because the formative experiences of Iraq's post-1958 political leadership centered on clandestine opposition activity, decision-making and government activity in general, customarily have been veiled in secrecy. Furthermore, because the country lacks deeply rooted national political institutions, a small elite - often bound by close family or tribal ties - frequently has monopolized political power.[65]

Saddam Hussein

Between the overthrow of the monarchy in 1958 and the emergence of Saddam Hussein in the mid-1970s, Iraqi history was, therefore, a chronicle of conspiracies, coup d'etats, countercoups and fierce Kurdish uprisings.[66]

---

[64] MacArthur (2003).

[65] *Ibid.*

[66] CountryWatch (2003a).

The 1958 coup d'etat brought Abd-al-Karim Qasim to power and made Iraq a republic. Abd-al-Salam Muhammad Arif then ousted Qasim in a coup d'etat in 1963, thus bringing the Ba'athists (Arab Socialist Resurrection Party) to power. Arif died and was succeeded by his brother in 1966. Then, in 1968, another coup d'etat took place, which resulted in the new presidency of Ahmad Hasan al-Bakr. A period of political and economic nationalization followed and in 1979, the president resigned and was succeeded by the Vice President, Saddam Hussein.[67]

The government of Iraq and the Shah of Iran signed the Algiers Agreement in 1975 and ended Iranian military support for the Kurds in Iraq; this arrangement brought Iraq an unprecedented period of stability.

Once he became president, Saddam Hussein effectively used rising oil revenues to fund large-scale development projects, to increase public sector employment, and to improve education and health care. This tied increasing numbers of Iraqis to the ruling Ba'ath (Arab Socialist Resurrection) Party. Consequently, for the first time in contemporary Iraqi history, an Iraqi leader successfully forged a national identity out of Iraq's diverse social structure.[68]

---

[67] Library of Congress (n.d.).
[68] CountryWatch (2003a).

Saddam Hussein's achievements and Iraq's general prosperity, however, did not last long. In September 1980, Iraqi troops crossed the border into Iran, embroiling the country in a costly war. The Iran-Iraq War permanently altered the course of Iraqi history. It strained Iraqi political and social life and led to severe economic dislocations. Viewed from a historical perspective, the outbreak of hostilities in 1980 was, in part, just another phase of the ancient Persian-Arab conflict fueled by 20th century border disputes.[69]

Many observers believe that Saddam Hussein's decision to invade Iran was a personal miscalculation based on ambition and a sense of vulnerability. Saddam Hussein, despite having made significant strides in forging an Iraqi nation-state, feared that Iran's new revolutionary leadership would threaten Iraq's delicate Sunni-Shi'a balance and would exploit Iraq's geo-strategic vulnerabilities (for example, its minimal access to the Persian Gulf). In this respect, Saddam Hussein's decision to invade Iran had historical precedent; the ancient rulers of Mesopotamia, fearing internal strife and foreign conquest, also engaged in frequent battles with the peoples of the highlands.[70]

By November 1980, the Iraqi offensive had lost its momentum. Rejecting an Iraqi offer to negotiate, Iran's leader, the Ayatollah

---

[69] *Ibid.*
[70] *Ibid.*

Khomeini, launched a series of counter-offensives in 1982, 1983, and 1984 that resulted in the recapture of the Iranian cities of Khorramshahr and Abadan. The destruction of huge oil facilities caused sharp declines in both states' oil revenues. Nonetheless, Iraq was able to obtain substantial financial aid from Saudi Arabia and other Gulf states, as well as from several Western states, including the United States, which viewed the new Islamic and anti-Western government in Iran as a threat.

In early 1986, an Iranian offensive across the Shatt al-Arab resulted in the fall of the Iraqi oil-loading port of Faw and the occupation of much of the Faw Peninsula almost to the Kuwait border. The Iranians, however, could not break out of the peninsula to threaten Al Basrah, and their last great offensive, which began in December 1986, was ultimately repelled with heavy losses. In the spring of 1988, the freshly equipped Iraqi ground and air forces succeeded in retaking the Faw Peninsula and, through a succession of frontal assaults, continued into Iran. Iranian battlefield losses, combined with Iraqi air and missile attacks on Iranian cities, forced Khomeini to accept a cease-fire, which took effect in August 1988.[71]

Peace in Iraq, however, was not long-lived, and within a few years, Iraq invaded Kuwait. The Gulf War followed soon thereafter, and the after-effects of the war continue to be felt.

---

[71] *Ibid.*

Political Landscape of Iraq Up to The War of 2003

The Attack on Kuwait

From the time of Saddam Hussein's emergence as the leader of Iraq and the expanded role played by the ruling Ba'ath Party, Iraq's sense of nationhood, as well as its general prosperity rose incrementally. The war between Iran and Iraq ensued in 1980, and when it finally ended in 1988, both countries had suffered massive destruction. Despite its huge losses in the Iran-Iraq War, Iraq was unchallenged as the most powerful military presence in the Gulf region. The Iraqi army was weakened, but still retained a significant offensive capability relative to its neighbors.

As a result of the war, the Iraqi economy was shattered. The war, in conjunction with lower international prices for crude oil, had contributed to the collapse of oil revenues. As a result, Iraq cut its imports and curtailed consumption. With many of the Iraqi population conscripted into military service in order to fight in the war against Iran, the economy became increasingly reliant on external labor sources. Remittances from these foreign workers were sent to their home countries, which adversely affected Iraq's balance of payments. Exacerbating the situation was the increase in military spending from less than $1 billion in 1970 to more than $25 billion in 1984 – an amount that far exceeded the value of Iraq's oil revenue. Ultimately, the war with Iran cost Iraq in excess of $450 billion in losses and the country had accrued $86 billion in foreign debt, although Iraq claims that about half the debt does not really exist, as they were "grants" from other countries. In the last decade, claims against the Iraqi government have increased monumentally and now stand in excess of $300 billion.[72]

Some observers believe that the need for a solution to these problems contributed to Iraq's revival of old territorial claims against oil rich Kuwait. Saddam Hussein called for the annexation of the Bubiyan and Warbah islands at the mouth of the Shatt al-Arab, which would give Iraq a clear passage to the Gulf. He also accused Kuwait of illegally siphoning off oil from the Rumaila field, one of the world's largest oil pools, which the two countries shared. Hussein threatened to use force against all Arab oil producers, (including Kuwait and the United Arab Emirates) who exceeded their oil quotas, and accused them of collaborating with the United States to strangle the Iraqi economy by flooding the market with low-priced oil.[73]

Although Iraq had accompanied its threats by moving troops to the border area, the world was largely taken by surprise when, on August 2, 1990, the Iraqi army invaded and occupied Kuwait. A force of about 120,000 soldiers and approximately 2,000 tanks and other armored vehicles met little resistance. The Kuwaiti army was not on the alert, and those troops at their posts could not mount an effective defense. Some aircraft operating from

---

[72] Rivlin (2003).
[73] CountryWatch (2003a).

southern Kuwait attacked Iraqi armored columns before their air base was overrun, and they sought refuge in Saudi Arabia. Of the 20,000 Kuwaiti troops, many were killed or captured, although up to 7,000 escaped into Saudi Arabia, taking with them about 40 tanks.[74]

Having completed the occupation of Kuwait, the Iraqi armored and mechanized divisions and the elite Republican Guard advanced south towards Kuwait's border with Saudi Arabia. Intelligence sources indicated that the Iraqis were positioning themselves for a subsequent drive toward the Saudi oil fields and shipping terminals, possibly continuing toward the other Gulf States.[75]

The American Coalition Retakes Kuwait

In the first of a series of resolutions condemning Iraq, the United Nations Security Council on August 2, 1990, called for Iraq's unconditional and immediate withdrawal from Kuwait. In the months following, a coalition force of more than 600,000 ground, sea, and air force personnel deployed to defend Saudi Arabia and to drive the Iraqis out of Kuwait.[76]

Command of the force was divided. Commander-in-Chief of the United States Central Command Gen. H. Norman Schwarzkopf

---

[74] *Ibid.*

[75] *Ibid.*

[76] *Ibid.*

headed American, British, and French units. Schwarzkopf's Saudi counterpart, Lt. Gen. Khalid ibn Sultan ibn Abd al-Aziz al-Saud, commanded units from 24 non-Western countries, including troops from Saudi Arabia, Egypt, Syria, Kuwait, and the other Gulf states. In addition to 20,000 Saudi troops and 7,000 Kuwaiti troops, an estimated 3,000 personnel from the other Gulf Cooperation Council states (Bahrain, Kuwait, Oman, Qatar, Saudi Arabia and the United Arab Emirates) took part in the land forces of the coalition offensive, known as Operation Desert Storm.[77]

In January 1991, Operation Desert Storm evolved into a full coalition offensive against Iraq by the Coalition Forces. Sanctioned by the United Nations Security Council, the conflict was then called the Gulf War. On February 26, 1991 Kuwait was officially liberated. An official cease-fire was established, international sanctions against Iraq were instituted, and carefully circumscribed provisions for peace were implemented, including enforced air-exclusion ("no fly") zones in southern and northern Iraq. The "no fly" zones were put into effect to protect the Shi'a Muslim and Kurdish minorities in those areas. Despite the existence of these agreed measures, Iraq was accused of acting against the peace concord by repeatedly violating the boundaries of the zones.[78]

---

[77] *Ibid.*

[78] *Ibid.*

The Kurdish Problem

In November 1994, a political conundrum erupted within the Kurdish area of Iraq. Two competing political entities, the Patriotic Union of Kurdistan, or PUK, and the Kurdish Democratic Party, or KDP, signed a peace agreement, which allowed elections to be held in May 1995. In January 1995, however, despite the existence of the peace agreement, fighting broke out and continued until May. The situation led to the postponement of the Kurdish National Assembly elections. Peace negotiations to resolve the conflict in northern Iraq amongst warring groups were made in October 1995, and resulted in an agreement stating that they would hold elections in May 1996.[79]

On August 31, 1996, Iraqi troops were deployed to the Kurdish region to give assistance to the KDP. With the aid of the Iraqi military, the KDP was able to capture three cities, thereby controlling all three Kurdish provinces. Subsequently, the Iraqi government offered amnesty to Kurdish insurgents. In September 1996, the KDP formed a coalition consisting of the Islamic Movement of Iraqi Kurdistan, or IMIK, the Kurdistan Communist Party, and Assyrian and Turkmen representatives. In October, PUK forces regained much of the terrain they had lost to the KDP.[80]

---

[79] *Ibid.*

[80] *Ibid.*

In May 1997, some 10,000 Turkish troops were deployed to the northern Kurdistan region where they attacked Kurdish Workers' Party, or PKK bases. The United Nations opposed the Turkish presence and demanded their withdrawal from the region. The Turkish forces complied, but later commenced air strikes on the PKK bases. The KDP withdrew from peace negotiations in March 1997. On October 12, 1997, the PUK instigated its strongest military assault to date against the KDP. A four-day cease-fire was negotiated beginning on October 17, 1997. The fighting, however, resumed shortly after the established cease-fire ended.[81]

On February 12, 1998, two delegations of KDP and PUK met in Shaqlawa. Participants at the meeting addressed the peace process and the recently exchanged peace plans. The meeting resulted in agreement that both sides uphold and respect the cease-fire; settle differences through discussions; avoid violence at all costs; use the media to promote the peace process; unconditionally release all prisoners; and form a joint commission to coordinate the public services in education, health, and energy.[82]

The internal divisions within the Kurdish population, although less contentious in recent years, may still prove to be a

---

[81] *Ibid.*
[82] *Ibid.*

complicating factor in efforts aimed at establishing a united and stable Iraq.

Internal Tensions with Islamic Factions

In the past decade, Iraq has experienced domestic tensions between the ruling minority Sunnis and the Shi'a majority. The killing of Ayatollah Sadeq al-Sadr -- a prominent Shi'a cleric -- on February 17, 1999, sparked violent demonstrations. Dozens of Islamic activists and security forces were killed, and several hundred people were arrested. Human rights organizations reported that hundreds of people, including political prisoners, were executed and large-scale arbitrary arrests of suspected political opponents took place. Torture and ill treatment of prisoners and detainees were widely reported.[83]

The Search for Weapons of Mass Destruction

In 1998, United Nations Special Commission, or UNSCOM, teams that were directed to investigate Iraqi military sites and facilities, and to destroy unauthorized Iraqi weapons systems, claimed that they had found evidence of chemical weapons production.

At the same time, Iraqi officials expressed their concern that the United States and their western allies controlled UNSCOM investigations. Iraqi officials also charged that the investigations

---

[83] *Ibid.*

constituted an unfairly prejudiced process. Presumably to make clear their outrage, the Iraqis intermittently closed off sites from UNSCOM inspection. The United States, in the interim, admitted it had, indeed, been involved in some clandestine investigations.

With inspections stymied, the Iraqi government in November of 1998 said it would be willing to resume the process. In December of 1998, however, the UNSCOM teams, headed at the time by Richard Butler, left Iraq stating that they were unable to perform their investigative duties. Air strikes against Iraq commenced soon thereafter. A protracted process of military proliferation and reflux in the Gulf resulted.[84]

In July 1999, arrangements were made for a team of experts to begin the removal of toxic substances in Iraq that were left by UNSCOM disarmament inspection teams. This team of experts included Russians, French and Chinese representatives, and excluded the original UNSCOM team. Since the launch of air strikes in December 1998, no weapons inspectors had been allowed back into Iraq.[85]

In December 1999, a new commission, the United Nations Monitoring, Verification and Inspection Commission for Iraq, or UNMOVIC, was established to replace UNSCOM. Iraq rejected the United Nations Security Council resolution that established

---

[84] *Ibid.*

[85] *Ibid.*

UNMOVIC. The new United Nations weapons inspection team for Iraq and its director, Hans Blix, were ready to begin work in Iraq, but the ongoing disagreement between Iraq and the United Nations prevented UNMOVIC from moving into Iraq.[86]

The No Fly Zone Incidents

In December 1998, American and British forces, bombed Iraqi targets. The United States and the United Kingdom stated that they were operating under the auspices of the United Nations Security Council Resolution 1154 (issued in March 1998) which threatened the "severest consequences" if Iraq failed to comply with the dictates of the United Nations. The United States and the United Kingdom explained that the bombing campaign was initiated as a result of Iraqi non-compliance with the stipulations of the existing post-Gulf War agreement.[87]

For the most part, the bombing campaign, referred to as "Operation Desert Fox," concentrated on the air-exclusion ("no fly") zones of the northern and southern parts of Iraq. The city of Mosul, the area of Al Basrah, and the Abu al-Khasib region all suffered civilian casualties as a consequence of the bombing campaign.[88]

---

[86] BBC News (2002).

[87] CountryWatch (2003a).

[88] *Ibid.*

Iraq was repeatedly accused of violating the "no fly" zone provisions. For its part, Iraq has never recognized the legitimacy of the "no fly" zones, since they were not specifically articulated in a given United Nations resolution. Thus, Iraq vowed to unrelentingly oppose the zones.[89]

Further, Iraqi officials explicitly blamed the United States and the United Kingdom for the bombing campaign, which they claimed targeted civilian installations, and resulted in deaths within the civilian population. Consequently, in the face of perceived aggression, Iraq hurled anti-aircraft fire back at allied aircraft activity. In this regard, the government of Iraq contended that because several Iraqi civilians were killed in attacks by allied forces, it had the right to protect its own people.[90]

The allied response, however, was that any indiscriminate anti-aircraft fire that might have been employed, in an attempt to bring down allied aircraft -- for whatever reason -- would be potentially detrimental to Iraqi civilians. American and British forces maintained that their presence in the Gulf was authorized by the existing United Nations Security Council Resolution 1154, as noted above. They also claimed that Saddam Hussein reportedly -- but not definitively -- had offered a bounty to anyone who successfully shot down any allied aircraft. From the

---

[89] *Ibid.*

[90] *Ibid.*

American and British perspective, this alleged statement was regarded as evidence supporting their actions of self-defense.[91]

Economic Sanctions

Meanwhile, increasing numbers of government and non-governmental organizations repeatedly criticized the economic sanctions program against Iraq and many called for their elimination. Indeed, the sanctions regime had not brought down Saddam Hussein and Iraq's political elite; the potential threat posed by Iraq still existed, as the country's weapons program was no longer under international surveillance.[92]

The sanctions' strict trade regulations had led to a lack of food as well as medication, not impacting the regime, as intended, but hurting the Iraqi population instead. The apparent suffering of civilians and the political shortcomings increased international criticism and defiance of the sanctions regime. In March 2000, Hans von Sponek resigned as Director of the United Nations Humanitarian Program in Iraq, in protest of the sanctions.[93] Previously, Denis Halliday, a coordinator of the Oil-for-Food Programme had also resigned after a 34-year-long career with the United Nations. Halliday warned that the sanctions were a

---

[91] *Ibid.*

[92] *Ibid.*

[93] American Friends Service Committee. (2000).

"bankrupt concept" and that they would breed resentment among Iraqis for a generation.[94]

In August 2000, the Saddam Hussein International Airport in Baghdad re-opened, 10 years after it was closed. A ceremony was held to mark the reopening of the airport, regarded as a fresh and bold move by Iraq to counter the United Nations ban on commercial flights to and from Iraq. Also in August, Venezuelan President Hugo Chavez became the first head of state to visit Iraq since the Gulf War. Since early 2000, numerous humanitarian, culture and trade delegations visited Iraq, underlining the increasingly international, and in particular Arab, opposition to the sanctions.[95]

Encouraged by the growing opposition to the sanctions, in October 2000, Iraq demanded that oil bought under the United Nations administered Oil-for-Food Programme be paid in euros instead of U.S. dollars. Since November 2000, Iraq had also attempted to charge its own "oil surcharge," demanding that oil lifters pay an additional 25-40 cents for each barrel of oil bought, as well as attempting to collect a 10 percent fee on import contracts. The Iraqi regime was already benefiting from unauthorized sales of oil, made possible by corrupt border police and international oil traders. An estimated 400,000 barrels per

---

[94] Halliday (1998).
[95] CountryWatch (2003a).

day (almost a quarter of the two million barrels per day allowed under the sanctions), was transported through Syrian, Jordanian and Iranian pipelines, and by trucks crossing over the Turkish border. The oil was sold in a clandestine international oil market, enriching Saddam Hussein and his entourage.[96]

Increased Tensions

On February 16, 2001, American and British forces bombed five Iraqi command and control centers around Baghdad. The bombings represented the most extensive attacks since December 1998 and the first attacks close to the Iraqi capital city. The operation, described as a "routine mission" by United States President George W. Bush, came in response to increasingly sophisticated Iraqi attacks on allied aircraft patrolling the "no fly" zone.[97]

Iraqi authorities claimed that two civilians were killed and more than 20 wounded in the attack, bringing the number of Iraqi civilians killed in allied bombings to over 300, and the number of people wounded to around 1,000 since December 1998. Large demonstrations took place in Baghdad the day after the raids. Iraqi press vowed to revenge the attack, and referred to President George W. Bush as "the son of the snake," accusing him of following his father's aggressive policy and hard stance towards

---

[96] *Ibid.*

[97] *Ibid.*

Iraq. Saddam Hussein's continued defiance of the United States made him a popular leader in many Arab countries where people believed that the United States was playing a too influential role in the region.[98]

Three permanent members of the United Nations Security Council -- Russia, China and France -- in addition to several other countries, criticized the raids. France, who helped set up the "no fly" zone, but withdrew in 1998, condemned the bombings, and criticized United States and United Kingdom authorities for not informing NATO allies about the attack.[99]

The February 2001 bombings again highlighted the shortcomings of the current sanctions regime. Renewed focus on the Iraq sanctions came amidst the Bush Administration's work on developing its policy towards not only Iraq, but the entire Middle East region as well. America's policy and reputation were repudiated in the region, while Hussein's regime remained more entrenched than ever, while reaping the benefits of international sympathy.[100]

Experts from International Atomic Energy Agency (IAEA), the United Nation's nuclear agency based in Vienna, had been in Iraq since 1998. In January 2001, IAEA experts praised Iraq for its

---

[98] *Ibid.*
[99] *Ibid.*
[100] *Ibid.*

willingness to cooperate, but refused to comment on the findings of their inspections. For its part, Iraq called for an end to the sanctions, claiming that it possessed no weapons of mass destruction. The United Nations hoped to see its weapons inspectors back in Iraq to verify compliance with United Nations resolutions, prior to the lifting of any sanctions.[101]

The United Nations Security Council's permanent members remained divided on the issue of the sanctions. Russia and China called for an end to the sanctions, France called for a change in the sanctions regime and the United States and the United Kingdom continued to remain skeptical about any changes. Various alterations of the sanctions regime were proposed. Movement towards the implementation of so-called "smart sanctions", focusing more tightly on arms control and removing controls on civilian goods, was considered, but no consensus was reached.[102]

On June 30, 2001, sanctions were extended for five more months. Iraq responded by withholding oil from the world market.[103]

The sanctions regime, the previous wars, and the intermittent bombing campaigns, as well as the Iraqi government's priorities, had left civilian infrastructure and oil installations in dire need of

---

[101] *Ibid.*

[102] *Ibid.*

[103] *Ibid.*

repair and upgrading. The country's power grids and water distribution networks were particularly affected, and ultimately had an effect on the population in terms of health (noted earlier).[104] The degradation of the basic infrastructure also had an effect on economic productivity since many Iraqis were simply unable to work and produce income for their families. This is one of the reasons attributed to the disturbing increase in the levels of child labor and prostitution in Iraq. As well, smuggling was normative and continued unchecked, to the benefit of neighboring countries. Another complication was the heavy burden of Iraq's foreign debt, in excess of $300 billion.

The November 2001 trade fair in Baghdad witnessed greater Arab interest in Iraqi markets and brethren. New measures to reform the sanctions were anticipated at the November 2001 United Nations General Assembly session.[105]

While it was widely expected that Russia would refuse to support the so-called smart sanctions, the events on Sept. 11, 2001 in the United States put the entire situation on hold. Iraq strongly condemned the terrorist attacks on the United States, but equally formidable wording was used to condemn the bombing of Afghanistan. Political developments on Iraq depended on progress in the United States-led campaign against terrorism.

---

[104] National Public Radio (2002).

[105] CountryWatch (2003a).

Although Iraq had not been implicated in the attacks, military moves were possible, as the United States accused Iraq of pursuing the development of weapons of mass destruction.[106]

Together, this assemblage of challenges constitutes the pre-conditions of Iraq's political and economic landscape. The economy and infrastructure of Iraq had already been degraded in the war with Iran; the Gulf War, the post-Gulf War bombing campaigns, and economic sanctions further devastated them. Meanwhile Iraq's foreign debt was exponentially increasing. Against this backdrop, Iraq's future was about to further be complicated by the effects of yet another war.

---

[106] *Ibid.*

II. The War of 2003 and the Transition to Stability

Prelude

This chapter is intended to cover the events leading up to the War of 2003, as well as the issues associated with the transition to Iraqi self-determination and autonomy. Though the first part of the chapter may be regarded as the history of recent developments in Iraq, the course to Iraqi self-government is ongoing. As such, the events delineated here remain an integral part of an ongoing development process, and should be viewed within the prism of the emerging moment.

Events Leading Up to the War of 2003

Preemption and the Axis of Evil

In January 2002, in his first State of the Union address following the terrorist attacks of September 11, 2001, United States President George W. Bush declared Iraq along with North Korea and Iran, to be a member of an "axis of evil."

The terrorist attacks in the United States had been carried out by a radical Islamic movement called al-Qaeda. At the time of these attacks, there was no expressed connection between this militant transnational entity and Iraq. Nevertheless, over the course of the next year, the Bush Administration would meld together the issues surrounding the terrorist attacks on September 11, 2001, the threat posed by rogue states like Iraq and their weapons of mass destruction, as well as the need for preemptive action against such possible threats. With time, discourses surrounding a United States-led offensive against Iraq intensified and the Bush Administration stated it would support a regime change in Iraq consistent with the national security strategy of preemption.

The United States also stepped up its financial support of Iraqi opposition to the country's leader, Saddam Hussein. State Department officials from the United States met with Iraqi Kurdish opposition leaders from late 2001 until the time of the War of 2003. It was believed that the strategy favored by the United States involved promoting instability within Iraq. This method was viewed as a possible alternative to direct military action in toppling the Hussein regime.

In response to the Bush Administration's threats, the green light was given by Saddam Hussein to Ba'ath party members to kill those people suspected of plotting to overthrow the government. Saddam Hussein also intensified security along the northern Kurdish enclave, a well-known spot for Iraqi dissidents.[1]

---

[1] CountryWatch (2003a).

Meanwhile, in the first part of 2002, Iraq extended several invitations to the United Nations to begin a dialogue about the implementation of United Nations Security Council resolutions. Iraq also invited a United Nations envoy to review the human rights situation in the country. In February 2002, Benon Sevan, the executive director of the United Nations Oil-for-Food Programme, recommended the organization make necessary and frequent adjustments to the program, in order to properly meet the needs of the Iraqi people. For its part, the Iraqi government complained to the United Nations Compensations Committee that the committee was accepting too many demands from individuals or organizations, rather than from countries as a whole. The Oil-for-Food Programme, which was quickly reaching expiration, was extended on May 14, 2002.[2]

Without external military intervention, Saddam Hussein's hold on power remained unchallenged. The Iraqi president had been rumored to suffer from cancer for some time, but on several occasions had appeared in public, reportedly, in good health. In addition to the power struggle that would follow either his death or defeat, serious domestic problems continued to be identified. There were divisions between Sunnis and Shi'as, and there was dissonance within the Kurdish areas in the northern part of Iraq. Despite the United States' financial and military support for

---

[2] *Ibid.*

opposition groups both inside and outside of Iraq (such as the Iraqi National Congress), there was little reason to expect regime change in Iraq.[3]

Human Rights in Iraq

The Iraqi regime continued to be one of the most repressive in the world. Amnesty International reported widespread use of torture, arrests of political opponents, forceful expulsions of Kurds, Turkmen and Assyrians, and hundreds of executions -- among them numerous political prisoners. Amnesty International, in its 2001 report, also recorded human rights abuses in Iraqi Kurdistan. The United Nations Commission on Human Rights issued a resolution condemning "systematic, widespread, and extremely grave violations of human rights and international humanitarian law by the government of Iraq."[4]

Whether United Nations sanctions were lifted or reformed, it was hoped that any contemplated changes would target and punish the Iraqi regime, alleviate the suffering of ordinary Iraqis, open up the country politically and economically, and in a longer-term perspective, facilitate political change from within.[5]

---

[3] CountryWatch (2003a) and see also Amnesty International (2001).

[4] CountryWatch (2003a) and see also United Nations (2003a).

[5] *Ibid.*

The United States Presses for "Regime Change"

Meanwhile, in late July 2002, reports surfaced surrounding the United States' plan to remove Saddam Hussein as leader of Iraq. While in the past, such plans had centered on mass assaults reminiscent of "Desert Storm" over a decade ago, newer strategies seemed to center on specific key targets in Iraq, and the subsequent isolation and collapse of Hussein's government. It was believed, consistent with the earlier conflict in Afghanistan, that a very light ground force, combined with indigenous opposition factions, might have been sufficient to defeat the Iraqi military.[6]

By late August 2002, voices in the Bush Administration were stridently calling for the removal of Saddam Hussein from power. The Bush team cited the need for preemptive action against Iraq, alleging that Iraq was not only developing weapons of mass destruction, but also allowing such weaponry to fall into the hands of international terrorist organizations. Unable to clearly link Iraq's alleged weapons program to identifiable terrorist groups, the Bush Administration, bolstered by Prime Minister Tony Blair of the United Kingdom, stated that the simple existence of a burgeoning nuclear program in Iraq, along with chemical and biological weapons capabilities, demanded preemptive action.[7]

---

[6] *Ibid.*

[7] *Ibid.*

The Coalition and the United Nations

International Dissent on Iraq

With international outcry against unilateral -- or even bilateral -- military action against Iraq burning in the background, United States President George W. Bush addressed the United Nations in September 2002 in an attempt to shore up support for his efforts. Specifically, he called for that international body to bring Iraq back into line with the dictates of a number of its resolutions against Iraq. Most of the resolutions mandated weapons inspections and the resumption of this program remained the procedure of choice among most of the global community.[8]

Although the majority of the international community wanted to ensure Iraq's compliance with the weapons inspections process, the United States government had been hoping instead for a strong resolution authorizing the use of force against Iraq. The Bush Administration believed that continued weapons inspections efforts would be useless, Iraq would not comply with any external dictates, and only regime change could assure the destruction of Iraq's alleged nuclear capacity. Detracting from this claim was the revelation that a report by the International Atomic Energy Agency (IAEA), which had been cited by

---

[8] *Ibid.*

President Bush in his warnings about Iraq's alleged nuclear capacity, did not actually exist.[9]

Meanwhile, United Kingdom Prime Minister Tony Blair addressed the parliament in London and outlined a dossier covering Iraq's alleged weapons of mass destruction and the tactics employed to deceive weapons inspectors. His speech was aimed at gaining public support for military action against Iraq.[10]

As the United States' Congress discussed and debated the provisions of a draft resolution empowering the Bush Administration to take military action against Iraq, the United Kingdom's government crafted a resolution delineating specific requirements for Iraq to fully comply with international weapons inspections. This resolution was to be formally offered to the United Nations; it would then have to be approved by the United Nations General Assembly and most importantly, by the Security Council itself.[11]

---

[9] In 2002, the International Atomic Energy Agency (IAEA) disputed President George W. Bush's citation of an IAEA report on Iraq, which allegedly stated that in 1998, Iraq was "six months away" from developing nuclear weapons. The IAEA has said that the report simply does not exist and no such report was ever issued from the agency. Curl (2002).

[10] CountryWatch (2003a).

[11] *Ibid.*

France and Russia, both permanent members of the Security Council, stated they did not see the need for another resolution. Instead, these two countries favored going ahead with inspections on the basis of prior resolutions. China, also a permanent member of the Security Council, expressed great reservations about the military option proposed by the United States and the United Kingdom. China warned that such action would portend dire consequences.[12]

To complicate matters even further, the Iraqi government rejected the resolution drafted by the United States and the United Kingdom. Iraq also stated that it sought to comply with weapons inspections in accordance with an earlier plan negotiated by United Nations Secretary General, Kofi Annan. This plan, in terms of specifics, timeline and stringency, did not neatly or easily coincide with the policies outlined by the Bush Administration on Iraq.[13]

The Weapons Inspection Debate

During the week of October 1, 2002, discussions were scheduled to commence between Iraqi officials and United Nations representatives in Austria regarding the re-admittance of weapons inspectors to Iraq. Under new arrangements, inspectors from the United Nations Monitoring, Verification and Inspection

---

[12] *Ibid.*

[13] *Ibid.*

Committee (UNMOVIC), headed by Hans Blix, would search for biological, chemical and ballistic weapons in Iraq. The new agreement would allow "special sites," such as mosques and government ministry buildings, to be inspected without either prior notice or restrictions.[14]

Around the same time, a small delegation of United States congressmen traveled to Iraq to lobby Saddam Hussein's government to allow the re-admittance of weapons inspections and to examine the humanitarian situation. Their efforts, not unlike those of former weapons inspector, Scott Ritter, were ridiculed by various voices in the United States' government. Opponents of the delegation believed direct military action, resulting in regime change, was the only workable solution to rid Iraq of its perceived weapons of mass destruction.[15]

These developments came after a week of intensified bombing by the United States and the United Kingdom in the "no fly zone." The bombing raids also included a civilian airport in the city of Al Basrah. Russian officials noted that these bombing raids would be detrimental to the success of any political or diplomatic solutions under negotiation with Iraq. The Russians, along with the French and the Chinese, continued to note that they favored a

---

[14] *Ibid.*

[15] *Ibid.*

resumption of weapons inspections as the preferred course of action in dealing with Iraq.[16]

For its part, Iraq denied the existence of any weapons of mass destruction and tentatively stated it would allow weapons inspections to resume. Members of the Arab community both individually and collectively eschewed military action against Iraq. Some Arabic countries, such as Saudi Arabia, stated that their support for military action could be gained if it was sanctioned by the United Nations. Later, however, Saudi Arabian officials cautioned that bases on Saudi Arabian soil could not be used for any such military action.[17]

Security Council Resolution on Iraq

Following President George W. Bush's October 2002 address to the American people on the Iraq situation, a resolution authorizing the use of force against Iraq was passed in both houses of Congress with significant majorities. Anti-war protests ensued across the world, including those in countries normally aligned with the United States.

---

[16] *Ibid.*

[17] *Ibid.*

A defiant declaration by Iraq's leader, Saddam Hussein, stated that he would not voluntarily relinquish power. Discussions then followed in the United Nations about a resolution on Iraq.[18]

An acrimonious debate in the United Nations Security Council took place concerning how to proceed against Iraq, the result of which was Resolution 1441 unanimously passing in November 2002 (see Appendix II.1 for text of Security Resolution 1441).[19]

This resolution demanded unfettered access for United Nations inspectors to search for weapons of mass destruction. Although the United States claimed that military force would follow any failure on Iraq's part to comply with the resolution, the United Kingdom noted that while disarmament was inevitable, conflict was not. Nevertheless, the United States appeared to be preparing for war, as demonstrated by a substantial troop deployment to the Persian Gulf, which would ultimately total 250,000.[20]

Saddam Hussein convened a special session of the Iraqi parliament to consider a response to the United Nations resolution. Meanwhile, there was an emergency meeting of the Arab League. Member states expressed support for the United Nations Security Council Resolution and encouraged Iraq to accept the stipulated demands. At the same time, members of the

---

[18] *Ibid.*
[19] *Ibid.*
[20] *Ibid.*

Arab League made it explicitly clear that they were opposed to an attack on Iraq, which they would regard as an attack against a fellow Arab country. The regional body also asked that Arabs be part of the inspection teams and that any provocation by inspection teams be prevented.[21]

The Weapons Inspection Process

Weapons Inspectors Return to Iraq

In mid-November 2002, weapons inspectors returned to Iraq for the first time in four years. Led by Chief United Nations weapons inspector Hans Blix, the weapons inspection team consisted of twenty-five persons, including representatives from the International Atomic Energy Agency (IAEA), and inspectors from the United Nations Monitoring and Verification Commissions (UNMOVIC). The head of the IAEA, Mohammed El Baradei, was also part of the team.[22]

By year's end, the team was expected to expand to 100 persons. Blix's team promised an objective and professional weapons inspection process, which would include well-formulated and rigorous inspections. The weapons inspection team would also be helped by the use of new technologies, which were capable of detecting even the most well hidden weapons. The Iraqi

---

[21] *Ibid.*

[22] *Ibid.*

government stated at the time it would fully comply with all United Nations dictates, "for the sake of the Iraqi people, the Middle East region, and the world".[23]

Official searches began on November 27, 2002. On December 8, 2002, as required by United Nations resolutions, Iraq provided what was supposed to be a full accounting of all proscribed weapons. The weapons inspectors' early assessment that their efforts appeared unencumbered was tempered by United Nations Secretary General Kofi Annan's cautionary words that it was too early to draw any conclusions. Striking a more pessimistic tone, United States President George W. Bush stated that the results of the inspections process were "not encouraging."[24]

These developments occurred just as Iraq released its required declaration on the country's weapons programs and capabilities. United Nations weapons experts began examining the 12,000-page document, while the five United Nations Security Council permanent members were given access to the documents as well.[25]

In late December 2002, just as United Nations nuclear specialists interviewed Iraqi scientists who might have had knowledge of critical information about the Iraqi weapons program, the United

---

[23] *Ibid.*

[24] *Ibid.*

[25] *Ibid.*

States military stated that Iraq shot down one of its unmanned drones. The plane -- a low cost craft that was used for surveillance in the southern "no fly" zone -- was shot at by Iraqi forces in that very region of the country. The United States Chairman of the Joint Chiefs of Staff, however, did not regard the incident as an escalation of tensions, since the Iraqi forces consistently shot at allied aircraft patrolling the "no fly" zone. In fact, the United States air force routinely trolled the skies in that area, presumably to garner Iraqi response and to gauge Iraqi defense capabilities.[26]

On the issue of Iraq's weapons and ongoing inspections, however, the United States' government stated that the Iraqi's declaration in December delineating its weapons capabilities and programs was not a full accounting, as had been required by the United Nations. Thus, the United States asserted that the Iraqis were technically in violation of the recent United Nations' Security Council resolution. Both the United States and the United Kingdom declared Iraq to be "in material breach" of United Nations Security Council Resolution 1441.[27] For its part, Iraq stated that the United States' accusation was levied for the sole purpose of setting the stage for an inevitable war against Iraq.

---

[26] *Ibid.*

[27] BBC News (2003b).

In the background of these two contentions was the fact that the United States viewed the entire weapons inspections process quite differently from other countries, including Iraq. For many countries, the weapons inspections process was intended to achieve disarmament. From the perspective of the United States, however, the weapons inspections were not intended to be a "search and find" mission, aimed at uncovering weapons of mass destruction and other proscribed weaponry. Rather, it was to be a verification process aimed at validating the removal or destruction of such weaponry, as dictated by United Nations Security Council resolutions. The crucial difference in interpretation of the resolution would continue to create divisions and dissonance between members of the United Nations Security Council, and their decisions regarding Iraq.

By January 2003, in a televised address in honor of Iraq's Army Day, Iraqi President Saddam Hussein claimed that United Nations weapons inspectors were functioning as intelligence operatives. While the Iraqi leader also expressed his desire for the avoidance of war, he called on the Iraqi people to be prepared for its inevitability. The Iraqi leader's defiant speech came shortly after two senior Iraqi officials reacted with anger to their detainment for several hours at a Baghdad compound, which was contained and searched by United Nations weapons inspectors. Although Iraqi officials described these activities as "uncivilized" and "intrusive," the procedures appear consistent with the provisions of United Nations Security Council Resolution 1441.[28]

Regardless of the uncomfortable tactics used by the weapons inspectors, if war was to be avoided, it was imperative that Iraq be viewed as fully compliant with the dictates of United Nations Security Resolution 1441 and the demands of the weapons inspectors. For their part, weapons inspectors rejected Saddam Hussein's claim that they were involved in intelligence work and referred to his comments as "unfortunate." They insisted that they were not "exceeding their United Nations mandate" as was charged by the Iraqi leader.[29]

In early 2003, with only three weeks left before the inspectors issued their report to the United Nations Security Council, analysts and correspondents in Iraq observed that no discernible evidence of chemical, biological or nuclear weapons had been found. Indeed, Hans Blix observed that while there were still many "unanswered questions" about Iraq's weapons programs, thus far, the inspectors had not found anything clearly incriminating.[30]

---

[28] CountryWatch (2003a).

[29] *Ibid.*

[30] BBC News (2003b).

Then, in mid-January 2003, 11 empty chemical warheads for artillery rounds were discovered in an Iraqi army depot by weapons inspectors. Officials reacted cautiously to the news. Dimitri Perricos, the head of the United Nations team in Baghdad, said the find "may not be a smoking gun" that indicated a violation of United Nations resolutions. Nevertheless, chief weapons inspector, Hans Blix, described the situation in Iraq as "very dangerous," and declared that Baghdad had illegally imported arms-related materials to the country. Representing the view of the Iraqi government, Hossam Amin, head of Iraq's National Monitoring Directorate, said the material found was simply "forgotten."[31]

Weapons Inspections Process Concessions

With a report by weapons inspectors to the United Nations looming ahead, it was apparent that Iraq had to intensify its efforts in complying with the dictates of the international body.

By January 20, 2003, Iraqi officials agreed to a 10-point concession accord established by Blix and El Baradei. The agreement was struck in the wake of the discovery of the empty chemical warheads, which were not accounted for in the 12,000-page weapons declaration document. The 10-point agreement included provisions to interview nuclear scientists outside of Iraq, possibly in Cyprus. Earlier, the Iraqis had not been pleased with

---

[31] CountryWatch (2003a).

the idea of private interviews. The stipulations of the agreement also required further documentation to be handed over by the Iraqis to the United Nations.[32]

For its part, Iraq said it would also offer an explanation of the issues surrounding its incomplete weapons declaration. As well, Iraq stated it would appoint a team to search for munitions that may not have been declared in the original accounting under Resolution 1441.[33]

Blix and El Baradei were both cautiously optimistic about the agreement, noting that it effectively resolved many practical issues.[34] It remained unknown as to whether or not the weapons inspectors would be able to verify that Iraq was complying with United Nations Security Council Resolution 1441.

Also on January 20, 2003, United Kingdom Defense Secretary Geoffrey Hoon announced that 26,000 British troops would be deployed in the region around the Persian Gulf.[35]

The First Major Weapons Assessment

On January 27, 2003, United Nations Chief Weapons Inspector Hans Blix told the United Nations that Iraq had reluctantly

---

[32] *Ibid.*

[33] *Ibid.*

[34] *Ibid.*

[35] CNN News (2003a).

complied with Security Resolution 1441. Blix also noted that many crucial issues, such as anthrax, VX nerve gas and Scud missiles, had not yet been adequately addressed, and the last set of documents from Iraq contained no new information. In addition, he cautioned that Iraq might still be in possession of biological agents and rockets, which could be used to deliver those very agents. He did, however, state that the Iraqis had been cooperative in providing access to all sites. On balance, however, Blix observed that Iraq had not arrived at "a genuine acceptance of the goal of disarmament." In specific terms, Blix expressed the belief that Iraq had agreed "in principle" to the dictates of Security Council Resolution 1441, which was aimed at disarmament, but in practice, Iraq had not acted on the substance of that principle.[36]

In regard to the nuclear component of weapons of mass destruction, Mohamed El Baradei, the head of the International Atomic Energy Agency, said there was no evidence that Iraq had resumed its nuclear program, which was reported to have been discontinued in the early 1990s. Notably, El Baradei disputed the alleged use of various high-strength aluminum tubes possessed by the Iraqis, which the United States claimed were to enrich uranium for a nuclear weapon. The IAEA inspection team found that the tubes were not directly suitable for uranium enrichment. Instead, their usage appeared consistent with the formulation of

---

[36] CountryWatch (2003a).

ordinary artillery rockets. This finding coincided, in fact, with Iraq's official explanation for the tubes. Nevertheless, El Baradei stated that his inspectors would need more time to continue their investigative efforts before reaching any absolute conclusions.[37]

The combined findings of Blix and El Baradei were unexpectedly negative in some regards. As such, Blix's statements in particular, were touted by the United States and the United Kingdom as proof that Iraq was not cooperating. Conversely, other countries, including those on the United Nations Security Council, argued that the findings of the report demonstrated that the inspectors needed more time to finish their work.

The January 27, 2003, assessment would bear upon any decision to take military action against Iraq. Both the United States and the United Kingdom had said that any failure to comply with the dictates of Security Council Resolution 1441 could result in war. Indeed, the White House spokesman, Ari Fleischer, stated that partial compliance by Iraq did not constitute compliance in the comprehensive sense. Other key United Nations Security Council members, however, were adamant that inspections should continue. Two traditional allies of the United States and the United Kingdom, France and Germany, said that they would not support military action at that time. They believed that the inspections process should be exhausted before moving toward

---

[37] *Ibid.*

war footing. Meanwhile, United Nations Secretary General Kofi Annan stated that more time was needed to continue inspections before any action should be taken.[38]

The United Nations Security Council met on January 29, 2003, to decide the next step in dealing with Iraq. Most parties concurred that Iraq needed to be more pro-active in its compliance with the Security Council Resolution 1441. Nevertheless, there was no consensus on whether or not Iraq's failure to fully comply should result in military action. Further, with no evidence of nuclear weaponry, there was a general sense of wariness about going to war against Iraq. The United States and the United Kingdom were the obvious exceptions in this regard. Still, in the case of the United Kingdom, Prime Minister Tony Blair noted that a new United Nations Security Council Resolution -- that is to say, an additional resolution beyond Security Council Resolution 1441, authorizing the use of force against Iraq -- would be needed before launching an attack.[39]

Powell Addresses the United Nations

Secretary of State Colin Powell delivered a speech on Iraq to the United Nations Security Council on February 5, 2003. The Bush Administration promised "compelling evidence" on Iraq's weapons programs and other such violations during that speech.

---

[38] *Ibid.*
[39] *Ibid.*

The substance of the speech, however, did not change minds on either side of the divide, although support for the war increased among Americans, based on the evidence presented.[40]

Ironically, some of the very evidence presented by the United States Secretary of State was from a British intelligence report, which was itself embarrassingly and remarkably discredited for being outdated, improperly altered and plagiarized. Those opposed to using military action against Iraq seized on this inaccuracy as evidence that the United States was "trumping up" intelligence in order to promote its case for war.[41]

Meanwhile, with the threat of war looming ahead, three key members of the United Nations Security Council -- France, Russia and China -- noted that they favored an intensified inspections regime to deal with Iraq, albeit noting that Iraq had much work to do in the realm of cooperation, compliance and disarmament. Germany and Belgium were also vocal in their reticence to go to war against Iraq. In this regard, France and Germany developed a disarmament proposal that was to be offered to the United Nations, while Belgium said it would veto a request by the United States to give NATO support to Turkey in the event of a war with Iraq.[42] Because the decision was at odds

---

[40] *Ibid.*

[41] *Ibid.*

[42] *Ibid.*

with the NATO charter, the incident briefly evoked discussions that the very existence of NATO might be threatened.

The Second Major Weapons Inspection Report

Chief Weapons Inspector Hans Blix and the head of the International Atomic Energy Agency (IAEA) Mohamed El Baradei delivered their report to the United Nations Security Council on Friday, February 14, 2003. The report addressed Iraqi cooperation with arms inspectors and general compliance on United Nations Security Council Resolution 1441. Blix and El Baradei offered mixed reviews of Iraq's cooperation and compliance, noting that there had been some improvement since the time of the last report, when Blix famously noted that Iraq had not genuinely accepted the objective of disarmament.[43]

Notably, U2 surveillance over flights had been cleared, interviews with scientists had ensued, and Iraq had agreed to consultative talks with South Africa regarding that country's process of disarmament. Both explained that no banned biological, chemical and nuclear weapons had been found, although they did not preclude the possibility that such weapons did, indeed, exist. Blix also made note of the fact that supplies of VX nerve agents and anthrax, as well as long-range missiles were

---

[43] *Ibid.*

yet to be accounted for. He also noted that one particular missile with extended range was in violation of Security Resolutions.[44]

El Baradei observed that he had been presented with new documentation on weaponry and although the material did not provide new evidence, the gesture of openness suggested a notable shift on the part of the Iraqis.[45]

Significantly, Blix and El Baradei expressed the belief that inspections had been helpful and should be allowed to continue. In an unexpected development, Blix challenged aspects of the evidence that had been cited by United States Secretary of State Colin Powell in his address to the United Nations. He stated that there was no evidence that the Iraqis had previous knowledge of inspections, and he also said that the illicit movement of arms had not been persuasively proven by satellite imagery.[46]

In tone and in terms of substance, this joint presentation of Blix and El Baradei was significantly more positive than the last. The presentation was followed by passionate responses by members of the United Nations Security Council as well as the Iraqi ambassador. The address by French Foreign Minister Dominique de Villepin, which advocated inspections and no military action, elicited a rare thunder of applause from United Nations members.

---

[44] *Ibid.*

[45] *Ibid.*

[46] *Ibid.*

Some plans were made for a new resolution on the use of force against Iraq, while French and other officials called for a follow-up report by the inspectors in early March.[47]

Meanwhile, the United States and the United Kingdom were both involved in a massive build-up of battle groups and carriers in the Persian Gulf. Although criticized for taking logistical measures in their movement toward war, some observers suggested that increased Iraqi compliance might have been advanced precisely because of the tangible threat of military action.

Interim Developments

In the days immediately following the February 14 inspections report, the major cities of the world saw massive protests against a possible war against Iraq. In New York City and Los Angeles protestors each numbered around three-quarters of a million, while rallies in London, Rome, and other European cities each ranged from several hundred thousand to over one and a half million. Australia saw a two-day rally as citizens railed against their country's involvement in a prospective war.[48]

By the end of February 2003, the United States and the United Kingdom introduced a new resolution to the United Nations Security Council stating that Iraq had failed to disarm in

---

[47] *Ibid.*

[48] *Ibid.*

accordance with United Nations Security Council Resolution 1441. While the new resolution warned of consequences for non-compliance, it stopped short of expressing an explicit date for military action.[49]

The Third Weapons Inspections Report

On March 7, 2003, Chief Weapons Inspector Hans Blix and the head of the International Atomic Energy Agency Mohamed El Baradei delivered another report to the United Nations Security Council.[50]

Hans Blix noted that while the inspections process was not free from friction, impromptu inspections and increased surveillance had taken place. Also, despite initial reluctance, Iraq had accepted the demand to destroy its proscribed Al Samoud missiles. In this regard, the destruction of the missiles began.[51]

Blix did observe, however, that Iraq, as a country with a highly developed administrative system, could have produced more documentary evidence regarding its weapons program. The Iraqis had provided some paperwork on anthrax, and had undertaken a significant effort to furnish information regarding biological weapons, which were reportedly destroyed in 1991. Thus, Blix

---

[49] *Ibid.*

[50] *Ibid.*

[51] *Ibid.*

deemed that the level of Iraqi cooperation had increased and he concluded that the complete verification and disarmament process would take months to complete.[52]

Mohamed El Baradei declared that 218 nuclear inspections had been conducted, and that nuclear inspectors had interviewed individuals and groups, in both scheduled and unscheduled inspections. El Baradei also took time to explain the IAEA's investigation of the United States' claims regarding Iraqi attempts to procure high-quality aluminum tubes, presumably for the purpose of developing nuclear weapons. Explaining that the investigative process had been "well documented," El Baradei said that the IAEA had concluded that the overtures to purchase aluminum tubes were unrelated to the attempted manufacturing of gas centrifuges, which are used in the enrichment of uranium. In regard to magnets suspected for use in nuclear endeavors, IAEA experts concluded that they could not be used to produce nuclear material.[53]

El Baradei also refuted allegations by the United States and the United Kingdom that Iraq tried to buy uranium from Niger. In fact, the IAEA found that the supporting documents provided by the United States and the United Kingdom were forgeries. On this matter, the Washington Post published a story about the

---

[52] *Ibid.*

[53] *Ibid.*

fabricated evidence, which was exposed through the discovery of incriminating errors, such as unmatched names and titles of officials.[54]

El Baradei noted that after three months of intrusive inspections, there was no evidence of a revived nuclear program in Iraq. In particular, he stated that there was no sign of resumed nuclear activity since 1988 and no suggestion that Iraq had attempted to import uranium after 1990.[55]

Several months later, on July 11, 2003, the Director of the United States Central Intelligence Agency (CIA), George Tenet, accepted responsibility for the error on the aforementioned Niger nuclear incident. His admission followed a statement by President Bush that the CIA had cleared his use of the Niger nuclear story in the State of the Union address.[56] The matter continued to be a source of great contention both in the United States and the United Kingdom. Questions abounded regarding the quality of intelligence used, the process by which it was cleared, and the individuals in the governments who might have been involved in the publication of faulty information.

---

[54] Warrick (2003).

[55] CountryWatch (2003a).

[56] Solomon (2003), see Royce (2003) and see also BBC News (2003j).

No Second Resolution

Returning to the developments preceding the war in Iraq, there were ongoing attempts to garner support for a second draft United Nations Security Council resolution.

Despite the promising tone of the reports by Blix and El Baradei, the United States and the United Kingdom intended to compel a vote on their new resolution, which augmented the existing United Nations Security Resolution 1441.[57]

In summary, the second draft resolution recalled previous United Nations Security Council Resolutions on Iraq and promised to secure full compliance with United Nations Security Council decisions. It also called for the restoration of international peace and security in the area (see Appendix II.2 for full text on the second draft Resolution).

The new resolution was co-sponsored by Spain. Bulgaria, a non-permanent member of the Security Council, also expressed support for both the new resolution, and the use of force against Iraq. Regardless, passage of the resolution required nine votes and no vetoes from the Security Council's five permanent members -- the United States, the United Kingdom, Russia, France and China. The latter three countries all expressed intense opposition to military action at this time.

---

[57] CountryWatch (2003a).

Diplomatic efforts by the United States to shore up support from non-permanent members of the Security Council were intensified, because of the widespread opposition to the new resolution. With the exceptions of Spain and Bulgaria, every other non-permanent Security Council member state -- Germany, Syria, Angola, Cameroon, Chile, Pakistan, Guinea and Mexico -- were either in doubt or opposed to immediate military action against Iraq.[58]

Despite initial misgivings that the new resolution would not pass in the Security Council, United States Secretary of State Colin Powell expressed optimism about its passage. Although he acknowledged that a positive outcome of the vote could be vacated by a veto from a permanent Security Council member, he expressed the belief that a plurality of votes in favor of the new resolution would ensure a "moral victory".[59]

Diplomatic negotiations collapsed nonetheless. Efforts to modify elements of the draft of a second United Nations Security Council Resolution failed, despite the overtures by the United Kingdom to create an agreement that would satisfy the misgivings of most of the non-permanent Security Council members. Many undecided non-permanent members wanted a clear set of reasonable

---

[58] *Ibid.*

[59] *Ibid.*

benchmarks that Iraqi disarmament efforts could objectively be measured against. Further, they also requested a 45-day period in which this assessment could be made before concluding that military action was required. The United States declared the 45-day timeframe to be "a non-starter" and later refused a compromise of a three-week period.[60]

Meanwhile, France and Russia disputed the provisions for an automatic trigger -- resulting in war -- if Iraq failed to accomplish various benchmarks in disarmament. Both France and Russia earlier warned that they would veto any resolution containing such language. In response, British Prime Minister Tony Blair stated that "People have got to decide whether they are going to allow any second resolution to have teeth, to make it clear that there is a real ultimatum in it."[61]

Following a meeting in the Azores on March 16, 2003, between the leaders of the United Kingdom, the United States and Spain (the sponsors of the existing United Nations Resolution 1441), Blair announced that there would be a final round of informal discussions to try to resolve the impasse between the three allies and the rest of the Security Council. A deadline of March 17, 2003, was given to the rest of the Security Council to decide on a possible course of action, before military force against Iraq would

---

[60] *Ibid.*

[61] *Ibid.*

be exerted. France's Ambassador to the United Nations Jean Marc de la Sabliere responded that in one-on-one discussions with council members, it was clearly apparent that most did not endorse a use of force against Iraq at that point.[62]

With no progress made in regard to a second resolution, or, in building consensus among the Security Council by the March 17 deadline, the United States, the United Kingdom and Spain reversed their original commitment to seek a vote on its passage in the Security Council and, instead, withdrew the draft resolution.[63]

During an earlier media conference, United States President George W. Bush had promised a vote in the Security Council, whether or not the resolution passed, stating that council members would have to "show their cards." In an effort to pursue military action without overt illegality, which the defeat of a second resolution would surely signify, the allies took cover under the original United Nations Security Council Resolution 1441, which augured "serious consequences" for Iraqi non-compliance. Experts on international jurisprudence, however, were not at all agreed on this reasoning.[64]

---

[62] CountryWatch (2003a) and see also BBC News (2003d).

[63] CountryWatch (2003a).

[64] *Ibid.*

Several hours after the withdrawal of the draft resolution, United Nations Secretary General Kofi Annan announced the withdrawal of United Nations personnel, including weapons inspectors, from Baghdad in preparation for an imminent war against Iraq.[65]

In an interview on CNN, French President Jacques Chirac said "We should pursue diplomacy until we've come to a dead end."[66] France also called for an emergency meeting at the United Nations to discuss peaceful disarmament and suggested giving Iraq 30 days to disarm. On United States television around the time of Chirac's statement, United States Vice President Dick Cheney said that it was difficult to take the French position seriously.[67]

In spite of Cheney's disparagement of France, many other countries expressed great dismay at the prospects of a war against Iraq. China said that the matter should be resolved through dialogue, within the parameters of the United Nations. Russia condemned military action against Iraq as illegal and noted that it

---

[65] *Ibid.*

[66] In an interview with *CNN's* Christiane Amanpour, French President Jacques Chirac said that although France is not a pacifist nation, he believed that the diplomatic process should be thoroughly exhausted. CNN (2003b).

[67] In response to the French position that diplomatic channels should be exhausted and an extended timetable of 30 days might be considered, United States Vice President Dick Cheney said that it was "difficult to take the French position seriously." He suggested that the French were simply interested in "delaying tactics." *CBS News* (2003a) and see also Hutcheson (2003).

would only jeopardize international security. Germany expressed alarm over the developments and closed its embassy in Baghdad. Greece, which held the European Union presidency, said that the United Kingdom, the United States and Spain were working outside the United Nations. The European Union had already warned that if action were taken outside of the United Nations, it would not provide support. Pope John Paul called for a peaceful resolution and offered the belief that there was still time left for peace. Nelson Mandela, former president of South Africa, denounced the prospect of war.[68]

For his part, Saddam Hussein warned that if Iraq were attacked, the battle would take place "wherever there is sky, land and water in the entire world." The Iraqi leader, however, was reported to have left Baghdad for another part of Iraq. In an interview on Arab television, the Iraqi Foreign Minister Naji Sabri said that tens of thousands of Iraqis were ready to become martyrs in a war against American enemies. Iraq had been divided into zones in preparation for the war, which was predicted to commence within days.[69]

---

[68] BBC News (2003d).
[69] CountryWatch (2003a).

The Failure of Diplomacy

With not even a "moral victory" materializing in the realm of diplomacy, discussions shifted to a vision of a post-war Iraq and analysis as to why diplomacy failed.[70]

In regard to the post-war vision, Tony Blair promised that Iraq's territorial integrity would be protected and its natural resources used for the benefit of Iraqis. President Bush said that the United States and its allies were committed to the goal of a democratic Iraq, complete with an interim authority and a representative government; however, no specific form or process was presented. Notably, a State Department report released at the time expressed grave doubts about the successful democratization of Iraq; instead, it cautioned that destabilization and chaos were more likely to follow military action and impending occupation. Humanitarian aid and the lifting of sanctions were also promised.[71]

The failure of diplomacy has been blamed on several issues:

The first is the matter of whether or not diplomacy was truly an option. Although the lack of diplomatic tact by members of the Bush Administration did not help the diplomatic efforts, many countries around the world believed that the United States was

---

[70] *Ibid.*

[71] *Ibid.*

never committed to either inspections or disarmament, and instead, viewed "regime change" and war as inevitable.

Indeed, the on-going military build-up in the Persian Gulf during the diplomatic phase might support this view. In spite of the claims that the deployments to the Persian Gulf by United States and United Kingdom forces may have helped to compel cooperation by Iraq with weapons inspectors (as was noted earlier), there remained a prevailing perception that the military build-up not only undermined the diplomatic process, but also demonstrated an underlying certainty that war -- and concomitant "regime change" -- would take place.

A three-part investigation by the Financial Times suggested that the Bush Administration had decided in December 2002 to go to war, following the submission of the 12,000-page declaration by Iraq on weapons of mass destruction.[72] The Financial Times investigation expressed the view that after Iraq's submission of the incomplete declaration (which was discussed earlier), there was no likelihood of a diplomatic solution, although the diplomatic process of garnering United Nations support and sanction continued.

---

[72] Graham (2003a), Graham (2003b) and see also Agence France-Presse (2003c).

The second matter is that of hegemony. In a world that generally respects sovereignty, many members of the international community view facilitating "regime change" negatively as a new form of hegemony. As such, France (in addition to other less powerful countries in the United Nations) made it clear that they would challenge this modality.[73]

Viewed as intransigence by the United States and the United Kingdom, France's steadfast adherence to a diplomatic solution has also been perceived as the only contestation of unbridled power by the United States and the United Kingdom.[74] In fact, early reports suggested that France was not opposed to military action against Iraq, but rather, wanted to see the process unfold under the aegis of the United Nations. As events unfolded in late 2002, however, there has been some suggestion that France changed its course, as the United States appeared more determined to go to war. Regardless, the United States and the United Kingdom blame France for diplomatic obstructionism in regard to Iraq.

It is worth noting that the governments of the United Kingdom and France have viewed the diplomatic process and the functions of relevant international bodies differently. While France generally holds a multilateralist view of international relations,

---

[73] CountryWatch (2003b).

[74] *Ibid.*

the current administration in the United States is often described as being unilateralist. A news story by the British Broadcasting Corporation (BBC) explained how France's President Jacques Chirac believes that geopolitical decision-making should exist within the context of international structures such as the United Nations, NATO and the G-8. Conversely United States President George W. Bush is believed to regard such international structures as "instruments".[75] The disconnection between these two perspectives is not simply a dichotomy of France and the United States, but rather, a symbol of two divergent approaches to contemporary international relations.

The third matter concerns credibility. In the fall of 2002, prior to the return of weapons inspectors to Iraq, senior government officials in the United States and the United Kingdom claimed to have new – and even superior – intelligence demonstrating that Iraq was once again developing weapons of mass destruction. During his speech in Cincinnati, Ohio, in October 2002, United States President George W. Bush said, "After 11 years during which we have tried containment, sanctions, inspections, even selected military action, the end result is that Saddam Hussein still has chemical and biological weapons and is increasing his capabilities to make more, and he is moving ever closer to

---

[75] Mason (2003b) and see also Galen (2003).

developing a nuclear weapon."[76] This claim would eventually be challenged.

By the time the original Security Resolution 1441 was passed unanimously in the Security Council, the United Kingdom and the United States respectively claimed an impressive dossier of Iraqi ills. Over time, however, that dossier has crumbled.[77]

First, United States Secretary of State Colin Powell continuously repeated the claim that Iraq was in possession of aluminum tubes that could be used for uranium enrichment, while the head of the International Atomic Energy Agency Mohammed El Baradei maintained that the tubing could only be used for the manufacture of conventional rockets.[78] According to the New York Times, Powell was advised to hold up the tube when making his case in front of the United Nations but declined to do so saying, "Why hold up the most controversial thing in the pitch?"[79]

Second, Powell also made much of unmanned drones that Chief United Nations Weapons Inspector Hans Blix did not mention in his last oral report to the United Nations. The drones turned out

---

[76] The White House (2002b).
[77] CountryWatch (2003b).
[78] *Ibid.*
[79] Risen (2003).

to have been incapable of any dire activities involving the spread of biological and chemical weapons.[80]

Third, a document used by both the United Kingdom and the United States to make their case regarding the threat posed by Saddam Hussein was discovered to have been plagiarized. The contents were copied without attribution from a graduate student's thesis, which actually dealt with opposition groups in Iraq, as well as from several articles in Jane's Intelligence Review. The writers of both sources claimed that their figures and research had been altered in the British government's document.[81]

Fourth, allegations of Iraq purchasing uranium from Niger were revealed to have been fabricated, and included a collection of forged documents. Despite the evaluation by the IAEA that the Niger claim was inaccurate, Vice President Cheney said in a television interviews on Meet the Press on March 16, 2003, "You'll find that the CIA, for example, and other key parts of our intelligence community disagree." Cheney went on to say, "We believe he [Saddam Hussein] has, in fact, reconstituted nuclear weapons. I think Mr. [Mohamed] El Baradei [the IAEA director], frankly, is wrong. And I think if you look at the track record of the International Atomic Energy Agency [on] this kind of issue,

---

[80] CountryWatch (2003b) and see also Lederer (2003).

[81] Jones (2003).

especially where Iraq's concerned, they have consistently underestimated or missed what it was Saddam Hussein was doing."[82] To date, this issue continues to plague the governments of the United States and the United Kingdom.[83]

Fifth, links between al-Qaeda and Iraq were discounted by the United States' own CIA. Meanwhile, the CIA issued reports denouncing such a connection.[84] Indeed, many experts dismissed the likelihood that Saddam Hussein would use biological or chemical weapons, noting that such a scenario would only transpire if Hussein's power were threatened.[85] The Cato Institute also published a number of commentaries criticizing a proposed war against Iraq and disparaging the notion of an al-Qaeda connection.[86] Even a leaked British Defense Intelligence Staff report said that there were no current links between Iraq and al-Qaeda; the report also claimed that al-Qaeda's ideological aims were in conflict with the scenario in present-day Iraq.[87]

---

[82] NBC News (2003) and see also Kristof (2003a).

[83] BBC News (2003c), see Kristof (2003b) and Kristof (2003c) and see also Grice (2003).

[84] Goldberg (2003).

[85] CountryWatch (2003b) and see also Mearsheimer (2002).

[86] The Cato Institute issued a regular offering of commentaries criticizing the proposed war against Iraq, and challenging the Bush administration's claims regarding the Iraq threat. See Eland (2003), Eland (2002), Galen (2003a) and see also Niskanen (2003).

[87] Rangwala (2003).

Sixth, the realization that the United States and the United Kingdom were wiretapping the United Nations, in order to gain some advantage in procuring favorable votes on its second draft resolution, diminished the two countries' credibility in the eyes of the international community.[88]

Seventh, the British claim that Iraq could deploy its weapons of mass destruction in 45 minutes was soon surrounded by doubt. It was eventually discovered to have been based on a single source and was thoroughly discredited, most recently at a parliamentary inquiry in the United Kingdom regarding the credibility of intelligence.[89]

Another contributor to the breakdown of diplomacy was the incongruous trail of rationales underlying military action against Iraq. While President George W. Bush called for "regime change," his closest ally, Prime Minister Tony Blair started his call for action against Iraq by telling British parliament that the objective was disarmament and not "regime change."[90] Similarly, the United Kingdom continued to offer human rights abuses as its rationale for taking action against Iraq. The litany of Saddam

---

[88] Bright (2003). The loss of credibility was a result of the marginal media coverage this story received in the United States media, see also Fairness and Accuracy in Reporting (2003).

[89] United Press International (2003). For more detailed information, see Milbank (2003). See also Rangwala (2003).

[90] CNN News (2003c).

Hussein's human rights abuses – as horrific as they were – often provided the lion's share of space in dossiers calling for action against Iraq, however, the underlying rationale for any military action was always stated as being the failure to verify disarmament. This confusing trajectory of logic did not help the United States and the United Kingdom in building a substantial coalition, which was expressly focused on the problem of weapons of mass destruction.[91]

A final contributor to the credibility chasm was the way in which the logic of Iraq's possession of weapons of mass destruction was sometimes conflated with the claim that Iraq had terrorist ties. Specifically, Iraq was said to be collaborating with al-Qaeda group responsible for the September 11, 2001 attacks in the United States, and there were fears that Iraq would furnish weaponry to terrorist organizations.[92] Although the connection was questioned by a myriad of individuals and groups, for the Bush Administration, the link seemed to be quite clear. The lack

---

[91] The strategic forecasting group, Stratfor, published the view that there may have been "no strategic plan behind the invasion of Iraq beyond the desire to do good." The account went on to state, "Iraq had nothing to do with al-Qaeda, except to prevent future collaboration. In fact, the best way to view Iraq is as a souped-up Kosovo, a grand humanitarian gesture against another evil dictator." While this rationale is laudable, it is at odds with the expressed reason for going to war with Iraq in the first place. See Stratfor (2003a).

[92] Following the war, a United Nations draft report showed no link between Iraq and al-Qaeda. See Appleby (2003) and see also Linzer (2003).

of consensus on the matter, however, did not help the case being made by the United States and the United Kingdom.

The credibility gap was not bridged even after the conclusion of the diplomatic process at the United Nations. In the aftermath of the War of 2003, United States intelligence officials as well as members of the Bush Administration acknowledged that they had gained little new evidence in the five years since United Nations inspectors left Iraq.[93]

Under fire for supposedly misleading the public and Congress in this regard, United States National Security Advisor Condoleezza Rice said, "The question of what is new after 1998 is not an interesting question; there is a body of evidence since 1991. You have to look at that body of evidence and say what does this require the United States to do? Then you are compelled to act."[94] Likewise, in a meeting with Congress in July 2003, United States Secretary of Defense Donald Rumsfeld said, "The coalition did not act in Iraq because we had discovered dramatic new evidence of Iraq's pursuit of weapons of mass murder," he said. "We acted because we saw the existing evidence in a new light, through the prism of our experience on Sept. 11."[95]

---

[93] Risen (2003).

[94] *Ibid.*

[95] *Ibid.*

These statements, however, appeared to contradict previous assertions by members of the Bush Administration. For example, Paul Wolfowitz, the deputy secretary of defense, characterized the intelligence on Iraq as both credible and recent. At the Council on Foreign Relations, Wolfowitz said, "It is a case grounded in current intelligence...current intelligence that comes not only from sophisticated overhead satellites and our ability to intercept communications, but from brave people who told us the truth at the risk of their lives. We have that; it is very convincing."[96]

The War Begins ... and Ends

Opening Rounds

Following the failure of diplomacy and a subsequent 48-hour ultimatum by United States President George W. Bush, Coalition Forces began strikes against Iraq on March 19, 2003. On the basis of actionable intelligence, initial strikes were launched against Saddam Hussein's leadership group in Baghdad.[97] The success of the strikes was unknown at the time. Then, several days later, the start of the "shock and awe" strategy commenced.

---

[96] *Ibid.*

[97] CountryWatch (2003a). For information about the presumed tactical approach of the war and the political imperatives see Reynolds (2003) and see also Stratfor (2003b).

While the original plan was to start with the "shock and awe" strategy, a strategic decision was made to attempt to bomb the top Iraqi leadership with precision munitions at the outset of hostilities. Some experts suggested that the strategic shift was made in order to determine how the Iraqi leadership would respond to the war. Others, however, explained that information on the location of Saddam Hussein came to light and inspired early strikes. Then, when some of the southern oil fields were set ablaze, the timetable for the ground assault was accelerated. The rationale notwithstanding, Coalition Forces made their way over the Kuwaiti border into Iraq

Coalition forces encountered much tougher resistance from the Iraqis than had been expected, however, the source of the resistance did not include the Iraqi Republican Guard units or the regular Iraqi army. Instead, local militias -- called the Fedayeen -- had organized and were resisting Coalition Forces. The towns of Al Basrah, Najaf, Umm Qasr and Nassariya were particularly hit with massive attacks from Coalition Forces, while those very forces encountered fierce Iraqi resistance on the ground. In the face of criticism about the war strategy, coalition commanders insisted that they had expected these developments and the war was going according to plan.[98] Mitigating this claim were

---

[98] Mason (2003a) and see also comments by Commander William Wallace in this article BBC News (2003e).

comments from the field expressing surprise at the intensity of the Fedayeen.

Saddam Hussein appeared on Iraqi television several times urging the Iraqi people to keep up the fight. His appearances quelled stories of possible injury, although there remained suspicion that the person broadcasting was actually a body double of the Iraqi leader. The Iraqi government predicted disaster and death for coalition fighters. In the face of overwhelming air strikes and bombings, Iraqi defenders responded with mortars, rocket propelled grenades and anti-aircraft fire.[99] Despite the coverage of such incidences as being "heroic" in the Arab media, these efforts were largely ineffectual against the military technology of Coalition Forces.

Several casualties on both sides were recorded among troops and also among the civilian population. Reports also registered the possible downing of one or two United States apache helicopters and British fighter pilots parachuting into Iraqi territory.[100] British forces, in particular, were badly hit by friendly fire incidences and mid-air accidents. In this regard, Prime Minister Blair warned of "difficult days ahead".[101]

---

[99] CountryWatch (2003b) and see also Ladki (2003).
[100] Ladki (2003).
[101] BBC News (Mar 2003f).

Several prisoners of war from the United States were shown on Arab television. The videotape, which Coalition Forces deem to be a violation of the Geneva Convention, also showed the bodies of coalition fighters killed in action or murdered. Critics, however, noted that the war on Iraq contravenes against the United Nations charter and so claims of violations of international accords were rather hypocritical. Nevertheless, United States President George W. Bush warned that inhumane treatment of captives would result in war crimes prosecution; the United States is not, however, a country which accepts International Criminal Court jurisdiction.[102]

The Air War Intensifies

Coalition convoys moved toward Baghdad and heavy bombardment of Iraqi forces by the United States and United Kingdom continued. As the war in Iraq raged on, air raids by Coalition Forces pounded Baghdad. Long range B1, B2 and B52 bombers were part of the attacks on communications and command centers in Baghdad. The assault of missiles and bombs was intended to erode Iraqi defenses before Coalition Forces arrived in the capital city. The presidential palace used by the son of Saddam Hussein was one of the key targets hit in aerial bombardment. The city's southern edge was particularly

---

[102] CountryWatch (2003b).

hammered by artillery and bombings, although explosions were also heard in the western parts of Baghdad.[103]

As Coalition Forces moved closer toward the capital city, within 50 miles (or 80 kilometers) of Baghdad, they increasingly battled Iraqi Republican Guard units on their approach. Once in Baghdad, however, the Coalition Forces found the Iraqi resistance to be less intense than originally expected. United States forces captured two presidential compounds in Baghdad, including the palace, which headquartered the Republican Guard units. The Iraqi information minister denied the capture of the compounds and instead claimed that Iraqi fighters were prevailing over United States forces. On Iraqi television, President Saddam Hussein called for a call to arms in the city and instructed fighters who could not reach their respective units to join any unit that could be located.[104]

While heavy bombardment of Baghdad continued, United States forces positioned tanks and Bradley fighting vehicles near the Information Ministry and the al-Rashid Hotel. For their part, Iraqi fighters blocked bridges over the Tigris and defended key government buildings with rocket grenades. Fedayeen militia members patrolled the streets. Urban warfare and street fighting

---

[103] CountryWatch (2003a).

[104] CountryWatch (2003a). See also an article delineating successful attacks on Iraqi targets by Coalition Forces, as well as developments in specific parts of Iraq: Chandrasekaran (Mar 2003).

commenced. One battle zone was reported to be in central Baghdad near a residential district. United States officials said that the activity in Baghdad was intended to be "a show of force" and not a full-scale take-over and occupation. It was hoped that the demonstration of military dominance would convey the futility of Iraqi resistance.[105]

The demonstration was something of a success as United States forces were able to take control of large portions of the city. After toppling a statue of Saddam Hussein in the capital city, the United States declared the regime of Saddam Hussein to have been toppled, although the fighting raged on.[106]

When the 3rd Infantry Division reached Baghdad, however, troop deployments were truncated. The United States' Secretary of Defense officials believed that only light forces would be necessary in the capital city, since Baghdadis would jubilantly celebrate their liberation by Coalition Forces. In fact, the toppling of Hussein's regime, in combination with only minimal forces in Baghdad, left a massive power vacuum. Consequently, looting, vandalism and a general state of chaos ensued. Insufficient troops in Baghdad also made it difficult to stabilize the situation.

---

[105] CountryWatch (2003a).

[106] *Ibid.*

Conditions Inside Iraq

Meanwhile, the most difficult challenge for civilians to deal with was the terribly degenerated state of the Baghdad hospital. The hospital was understaffed because doctors and nurses were unable to safely travel the streets of Baghdad to get to work. Insufficient medical supplies exacerbated the problem as patients arrived by the hundreds every hour. Power supplies were affected as was the water supply and other basic services. Several months later, power and water was yet to be restored in various parts of Iraq, although Baghdad was most acutely affected.[107]

United States forces pounded on Saddam Hussein's stronghold of Tikrit. Although fierce battles ensued between remaining Iraqi army units in Tikrit, the majority of Iraqi forces had fled the town, most recently when Baghdad fell to United States forces.[108]

In Baghdad, even though it became evident that the Hussein regime had lost power, pockets of resistance continued to engage with United States forces and widespread looting characterized a general climate of lawlessness.[109] The Iraqi National Museum was hard hit in the looting; artifacts dating back to the earliest records of humankind were either destroyed or stolen. Joint patrols by United States forces and Iraqi civilian leaders were

---

[107] *Ibid.*

[108] *Ibid.*

[109] CountryWatch (2003a) and see *PBS* (2003).

launched to combat the problem. Similarly, Iraqi police joined British forces in an attempt to restore security and calm to the southern town of Al Basrah.

Violence raged in Najaf when mobs of people hacked to death two Shi'ite Muslim clerics who had aligned themselves with the United States-led war. Shi'ite factions also surrounded the home of another Shi'ite cleric and gave him forty-eight hours to leave Najaf.[110]

Meanwhile, the head of Iraq's scientific program was taken into United States custody; he stated that Iraq had no biological and chemical weapons and declared the war to be unnecessary. Saddam Hussein's brother was also captured close to the Syrian border.[111] Since that time, several captures of high level Iraqi officials have taken place, and Saddam Hussein's sons were killed.[112]

In Nasiriya, a meeting of Iraqis was scheduled to take place about the future of the country. Ahmad Chalabi, the head of the exile group, Iraqi National Congress, was to be present for the meeting. Chalabi, at the time, was the United States' choice for

---

[110] CountryWatch (2003a).

[111] *Ibid.*

[112] A list of the high level officials of Hussein's regime is available by reading BBC News (2003a). For more details about the deaths of Saddam Hussein's sons, see Tyson (2003).

running post-war Iraq. Chalabi's reception in Iraq, however, was less than enthusiastic and his group had little popular backing in Iraq.[113]

In a stunning positive development for United States forces, in the midst of all the military activity, missing prisoners of war were subsequently found alive. Jessica Lynch, a wounded United States Army private, was located in an Iraqi hospital in an Iraqi controlled area and then rescued by United States special operations troops based on information from Iraqi citizens. Months later, it would be revealed that Lynch's injuries were sustained in a vehicle crash. Local medical staff had tried to return her to the care of United States forces after Iraqi forces pulled out of the hospital, but the doctors were forced to turn back when United States troops opened fire on them. The Special Forces actually encountered no resistance despite the appearance of a daring rescue mission.[114]

By the end of July 2003, 280 coalition fighters had been killed (237 from the United States and 43 from the United Kingdom). The numbers of Iraqi fighters killed were inconclusive and contradictory, ranging from 2,000 to 10,000 according to various sources. Estimates for Iraqi civilian casualties suggest that over

---

[113] CountryWatch (2003b).

[114] CountryWatch (2003b), and see Kamfner (2003) and see Rulon (2003).

7,000 Iraqis had been killed and 5,000 wounded, according to some Iraqi sources.[115]

Meanwhile, by mid-April 2003, it was clear that Coalition Forces had control of Iraq and Saddam Hussein's rule of the country was over. However, there was no confirmation that Saddam Hussein had been killed and he certainly had not been captured. Moreover, as of the end of July 2003, ambushes and attacks against the coalition soldiers continued.[116]

As noted above, on May 1, 2003 President Bush, in a speech on the U.S. aircraft carrier Abraham Lincoln, declared major combat operations in Iraq over.[117]

Transition to Stability: The Immediate Aftermath

The United States and the United Kingdom agreed immediately after the cessation of major military hostilities to the fundamentals of a preliminary three-stage plan for administering a post-war Iraq.

1. Coalition forces would maintain security, infrastructure and aid, reporting to the United States Secretary of Defense through General Tommy Franks. Military forces in Iraq would remain

---

[115] Reuters (2003a).

[116] Washington Post (2003) and see also McLeod (2003).

[117] The White House (2003).

under the command of General Franks, head of the United States central command. Retired General Jay Garner, who headed the Pentagon's office of reconstruction and humanitarian relief, would have initial responsibility for reconstruction efforts, and report to General Franks.

2. A broad-based, multi-ethnic interim Iraqi administration would be formed with the United States retaining control of external defense and internal security for some time.

3. Iraq would be eventually transitioned to a representative democratic government; the country's oil wealth would be used to rebuild the country, along with international aid and assistance.[118]

Some time after Garner's arrival in Iraq, a former diplomat and United States Department of State official, L. Paul Bremer III, arrived in Iraq and became the senior civilian official in Iraq, effectively outranking Garner. The shift was intended to signify a symbolic transition, with the military portrayed in a subordinate role. Still, Bremer was an ally of the United States Secretary of Defense Donald Rumsfeld and he would report directly to the head of the Pentagon.[119]

---

[118] Reuters (2002) and see also Observer (2003). For more information about Jay Garner see CBS News (2003b).

[119] For information about the transition from Garner to Bremer, see Stoullig (2003) and for more information about Paul L. Bremer III see BBC News (2003).

Military operations in Iraq were turned over to the jurisdiction of Lieutenant General John Abizaid, a Lebanese-American. Fluent in Arabic and with a Master's Degree in Middle Eastern Studies, it was hoped that Abizaid's presence would be well received on the ground in Iraq. Skeptics have said that his effectiveness will be more important than his ethnicity or background.[120]

Meanwhile, the efforts to create some sort of indigenous ruling authority in Iraq took off to an uncertain start. The initial meetings to convene an interim authority during the first weeks of Garner's arrival were halted when Bremer took the reins. Bremer announced initially that no such interim authority would exist for some time. Soon, however, he announced a return to the plan for an interim authority, with limited executive power. Bremer also said that the interim body would have to write a constitution as well as the framework for democratic elections. To date, there has been no decisive timetable for a handover to full Iraqi rule although an initial meeting of a Governing Council has taken place -- the details of which are discussed later in this chapter.

[120] For a profile of John Abizaid, see BBC News (2003).

The Role of the United Nations

The Post-war United Nations Debate

Many of the important details in regard to this plan are cause for disagreement between the United States and the United Kingdom. Although both countries agreed to United States control of Iraq immediately following the conclusion of the war, and an eventual transition of authority to Iraqis, the most significant differences appeared to be in regard to the role of the United Nations in this process, as well as the overall timing of the elements of the plan.

The United States had envisioned a far more limited role for the United Nations, mostly in the realm of humanitarian activities. This view was in contrast with that of the United Kingdom. There were mixed messages coming out of Washington on the issue. United States National Security Adviser Condoleezza Rice stated that those Coalition Forces who had expended the "life and blood" in the liberation of Iraq would have the principal role. Significantly, in the days following the fall of Saddam Hussein's regime, she also noted that a United Nations' role was not even under discussion.[121]

United States President George W. Bush assured United Kingdom Prime Minister Tony Blair that there would be a role

---

[121] CountryWatch (2003b).

for the United Nations. On the record, however, Bush did not specify what that role might be. United States Secretary of State Colin Powell suggested that discussions about the role of the United Nations were underway. He also hinted at greater United Nations involvement than was allowed by the National Security Advisor. Powell expressed the view that the United Nations would be integral, not only in supervising humanitarian aid, but also in regard to developing the interim civilian authority. Later, however, Powell said that the bulk of the control would lie in United States hands, roughly mirroring words spoken by Condoleezza Rice.[122]

In this way, the Bush Administration has sent out mixed signals. First, it did not specify a difference between a "vital" or "crucial" role for the United Nations in public speeches with its ally, the United Kingdom. Yet, the United States also made it clear that the central control of Iraq would be under United States jurisdiction. Although it indicated that Iraqis would participate in an interim administration, Washington has also said it would continue to oversee the defense and security of Iraq in Stage Two of the proposed plan. Officials in Washington suggested that the restructuring of the Iraq army would drive the defense and security phase-out stage.[123]

---

[122] *Ibid.*

[123] *Ibid.*

For its part, the United Kingdom expressed the desire to have the United Nations take charge of a conference in which Iraqis would decide upon their new leaders. In this formulation, the United Nations would play a key facilitator role and would also be charged with coordinating and supervising the process.[124]

The difference in vision between the two coalition partners was based on the desires of United Kingdom Prime Minister Tony Blair to have the United Nations involved not only in humanitarian endeavors, but also in reconstruction efforts, and, most significantly, in the establishment of a new Iraqi government (as aforementioned). The United Kingdom also wanted a new United Nations Security Council resolution which would set forth the depth of these respective roles, thus offering some degree of endorsement for a new representative Iraqi state.[125]

In hoping for crucial involvement by the United Nations, the United Kingdom was hopeful that three European Security Council countries that opposed the war -- France, Germany and Russia -- would take on collaborative roles. These countries had stressed the importance of United Nations involvement. Indeed, Russian Foreign Minister Igor Ivanov observed that the governments of these three key countries believed that the United

---

[124] *Ibid.*

[125] *Ibid.*

Nations was the only organization that could play a "central role." French President Jacques Chirac emphatically expressed the view that the United Nations should play a key role in rebuilding Iraq. He declared, "It is up to the United Nations -- and it alone -- to take on the political, economic, humanitarian and administrative reconstruction of Iraq."[126]

For its part, however, the Bush Administration was adamant that it would retain control over the developments in Iraq, since the credibility of the United States was at stake.

European Post-Mortem

The leaders of France, Germany and Russia met in St. Petersburg, Russia, to discuss post-war Iraq. Dubbed the "summit of losers" by a Russian daily newspaper, the meeting was held to discuss plans for the United Nations to play a "central role" in the development of a stable post-war Iraq. As noted above, however, the United States, while stating that the United Nations would play a "vital role" in a post-war Iraq, made it clear that control of Iraq would not be given to that international organization.[127]

Although the governments of France, Germany and Russia had expressed the hope for reconciliation with the United States, and

---

[126] CountryWatch (2003b) and see also Agence France-Presse. (2003a). For information about how the United Nations might fit into the post-war plan for Iraq see Baldauf (2003).

[127] CountryWatch (2003b) and see also Holley (2003).

the desire to collaborate in rebuilding Iraq, wide divisions remained on how this might have been achieved, and most significantly, on the role of international instruments and bodies, such as the United Nations. Complicating matters were the divisions within the European Union over Europe's relationship with the United States. The respective positions of France, Germany and Russia on Iraq created a split within Europe, thus spurring something of a shift in post-World War II trans-Atlantic alliances and policies.[128]

The stance favoring diplomatic resolution of the Iraq issue over military action was not simply a counterweight to the United States and the United Kingdom. Indeed, the differences over the Iraq issue were rooted neither in ideology nor in the simple desire to check the might of the United States. Indeed, many analysts have suggested that the differences over Iraq represent internal debates over the European identity, and how the relationship with the United States plays into that conception.[129]

Specifically, while the United Kingdom Prime Minister Tony Blair has pursued an aggressive policy of engagement with the United States, Germany's Chancellor Gerhardt Schroeder has mentioned "emancipating" Germany from its decades-long relationship with the United States. Meanwhile, many of the

---

[128] CountryWatch (2003b).
[129] *Ibid.*

former communist nation states of Europe have supported coalition efforts in Iraq, and have endeavored to strengthen ties with the United States. Dubbed the "New Europe" by United States Secretary of Defense Donald Rumsfeld, it is clear that these emerging democracies have their own reasons -- among them the economic benefits -- for aligning themselves with the United States. These competing approaches have their own set of consequences and implications on the European continent.[130]

In this way, the debate about Iraq has not been simply about how to deal with American power. It is simultaneously, and possibly, more significantly, about how the relationship with the United States shapes the European identity and position in the world.[131]

It remains to be seen if the schisms over Iraq will become solidified in the realm of international relations. It is generally believed that the first test in this regard will be whether or not the United States/United Kingdom coalition can find common ground with France, Germany and Russia in regard to a role for the United Nations in a post-war Iraq.[132]

---

[130] *Ibid.*

[131] *Ibid.*

[132] *Ibid.*

The Continued Call for United Nations Involvement

Many other countries, regional bodies and key United Nations Security Council members, such as Chile, have said that it is important that the United Nations play a leading role, or a post-war Iraq would risk legitimacy and recognition by international institutions. The French Foreign Minister Dominique de Villepin said the principle of "international legitimacy" was crucial, thus conferring the view that only United Nations involvement could confer this legitimacy. The European Union has said it cannot be involved in any post-war efforts in Iraq without sanction from the United Nations, however, Greek Foreign Minister George Papandreou, whose country held the European Union's presidency, stated that signs of a consensus on the matter were emerging. NATO Secretary Lord Robertson said that NATO requires and expects consensus in regard to dealing with a post-war Iraq.[133]

Complicating matters has been the fact that the United States does not wish to be financially responsible for the entire post-war efforts in Iraq. Although the United States wants assistance from the United Nations and single states, it is unlikely that either the United Nations or any single state will agree to pay for the reconstruction of Iraq in the aftermath of a war that was never fully endorsed by the international body in the first place. The international community will likely require reassurances from the

---

[133] CountryWatch (2003b) and see also Papandreou (2003).

United States and the United Kingdom before agreeing to any substantial financial contributions.[134]

Final Decisions … United Nations Resolution 1483

After weeks of discussion, resolution of some of the Iraqi post-war questions were settled with the passage of United Nations Resolution 1483 on May 22, 2003 by a vote of 14-0. The Syrian government boycotted the vote. This resolution recognized the United States and the United Kingdom as occupying powers ("the Authorities") with the specific authorities, responsibilities, and obligations as applicable under international law.

The resolution outlined the initial steps with respect to United Nations activities and the reconstruction activities in Iraq. In addition, the resolution lifted sanctions on international commercial dealings with Iraq; phased out the United Nations Oil-for-Food Programme over a period of six months; requested that the Secretary General of the United Nations appoint a Special Representative to coordinate United Nations efforts in Iraq; and set up a $1 billion Development Fund for Iraq to be used for humanitarian needs and for reconstruction efforts (see Appendix II.3 for the full text of this resolution).

---

[134] CountryWatch (2003b).

Resolution 1483 signaled international acquiescence to actions by the United States and the United Kingdom and set the stage for certain United Nations activities with respect to reconstruction.[135]

Post-Script on the United Nations Involvement

The fact that post-war Iraq in mid-2003 was not fully stabilized evoked calls for greater United Nations involvement by a number of sources. Although the Bush Administration eschewed United Nations involvement beyond the provisions of United Nations Security Council Resolution 1483, it has become clear that with so few coalition troops in Iraq, international peacekeepers would be needed to establish peace and security in Iraq.[136]

The United States had hoped that India might provide additional troop support in Iraq. India -- home to the world's fourth largest military -- declined the request. The government of Prime Minister Atal Behari Vajpayee was unable to build consensus on the matter in the Indian parliament. The Indian government said that although it would contribute to the rebuilding of Iraq's infrastructure and various civilian needs, it would not send peacekeeping troops to Iraq without an expressed United Nations mandate. Members of opposition parties and the prime minister's own Hindu nationalist coalition concurred in saying that without

---

[135] *Ibid.*

[136] McMahon (2003).

a United Nations mandate, Indian troops would not become part of an "occupying force."[137]

Some observers have suggested that whether or not it is the preference of the United States government to limit the role of the United Nations, it could be forced to request burden sharing assistance from that international body as a result of the extremely high cost of post-war operations in Iraq (close to $4 billion per month) as well as the requirement to maintain large numbers of troops on the ground in Iraq. Already, British troops in Iraq have been significantly reduced in strength, thus increasing the potential burden to U.S. forces. To date, however, reconstruction in Iraq has been an effort dictated by the Coalition Forces.

Note on Kurdistan and Turkey

Other issues related to a post-war Iraq involved the Kurdish question and the role of Turkey. In the north, Kurdish "pershmerga" fighters took control of oil-rich cities such as Mosul and Kirkuk, as the Iraqi fighting troops disintegrated. The United States brokered a deal in which the "pershmerga" would control these cities until Coalition Forces were able to ensure security, while at the same time, preventing Turkish troops from entering Iraq.[138]

---

[137] Baruah (2003).

[138] CountryWatch (2003b).

Turkey has been uneasy about the increasing autonomy achieved by Kurds in Iraq since the 1991 Gulf War. The Turks fear that the establishment of a Kurdish state will create instability within the Kurdish factions of Turkey. For its part, the Kurds have agreed not to declare independence (which could potentially spawn Turkish military action), as long as they are granted extensive autonomy within a federal system that preserves Iraq's territorial integrity. Leaders within the Kurdistan Regional Government have said that federalism is the necessary compromise needed in lieu of independence. They have demanded a federal system as compensation for helping the United States.[139]

Turkey, which is itself a centralized state, has balked at the idea of a federal system allowing Kurdish autonomy in Iraq. However, the Kurdish leadership has stated that if federalism were not pursued, all other options ensuring the interests of the Kurdish people would be explored.[140]

Iraqi Leadership Possibilities

On July 11, 2003, after weeks of negotiations with the American and British occupation powers, it was reported that a Governing Council of 21-25 members would be appointed setting up the first interim post-war government in Iraq.

---

[139] *Ibid.*
[140] *Ibid.*

The council would include representatives of the major political, ethnic and religious groups in Iraq and would include, not only resident politicians, but also exile leaders coming home.

Sergio Vieira de Mello, the Special Representative of the United Nations Secretary General Kofi Annan indicated his desire to have the interim Governing Council recognized by the United Nations Security Council so as to give it international legitimacy.[141]

A key issue, which was resolved just prior to the decision on forming the Governing Council, was to make the majority of the representatives on the council Shi'a Muslims reflecting their majority position in the general population. Also, Mr. Bremer, the American Administrator, would guarantee the executive powers of the Governing Council in writing.

Initial representatives of the Governing Council included Abdul Aziz al-Hakim, brother of the Ayatollah Muhammad Bakr al-Hakim the spiritual leader of the Council of the Islamic Revolution in Iraq, Massoud Barzani and Jalal Talabani, leaders of the two main Kurdish factions in Iraq, Ahmad Chalabi, leader of the Iraqi National Congress, Iyad Alawi, head of the Iraqi National Accord, Nasir Kamel Chadirchy, son of the founder of

---

[141] Aita (2003).

the first democratic political party in Iraq, Ibrahim Jafari of the Shi'a Daawa Party, and Adnan Pachachi, formerly Iraq's ambassador to the United Nations in the 1960's. In addition it was reported that Lena Aboud, a woman's rights activist was being asked to participate along with a Chaldean Christian and a Turkmen representative.[142]

Two days later, Iraq held its inaugural meeting of the country's new Governing Council on July 13, 2003. The meeting signified Iraq's first major step toward autonomy in the aftermath of the war, and following several months of coalition rule. The council will function as a predecessor to a new sovereign and democratic government. The council will have the authority to appoint and/or remove cabinet ministers, draft the budget and create a new constitution.[143]

Because the council will exist under the aegis of the Coalition Provisional Authority (CPA), some observers have referred to the structure and system as being similar to that of a constitutional monarchy, in which the crown ratifies legislation and certifies policies that are developed. Conversely, critics have warned that the council might be a perfunctory entity, charged only with endorsing the programs and plans of the Coalition Forces.[144]

---

[142] BBC News (2003i).

[143] CountryWatch (2003b).

[144] *Ibid.*

Several members of the council vocalized their intent to wield their new powers without pressure from the United States and the United Kingdom. Still others called for the immediate expulsion of Coalition Forces. Most, however, focused their energies on the council's governmental functions and duties.[145]

Included in the new council were several representatives from the Shi'a communities. The Shi'a representatives decided to participate in the new council at the last minute, presumably opting to be engaged in the political process of Iraq, rather than be left out altogether. Shi'ites comprise about 60 percent of the total Iraqi population and hold over half the seats in the council.[146]

The significance of the participation of Shi'as in the council is yet unknown. As with all communities, Shi'as are not monolithic and there are many who eschew the council as a symbol of foreign rule and call for Iraq to become an Islamic theocracy. There are some Shi'as who want some sort of symbiotic linkage between Islam and the state and look to Iran as a model. Still others worry about the failure of Iran's revolution and its attempt to build a democratic Islamic state. For them, they want Islam to be respected within the context of a secular Iraqi democracy. They do not wish to replace one form of dictatorship with

---

[145] *Ibid.*

[146] *Ibid.*

another. Thus, in the early days, it is difficult to determine how these internal Shi'a factions will play against -- or in tandem with -- one another.[147]

Other groups in the council include Kurdish organizations, however, exile groups hold almost all of the remaining seats in the council. There are three women represented, as well as a judge who gained notoriety for declaring Saddam Hussein's land confiscation scheme to be unconstitutional.[148]

The formation of the council was orchestrated by the CPA, which held consultations with prominent Iraqis to determine candidates to become council members. Membership on the council was offered by invitation and there were no refusals registered. Some critics say that the domination of Shi'ites and exiles in the council will inevitably result in challenges, while other observers believe that the council's makeup is highly representative of Iraq's general population. Regardless of these competing views, it is agreed that time and effort will have to be expended before the new political leaders can properly connect with the Iraqi populace.[149]

---

[147] Steele (2003).

[148] CountryWatch (2003b).

[149] *Ibid.*

The Iraqi Governing Council

- Ahmed Chalabi, founder of Iraqi National Congress, Shi'ite

- Abdel Aziz al-Hakkim, a leader of the Supreme Council for the Islamic Revolution, Shi'ite

- Ibrahim al-Jaafari, Dawa Islamic Party, Shi'ite

- Nasir al-Chadirch, National Democratic Party, Sunni

- Jalal Talabani, Patriotic Union of Kurdistan, Sunni Kurd

- Massoud Barzani, Kurdistan Democratic Party, Sunni Kurd

- Iyad Alawi, leader of the Iraqi National Accord, Shi'ite

- Ahmed al-Barak, human rights activist, Shi'ite

- Adnan Pachachi, former foreign minister, Sunni

- Aquila al-Hashimi, female, foreign affairs expert, Shi'ite

- Raja Habib al-Khuzai, female, maternity hospital director in south, Shi'ite

- Hamid Majid Moussa, Communist Party, Shi'ite

- Mohammed Bahr al-Uloum, cleric from Najaf, Shi'ite

- Ghazi Mashal Ajil al-Yawer, northern tribal chief, Sunni

- Mohsen Abdel Hamid, Iraqi Islamic Party, Sunni

- Samir Shakir Mahmoud, Sunni

- Mahmoud Othman, Sunni Kurd

- Salaheddine Bahaaeddin, Kurdistan Islamic Union, Sunni Kurd

- Younadem Kana, Assyrian Christian

- Mouwafak al-Rabii, Shi'ite

- Dara Noor Alzin, judge

- Sondul Chapouk, female, Turkoman

- Wael Abdul Latif, Al Basrah governor, Shi'ite

- Abdel-Karim Mahoud al-Mohammedawi, member of Iraqi political party Hezbollah, Shi'ite

- Abdel-Zahraa Othman Mohammed, Dawa Party, Shi'ite

Democracy in Iraq

Most experts concur that the greatest challenge to creating a democratic Iraq lies in the authoritarian legacy of Saddam Hussein.

The optimistic vision espoused by neo-conservative thinkers in the United States has been that Iraq, in the throes of joyful liberation, would naturally gravitate toward unchallenged democratic rule. For them, Iraq would be a model of democracy in the Middle East, and a formula for emulation across the region.

This idealist vision has been countered by realist contentions, which hope -- at best -- for a stable Iraq and the resumption of the rule of law. At worst, the realists, as exemplified by a recent report by the United States Department of State, have warned of chaos in Iraq. The State Department report also noted that there was very little likelihood of a "democratic domino" effect in the Middle East.

Iraqi sociologist, Faleh A. Jabar, has suggested that it may be possible to achieve a scenario in Iraq that encompasses some of the idealist vision along with the pragmatism of the realists.

Still, the fact that Iraq has emerged out of a colonial past as a product of post-colonial nationalism, into being a country largely untouched by democracy or democratic ideals, should not be ignored. In fact, history shows that while authoritarianism was under attack by Islamists in the region during the late 1960s, Iraq was about to come under control by the political elite that brought Saddam Hussein to power. Notably, the Ba'ath Regime took root in the same period of history when the autocratic model of rule was eroding elsewhere across the globe. Thus, it is clear that Iraq has not politically conformed with regional or global trends.[150]

The command economy of Iraq -- an oil rentier economy, in fact -- removed all semblance of freedom from the economic sphere of production. The vast oil wealth in the command economy was used to finance massive state structures, including the military, the education system and the health care system.[151] In this way, basic services and income were controlled by the ruling political entity. Although Iraq developed into being a middle class dominated society during that period from the 1960s to the 1980s, it set the tone for a political paradigm that the Ba'athists would exploit. That is, Iraqi people were provided with food, education, employment and the basics of life in lieu of political freedom and democracy.

---

[150] Jabar (2003). Jabar, a sociologist, delineated his observations about the specific circumstances needed for democracy and the culture of Iraq, in a piece published by BBC News.

[151] *Ibid.*

Jabar notes that the social and political structure was not free from cultural influence. Tribal networks -- mostly associated with the leadership of the Ba'ath regime -- as well as preferred clans from traditional institutions were incorporated into a new political elite. The political culture itself has been described as one dominated by clan connections.[152]

These structures within the single-party system of Iraq will not be easily dismantled since they have become entrenched as part of the normative civil society. The destruction of social associations will have an effect on the very fabric of Iraqi culture and society. It is inevitable that Iraq's economic and political spheres be separated, just as it is clear that the old social structures will not easily apply in a post-war Iraq. Still, the process by which these changes are made has to be considered carefully and with a clear plan of action.

In addition to the local consideration of cultural systems, there are other considerations with regard to the democratization of Iraq, or indeed, any country. As noted by the Cato Institute, political trust, social tolerance, economic development, support of gender equality, and a priority on freedom of speech, as well as popular participation, form the fulcrum of ingredients needed

---

[152] *Ibid.*

to ensure a democratic system.[153] Even with the implementation of a constitution to enshrine these precepts, it is unlikely that Iraq will be transformed automatically. Like many emerging democracies, Iraq will experience an ongoing transitory state if all goes well.

In regard to democratization in Iraq, there are three considerations that should be noted:

First, the fact remains that many elements of the Arab street are demanding greater representation and participation in the policies that affect daily life. Small cadres of leaders who have typically ruled Arab countries wield less power and influence than in the past. The political strife in several Arab countries, such as Algeria, the emergence of more progressive forms of government, as in Lebanon and Turkey, as well as the political reforms that have been implemented in countries such as Jordan, all suggest that there is a desire for change in the way Arab governments have traditionally functioned. Consequently, despite the obvious challenges that are associated with the democratization of Iraq (noted earlier), there are also favorable trends to be considered.[154]

---

[153] Basham (2003). The Cato Institute's Patrick Basham does not hold out hope for the successful democratization of Iraq. Nevertheless, he spells out many of the conditions for democracy.

[154] Ghabra (2001).

Second, in practical terms, the formation of the new Iraqi Governing Council can, in some ways, be regarded as a power-sharing government. The power-sharing modality of inclusive government has been used in various countries with diverse populations with some degree of success. The balkanization of Eastern Europe after the fall of communism has involved ethnic strife, however, it has also included complex paradigms of inclusive government. In Slovenia, for example, seats in the legislature are filled according to proportional representation, with certain seats reserved for ethnic minorities. Within the Middle East, Lebanon's constitutional and republican style of government, with its sectarian provisions, is another example of a complex representative form of government. These types of models can be transformed to meet the needs of the Iraqi population within the context of representative democratic government.

Third, Kurdistan's autonomy within Iraqi sovereignty suggests that there is already a foundation for the federal formula of political administration. The Swiss model of coexisting autonomous regions has allowed for local control, along with a sense of national identity. Likewise, the Belgian model, which recognizes distinct ethno-linguistic communities and divides the country into three distinct "regions," similarly respects the country's diversity, allows for representation of various groups, and also offers limited autonomy to such groups. While these examples are clearly distinct -- historically, culturally and politically -- from Iraq, they suggest that a federal system would not be beyond the realm of possibility in Iraq.

Democracy, along with the various instruments and structures of democratic government, however, will have little chance of flourishing in Iraq without sound economic development. Economic development and political development will have to be realized together in a post-war Iraq.

APPENDIX II.1: UNSC Resolution 1441

United Nations Security Council 1441

Adopted by the Security Council at its 4644th meeting, on November 8, 2002

Explanatory Summary: This resolution was drafted by the United States and the United Kingdom. In general, it states that Iraq "has been and remains in material breach of its obligations" under previous resolutions, and it demanded that "Iraq cooperate immediately, unconditionally, and actively with UNMOVIC and IAEA." All countries of the United Nations Security Council adopted the resolution unanimously. The United States has argued that Security Council Resolution 1441 provided authority for military action against Iraq. Various other members of the United Nations Security Council have been adamant in stating that the resolution does not allow for the automatic use of force against Iraq. The full text of resolution 1441 (2002) reads, as follows:

"The Security Council,

"Recalling all its previous relevant resolutions, in particular its resolutions 661 (1990) of 6 August 1990, 678 (1990) of 29 November 1990, 686 (1991) of 2 March 1991, 687 (1991) of 3 April 1991, 688 (1991) of 5 April 1991, 707 (1991) of 15 August 1991, 715 (1991) of 11 October 1991, 986 (1995) of 14 April 1995, and 1284 (1999) of 17 December 1999, and all the relevant statements of its President,

"Recalling also its resolution 1382 (2001) of 29 November 2001 and its intention to implement it fully,

"*Recognizing* the threat Iraq's non-compliance with Council resolutions and proliferation of weapons of mass destruction and long-range missiles poses to international peace and security,

"*Recalling* that its resolution 678 (1990) authorized Member States to use all necessary means to uphold and implement its resolution 660 (1990) of 2 August 1990 and all relevant resolutions subsequent to resolution 660 (1990) and to restore international peace and security in the area,

"*Further recalling* that its resolution 687 (1991) imposed obligations on Iraq as a necessary step for achievement of its stated objective of restoring international peace and security in the area,

"*Deploring* the fact that Iraq has not provided an accurate, full, final, and complete disclosure, as required by resolution 687 (1991), of all aspects of its programmes to develop weapons of mass destruction and ballistic missiles with a range greater than one hundred and fifty kilometers, and of all holdings of such weapons, their components and production facilities and locations, as well as all other nuclear programmes, including any which it claims are for purposes not related to nuclear-weapons-usable material,

"*Deploring further* that Iraq repeatedly obstructed immediate, unconditional, and unrestricted access to sites designated by the United Nations Special Commission (UNSCOM) and the International Atomic Energy Agency (IAEA), failed to cooperate fully and unconditionally with UNSCOM and IAEA weapons inspectors, as required by resolution 687 (1991), and ultimately ceased all cooperation with UNSCOM and the IAEA in 1998,

"*Deploring* the absence, since December 1998, in Iraq of international monitoring, inspection, and verification, as required by relevant resolutions, of weapons of mass destruction and ballistic missiles, in spite of the Council's repeated demands that Iraq provide immediate, unconditional, and unrestricted access to the United Nations Monitoring, Verification and Inspection Commission (UNMOVIC), established in resolution 1284 (1999) as the successor organization to UNSCOM, and the IAEA, and regretting the consequent prolonging of the crisis in the region and the suffering of the Iraqi people,

"*Deploring also* that the Government of Iraq has failed to comply with its commitments pursuant to resolution 687 (1991) with regard to terrorism, pursuant to resolution 688 (1991) to end repression of its civilian population and to provide access by international humanitarian organizations to all those in need of assistance in Iraq, and pursuant to resolutions 686 (1991), 687 (1991), and 1284 (1999) to return or cooperate in accounting for Kuwaiti and third country nationals wrongfully detained by Iraq, or to return Kuwaiti property wrongfully seized by Iraq,

"*Recalling* that in its resolution 687 (1991) the Council declared that a ceasefire would be based on acceptance by Iraq of the provisions of that resolution, including the obligations on Iraq contained therein,

"*Determined* to ensure full and immediate compliance by Iraq without conditions or restrictions with its obligations under resolution 687 (1991) and other relevant resolutions and recalling that the resolutions of the Council constitute the governing standard of Iraqi compliance,

"*Recalling* that the effective operation of UNMOVIC, as the successor organization to the Special Commission, and the IAEA is essential for the implementation of resolution 687 (1991) and other relevant resolutions,

"*Noting* the letter dated 16 September 2002 from the Minister for Foreign Affairs of Iraq addressed to the Secretary-General is a necessary first step toward rectifying Iraq's continued failure to comply with relevant Council resolutions,

"*Noting further* the letter dated 8 October 2002 from the Executive Chairman of UNMOVIC and the Director-General of the IAEA to General Al-Saadi of the Government of Iraq laying out the practical arrangements, as a follow-up to their meeting in Vienna, that are prerequisites for the resumption of inspections in Iraq by UNMOVIC and the IAEA, and expressing the gravest concern at the continued failure by the Government of Iraq to provide confirmation of the arrangements as laid out in that letter,

"*Reaffirming* the commitment of all Member States to the sovereignty and territorial integrity of Iraq, Kuwait, and the neighboring States,

"*Commending* the Secretary-General and members of the League of Arab States and its Secretary-General for their efforts in this regard,

"*Determined* to secure full compliance with its decisions,

"*Acting* under Chapter VII of the Charter of the United Nations,

"1. *Decides* that Iraq has been and remains in material breach of its obligations under relevant resolutions, including resolution 687 (1991), in particular through Iraq's failure to cooperate with United Nations inspectors and the IAEA, and to complete the actions required under paragraphs 8 to 13 of resolution 687 (1991);

"2. *Decides*, while acknowledging paragraph 1 above, to afford Iraq, by this resolution, a final opportunity to comply with its disarmament obligations under relevant resolutions of the Council; and accordingly decides to set up an enhanced inspection regime with the aim of bringing to full and verified completion the disarmament process established by resolution 687 (1991) and subsequent resolutions of the Council;

"3. *Decides* that, in order to begin to comply with its disarmament obligations, in addition to submitting the required biannual declarations, the Government of Iraq shall provide to UNMOVIC, the IAEA, and the Council, not later than 30 days from the date of this resolution, a currently accurate, full, and complete declaration of all aspects of its programs to develop chemical, biological, and nuclear weapons, ballistic missiles, and other delivery systems such as unmanned aerial vehicles and dispersal systems designed for use on aircraft, including any holdings and precise locations of such weapons, components, sub-components, stocks of agents, and related material and equipment, the locations and work of its research, development and production facilities, as well as all other chemical, biological, and nuclear programs, including any which it claims are for purposes not related to weapon production or material;

"4. *Decides* that false statements or omissions in the declarations submitted by Iraq pursuant to this resolution and failure by Iraq at any time to comply with, and cooperate fully in the implementation of, this resolution shall constitute a further material breach of Iraq's obligations and will be reported to the Council for assessment in accordance with paragraphs 11 and 12 below;

"5. *Decides* that Iraq shall provide UNMOVIC and the IAEA immediate, unimpeded, unconditional, and unrestricted access to any and all, including underground, areas, facilities, buildings, equipment, records, and means of transport which they wish to inspect, as well as immediate, unimpeded, unrestricted, and private access to all officials and other persons whom UNMOVIC or the IAEA wish to interview in the mode or location of UNMOVIC's or the IAEA's choice pursuant to any aspect of their mandates; further decides that UNMOVIC and the IAEA may at their discretion conduct interviews inside or outside of Iraq, may facilitate the travel of those interviewed and family members outside of Iraq, and that, at the sole discretion of UNMOVIC and the IAEA, such interviews may occur without the presence of observers from the Iraqi Government; and instructs UNMOVIC and requests the IAEA to resume inspections no later than 45 days following adoption of this resolution and to update the Council 60 days thereafter;

"6. *Endorses* the 8 October 2002 letter from the Executive Chairman of UNMOVIC and the Director-General of the IAEA to General Al-Saadi of the Government of Iraq, which is annexed hereto, and decides that the contents of the letter shall be binding upon Iraq;

"7. *Decides further* that, in view of the prolonged interruption by Iraq of the presence of UNMOVIC and the IAEA and in order for them to accomplish the tasks set forth in this resolution and all previous relevant resolutions and notwithstanding prior understandings, the Council hereby establishes the following revised or additional authorities, which shall be binding upon Iraq, to facilitate their work in Iraq:

-- UNMOVIC and the IAEA shall determine the composition of their inspection teams and ensure that these teams are composed of the most qualified and experienced experts available;

-- All UNMOVIC and IAEA personnel shall enjoy the privileges and immunities, corresponding to those of experts on mission, provided in the Convention on Privileges and Immunities of the United Nations and the Agreement on the Privileges and Immunities of the IAEA;

-- UNMOVIC and the IAEA shall have unrestricted rights of entry into and out of Iraq, the right to free, unrestricted, and immediate movement to and from inspection sites, and the right to inspect any sites and buildings, including immediate, unimpeded, unconditional, and unrestricted access to Presidential Sites equal to that at other sites, notwithstanding the provisions of resolution 1154 (1998);

-- UNMOVIC and the IAEA shall have the right to be provided by Iraq the names of all personnel currently and formerly associated with Iraq's chemical, biological, nuclear, and ballistic missile programmes and the associated research, development, and production facilities;

-- Security of UNMOVIC and IAEA facilities shall be ensured by sufficient United Nations security guards;

-- UNMOVIC and the IAEA shall have the right to declare, for the purposes of freezing a site to be inspected, exclusion zones, including surrounding areas and transit corridors, in which Iraq will suspend ground and aerial movement so that nothing is changed in or taken out of a site being inspected;

-- UNMOVIC and the IAEA shall have the free and unrestricted use and landing of fixed- and rotary-winged aircraft, including manned and unmanned reconnaissance vehicles;

-- UNMOVIC and the IAEA shall have the right at their sole discretion verifiably to remove, destroy, or render harmless all prohibited weapons, subsystems, components, records, materials, and other related items, and the right to impound or close any facilities or equipment for the production thereof; and

-- UNMOVIC and the IAEA shall have the right to free import and use of equipment or materials for inspections and to seize and export any equipment, materials, or documents taken during inspections, without search of UNMOVIC or IAEA personnel or official or personal baggage;

"8. *Decides further* that Iraq shall not take or threaten hostile acts directed against any representative or personnel of the United Nations or the IAEA or of any Member State taking action to uphold any Council resolution;

"9. *Requests* the Secretary-General immediately to notify Iraq of this resolution, which is binding on Iraq; demands that Iraq confirm within seven days of that notification its intention to comply fully with this resolution; and demands further that Iraq cooperate immediately, unconditionally, and actively with UNMOVIC and the IAEA;

"10. *Requests* all Member States to give full support to UNMOVIC and the IAEA in the discharge of their mandates, including by providing any information related to prohibited programs or other aspects of their mandates, including on Iraqi attempts since 1998 to acquire prohibited items, and by recommending sites to be inspected, persons to be interviewed, conditions of such interviews, and data to be collected, the results of which shall be reported to the Council by UNMOVIC and the IAEA;

"11. *Directs* the Executive Chairman of UNMOVIC and the Director-General of the IAEA to report immediately to the Council any interference by Iraq with inspection activities, as well as any failure by Iraq to comply with its disarmament obligations, including its obligations regarding inspections under this resolution;

"12. *Decides* to convene immediately upon receipt of a report in accordance with paragraphs 4 or 11 above, in order to consider the situation and the need for full compliance with all of the relevant Council resolutions in order to secure international peace and security;

"13. *Recalls*, in that context, that the Council has repeatedly warned Iraq that it will face serious consequences as a result of its continued violations of its obligations;

"14. *Decides* to remain seized of the matter."[1]

---

[1] United Nations Security Council (2002).

APPENDIX II.2: Draft Resolution of March 7, 2003

Draft Resolution by the United States, the United Kingdom and Spain on Iraq March 7, 2003

Explanatory Summary: The original draft resolution by the United States, the United Kingdom and Spain was later amended by the United Kingdom. In summary, it declares that, "Iraq will have failed to take the final opportunity afforded by resolution 1441 (2002) unless, on or before March 17, 2003, the Council concludes that Iraq has demonstrated full, unconditional, immediate and active cooperation." As such, the draft calls for the approval of military action against Iraq. Because of the lack of support for the terms of the draft resolution, it was withdrawn on March 17, 2003. The full text of the draft resolution (2003) reads, as follows:

The Security Council,

Recalling all its previous relevant resolutions, in particular its resolutions 661 (1990) of August 1990, 678 (1990) of 29 November 1990, 686 (1991) of 2 March 1991, 687 (1991) of 3 April 1991, 688 (1991) of 5 April 1991, 707 (1991) of 15 August 1991, 715 (1991) of 11 October 1991, 986 (1995) of 14 April 1995, 1284 (1999) of 17 December 1999 and 1441 (2002) of 8 November 2002, and all the relevant statements of its President,

Recalling that in its resolution 687 (1991) the Council declared that a ceasefire would be based on acceptance by Iraq of the provisions of that resolution, including the obligations on Iraq contained therein,

Recalling that its resolution 1441 (2002), while deciding that Iraq has been and remains in material breach of its obligations, afforded Iraq a final opportunity to comply with its disarmament obligations under relevant resolutions,

Recalling that in its resolution 1441 (2002) the Council decided that false statements or omissions in the declaration submitted by Iraq pursuant to that resolution and failure by Iraq at any time to comply with, and cooperate fully in the implementation of, that resolution, would constitute a further material breach,

Noting, in that context, that in its resolution 1441 (2002), the Council recalled that it has repeatedly warned Iraq that it will face serious consequences as a result of its continued violations of its obligations,

Noting that Iraq has submitted a declaration pursuant to its resolution 1441 (2002) containing false statements and omissions and has failed to comply with, and cooperate fully in the implementation of, that resolution,

Reaffirming the commitment of all Member States to the sovereignty and territorial integrity of Iraq, Kuwait, and the neighboring States,

Mindful of its primary responsibility under the Charter of the United Nations for the maintenance of international peace and security,

Recognizing the threat Iraq's non-compliance with Council resolutions and proliferation of weapons of mass destruction and long-range missiles poses to international peace and security,

Determined to secure full compliance with its decisions and to restore international peace and security in the area,

Acting under Chapter VII of the Charter of the United Nations,

1. *Reaffirms* the need for full implementation of resolution 1441 (2002);

2. *Calls on* Iraq immediately to take the decisions necessary in the interests of its people and the region;

3. *Decides* that Iraq will have failed to take the final opportunity afforded by resolution 1441 (2002) unless, on or before 17 March 2003, the Council concludes that Iraq has demonstrated full, unconditional, immediate and active cooperation in accordance with its disarmament obligations under resolution 1441 (2002) and previous relevant resolutions, and is yielding possession to UNMOVIC and the IAEA of all weapons, weapon delivery and support systems and structures, prohibited by resolution 687 (1991) and all subsequent relevant resolutions, and all information regarding prior destruction of such items;

4. *Decides* to remain seized of the matter.[1]

---

[1] United Nations Security Council (2003a).

APPENDIX II.3: UNSC Resolution 1483

United Nations Security Council 1483

Adopted by the Security Council at its 4761st meeting, on May 22, 2003

Explanatory Summary: This resolution was adopted 14-0 in the Security Council. Syria was absent for the vote. The resolution gave the United States and United Kingdom control of Iraq as the "occupying powers" or "Authority" and removed the sanctions that had been in place against Iraq for over a decade. Although the United States and the United Kingdom viewed the resolution as a legitimization of Coalition Forces' actions in Iraq, other members of the council viewed the resolution differently. The full text of resolution 1483 (2003) reads, as follows:

The Security Council,

Recalling all its previous relevant resolutions,
Reaffirming the sovereignty and territorial integrity of Iraq,
Reaffirming also the importance of the disarmament of Iraqi weapons of mass destruction and of eventual confirmation of the disarmament of Iraq,

Stressing the right of the Iraqi people freely to determine their own political future and control their own natural resources, welcoming the commitment of all parties concerned to support the creation of an environment in which they may do so as soon as possible, and expressing resolve that the day when Iraqis govern themselves must come quickly,

Encouraging efforts by the people of Iraq to form a representative government based on the rule of law that affords equal rights and justice to all Iraqi citizens without regard to ethnicity, religion, or gender, and, in this connection, recalls resolution 1325 (2000) of 31 October 2000,

Welcoming the first steps of the Iraqi people in this regard, and noting in this connection the 15 April 2003 Nasiriya statement and the 28 April 2003 Baghdad statement,

Resolved that the United Nations should play a vital role in humanitarian relief, the reconstruction of Iraq, and the restoration and establishment of national and local institutions for representative governance,

Noting the statement of 12 April 2003 by the Ministers of Finance and Central Bank Governors of the Group of Seven Industrialized Nations in which the members recognized the need for a multilateral effort to help rebuild and develop Iraq and for the need for assistance from the International Monetary Fund and the World Bank in these efforts,

Welcoming also the resumption of humanitarian assistance and the continuing efforts of the Secretary-General and the specialized agencies to provide food and medicine to the people of Iraq,
Welcoming the appointment by the Secretary-General of his Special Adviser on Iraq,

Affirming the need for accountability for crimes and atrocities committed by the previous Iraqi regime,

Stressing the need for respect for the archaeological, historical, cultural, and religious heritage of Iraq, and for the continued protection of archaeological, historical, cultural, and religious sites, museums, libraries, and monuments,

Noting the letter of 8 May 2003 from the Permanent Representatives of the United States of America and the United Kingdom of Great Britain and Northern Ireland to the President of the Security Council

(S/2003/538) and recognizing the specific authorities, responsibilities, and obligations under applicable international law of these states as occupying powers under unified command (the "Authority"),

Noting further that other States that are not occupying powers are working now or in the future may work under the Authority,
Welcoming further the willingness of Member States to contribute to stability and security in Iraq by contributing personnel, equipment, and other resources under the Authority,

Concerned that many Kuwaitis and Third-State Nationals still are not accounted for since 2 August 1990,

Determining that the situation in Iraq, although improved, continues to constitute a threat to international peace and security,

Acting under Chapter VII of the Charter of the United Nations,

1. *Appeals* to Member States and concerned organizations to assist the people of Iraq in their efforts to reform their institutions and rebuild their country, and to contribute to conditions of stability and security in Iraq in accordance with this resolution;

2. *Calls upon* all Member States in a position to do so to respond immediately to the humanitarian appeals of the United Nations and other international organizations for Iraq and to help meet the humanitarian and other needs of the Iraqi people by providing food, medical supplies, and resources necessary for reconstruction and rehabilitation of Iraq's economic infrastructure;

3. *Appeals* to Member States to deny safe haven to those members of the previous Iraqi regime who are alleged to be responsible for crimes and atrocities and to support actions to bring them to justice;

4. *Calls upon* the Authority, consistent with the Charter of the United Nations and other relevant international law, to promote the welfare of the Iraqi people through the effective administration of the territory, including in particular working towards the restoration of conditions of security and stability and the creation of conditions in which the Iraqi people can freely determine their own political future;

5. *Calls upon* all concerned to comply fully with their obligations under international law including in particular the Geneva Conventions of 1949 and the Hague Regulations of 1907;

6. *Calls upon* the Authority and relevant organizations and individuals to continue efforts to locate, identify, and repatriate all Kuwaiti and Third-State Nationals or the remains of those present in Iraq on or after 2 August 1990, as well as the Kuwaiti archives, that the previous Iraqi regime failed to undertake, and, in this regard, directs the High-Level Coordinator, in consultation with the International Committee of the Red Cross and the Tripartite Commission and with the appropriate support of the people of Iraq and in coordination with the Authority, to take steps to fulfill his mandate with respect to the fate of Kuwaiti and Third-State National missing persons and property;

7. *Decides* that all Member States shall take appropriate steps to facilitate the safe return to Iraqi institutions, of Iraqi cultural property and other items of archaeological, historical, cultural, rare scientific, and religious importance illegally removed from the Iraq National Museum, the National Library, and other locations in Iraq since the adoption of resolution 661 (1990) of 2 August 1990, including by establishing a prohibition on trade in or transfer of such items and items with respect to which reasonable suspicion exists that they have been illegally removed, and calls upon the United Nations Educational, Scientific, and Cultural Organization, Interpol, and other international organizations, as appropriate, to assist in the implementation of this paragraph;

8. *Requests* the Secretary-General to appoint a Special Representative for Iraq whose independent responsibilities shall involve reporting regularly to the Council on his activities under this resolution, coordinating activities of the United Nations in post-conflict processes in Iraq, coordinating among United Nations and international agencies engaged in humanitarian assistance and reconstruction activities in Iraq, and, in coordination with the Authority, assisting the people of Iraq through:

(a) *coordinating* humanitarian and reconstruction assistance by United Nations agencies and between United Nations agencies and non-governmental organizations;

(b) *promoting* the safe, orderly, and voluntary return of refugees and displaced persons;

(c) *working* intensively with the Authority, the people of Iraq, and others concerned to advance efforts to restore and establish national and local institutions for representative governance, including by working together to facilitate a process leading to an internationally recognized, representative government of Iraq;

(d) *facilitating* the reconstruction of key infrastructure, in cooperation with other international organizations;

(e) *promoting* economic reconstruction and the conditions for sustainable development, including through coordination with national and regional organizations, as appropriate, civil society, donors and the international financial institutions;

(f) *encouraging* international efforts to contribute to basic civilian administration functions;

(g) *promoting* the protection of human rights;

(h) *encouraging* international efforts to rebuild the capacity of the Iraqi civilian police force; and

(i) *encouraging* international efforts to promote legal and judicial reform;

9. *Supports* the formation, by the people of Iraq with the help of the Authority and working with the Special Representative, of an Iraqi interim administration as a transitional administration run by Iraqis,

until an internationally recognized, representative government is established by the people of Iraq and assumes the responsibilities of the Authority;

10. *Decides* that, with the exception of prohibitions related to the sale or supply to Iraq of arms and related materiel other than those arms and related materiel required by the Authority to serve the purposes of this and other related resolutions, all prohibitions related to trade with Iraq and the provision of financial or economic resources to Iraq established by resolution 661 (1990) and subsequent relevant resolutions, including resolution 778 (1992) of 2 October 1992, shall no longer apply;

11. *Reaffirms* that Iraq must meet its disarmament obligations, encourages the United Kingdom of Great Britain and Northern Ireland and the United States of America to keep the Council informed of their activities in this regard, and underlines the intention of the Council to revisit the mandates of the United Nations Monitoring and Verification Commission and the International Atomic Energy Agency as set forth in resolutions 687 (1991) of 3 April 1991, 1284 (1999) of 17 December 1999, and 1441 (2002) of 8 November 2002;

12. *Notes* the establishment of a Development Fund for Iraq to be held by the Central Bank of Iraq and to be audited by independent public accountants approved by the International Advisory and Monitoring Board of the Development Fund for Iraq and looks forward to the early meeting of that International Advisory and Monitoring Board, whose members shall include duly qualified representatives of the Secretary-General, of the Managing Director of the International Monetary Fund, of the Director-General of the Arab Fund for Social and Economic Development, and of the President of the World Bank;

13. *Notes further* that the funds in the Development Fund for Iraq shall be disbursed at the direction of the Authority, in consultation with the Iraqi interim administration, for the purposes set out in paragraph 14 below;

14. *Underlines* that the Development Fund for Iraq shall be used in a transparent manner to meet the humanitarian needs of the Iraqi people, for the economic reconstruction and repair of Iraq's infrastructure, for the continued disarmament of Iraq, and for the costs of Iraqi civilian administration, and for other purposes benefiting the people of Iraq;

15. *Calls upon* the international financial institutions to assist the people of Iraq in the reconstruction and development of their economy and to facilitate assistance by the broader donor community, and welcomes the readiness of creditors, including those of the Paris Club, to seek a solution to Iraq's sovereign debt problems;

16. *Requests* also that the Secretary-General, in coordination with the Authority, continue the exercise of his responsibilities under Security Council resolution 1472 (2003) of 28 March 2003 and 1476 (2003) of 24 April 2003, for a period of six months following the adoption of this resolution, and terminate within this time period, in the most cost effective manner, the ongoing operations of the Oil-for-Food Programme (the "Program"), both at headquarters level and in the field, transferring responsibility for the administration of any remaining activity under the Program to the Authority, including by taking the following necessary measures:
(a) *to facilitate* as soon as possible the shipment and authenticated delivery of priority civilian goods as identified by the Secretary-General and representatives designated by him, in coordination with the Authority and the Iraqi interim administration, under approved and funded contracts previously concluded by the previous Government of Iraq, for the humanitarian relief of the people of Iraq, including, as necessary, negotiating adjustments in the terms or conditions of these contracts and respective letters of credit as set forth in paragraph 4 (d) of resolution 1472 (2003);
(b) *to review*, in light of changed circumstances, in coordination with the Authority and the Iraqi interim administration, the relative utility of each approved and funded contract with a view to determining whether

such contracts contain items required to meet the needs of the people of Iraq both now and during reconstruction, and to postpone action on those contracts determined to be of questionable utility and the respective letters of credit until an internationally recognized, representative government of Iraq is in a position to make its own determination as to whether such contracts shall be fulfilled;

(c) *to provide* the Security Council within 21 days following the adoption of this resolution, for the Security Council's review and consideration, an estimated operating budget based on funds already set aside in the account established pursuant to paragraph 8 (d) of resolution 986 (1995) of 14 April 1995, identifying:

(i) all known and projected costs to the United Nations required to ensure the continued functioning of the activities associated with implementation of the present resolution, including operating and administrative expenses associated with the relevant United Nations agencies and programs responsible for the implementation of the Program both at Headquarters and in the field;

(ii) all known and projected costs associated with termination of the Program;

(iii) all known and projected costs associated with restoring Government of Iraq funds that were provided by Member States to the Secretary-General as requested in paragraph 1 of resolution 778 (1992) of 2 October 1992; and

(iv) all known and projected costs associated with the Special Representative and the qualified representative of the Secretary-General identified to serve on the International Advisory and Monitoring Board, for the six month time period defined above, following which these costs shall be borne by the United Nations;

(d) *to consolidate* into a single fund the accounts established pursuant to paragraphs 8 (a) and 8 (b) of resolution 986 (1995);

(e) *to fulfill* all remaining obligations related to the termination of the Program, including negotiating, in the most cost effective manner, any necessary settlement payments, which shall be made from the escrow accounts established pursuant to paragraphs 8 (a) and 8 (b) of resolution 986 (1995), with those parties that previously have entered into contractual obligations with the Secretary-General under the Program, and to determine, in coordination with the Authority and the Iraqi interim administration, the future status of contracts undertaken by the United Nations and related United Nations agencies under the accounts established pursuant to paragraphs 8 (b) and 8 (d) of resolution 986 (1995);

(f) *to provide* the Security Council, 30 days prior to the termination of the Program, with a comprehensive strategy developed in close coordination with the Authority and the Iraqi interim administration that would lead to the delivery of all relevant documentation and the transfer of all operational responsibility of the Program to the Authority;

17. *Requests* further that the Secretary-General transfer as soon as possible to the Development Fund for Iraq 1 billion United States dollars from unencumbered funds in the accounts established pursuant to paragraphs 8 (a) and 8 (b) of resolution 986 (1995), restore Government of Iraq funds that were provided by Member States to the Secretary-General as requested in paragraph 1 of resolution 778 (1992), and decides that, after deducting all relevant United Nations expenses associated with the shipment of authorized contracts and costs to the Program outlined in paragraph 16 (c) above, including residual obligations, all surplus funds in the escrow accounts established pursuant to paragraphs 8 (a), 8 (b), 8 (d), and 8 (f) of resolution 986 (1995) shall be transferred at the earliest possible time to the Development Fund for Iraq;

18. *Decides to* terminate effective on the adoption of this resolution the functions related to the observation and monitoring activities undertaken by the Secretary-General under the Program, including the monitoring of the export of petroleum and petroleum products from Iraq;

19. *Decides* to terminate the Committee established pursuant to paragraph 6 of resolution 661 (1990) at the conclusion of the six

months period called for in paragraph 16 above and further decides that the Committee shall identify individuals and entities referred to in paragraph 23 below;

20. *Decides* that all export sales of petroleum, petroleum products, and natural gas from Iraq following the date of the adoption of this resolution shall be made consistent with prevailing international market best practices, to be audited by independent public accountants reporting to the International Advisory and Monitoring Board referred to in paragraph 12 above in order to ensure transparency, and decides further that, except as provided in paragraph 21 below, all proceeds from such sales shall be deposited into the Development Fund for Iraq, until such time as an internationally recognized, representative government of Iraq is properly constituted;

21. *Decides* further that 5 percent of the proceeds referred to in paragraph 20 above shall be deposited into the Compensation Fund established in accordance with resolution 687 (1991) of 3 April 1991 and subsequent relevant resolutions and that, unless an internationally recognized, representative government of Iraq and the Governing Council of the United Nations Compensation Commission, in the exercise of its authority over methods of ensuring that payments are made into the Compensation Fund, decide otherwise, this requirement shall be binding on a properly constituted, internationally recognized, representative government of Iraq and any successor thereto;

22. *Noting* the relevance of the establishment of an internationally recognized, representative government of Iraq and the desirability of prompt completion of the restructuring of Iraq's debt as referred to in paragraph 15 above, further decides that, until December 31, 2007, unless the Council decides otherwise, petroleum, petroleum products, and natural gas originating in Iraq shall be immune, until title passes to the initial purchaser, from legal proceedings against them and not be subject to any form of attachment, garnishment, or execution, and that all States shall take any steps that may be necessary under their

respective domestic legal systems to assure this protection, and that proceeds and obligations arising from sales thereof, as well as the Development Fund for Iraq, shall enjoy privileges and immunities equivalent to those enjoyed by the United Nations except that the above-mentioned privileges and immunities will not apply with respect to any legal proceeding in which recourse to such proceeds or obligations is necessary to satisfy liability for damages assessed in connection with an ecological accident, including an oil spill, that occurs after the date of adoption of this resolution;

23. *Decides* that all Member States in which there are:
(a) funds or other financial assets or economic resources of the previous Government of Iraq or its state bodies, corporations, or agencies, located outside Iraq as of the date of this resolution, or
(b) funds or other financial assets or economic resources that have been removed from Iraq, or acquired, by Saddam Hussein or other senior officials of the former Iraqi regime and their immediate family members, including entities owned or controlled, directly or indirectly, by them or by persons acting on their behalf or at their direction,
(c) shall freeze without delay those funds or other financial assets or economic resources and, unless these funds or other financial assets or economic resources are themselves the subject of a prior judicial, administrative, or arbitral lien or judgment, immediately shall cause their transfer to the Development Fund for Iraq, it being understood that, unless otherwise addressed, claims made by private individuals or non-government entities on those transferred funds or other financial assets may be presented to the internationally recognized, representative government of Iraq; and decides further that all such funds or other financial assets or economic resources shall enjoy the same privileges, immunities, and protections as provided under paragraph 22;

24. *Requests* the Secretary-General to report to the Council at regular intervals on the work of the Special Representative with respect to the implementation of this resolution and on the work of the International

Advisory and Monitoring Board and encourages the United Kingdom of Great Britain and Northern Ireland and the United States of America to inform the Council at regular intervals of their efforts under this resolution;

25. *Decides* to review the implementation of this resolution within twelve months of adoption and to consider further steps that might be necessary;

26. *Calls upon* Member States and international and regional organizations to contribute to the implementation of this resolution;

27. *Decides* to remain seized of this matter. [1]

---

[1] United Nations Security Council (2003b).

APPENDIX II.4: Significant UNSC Resolutions on Iraq

Significant United Nations Security Council Resolutions related to post-war Iraq and the removal of Saddam Hussein from power:

UNSC 1483 (May 22, 2003): lifted non-military sanctions, recognized Britain and the United States as occupying powers ('The Authority'); called on them to attempt to improve security and stability, and provide opportunities for the Iraqis to determine their political future; created the position of United Nations Special Representative to Iraq; and called for establishment of a Development Fund for Iraq.

UNSC 1476 (April 24, 2003): extended the provisions contained in paragraph 4 of resolution 1472 (2003) until 3 June 2003.

UNSC 1472 (March 28, 2003): gave United Nations increased authority to administer the Oil-for-Food Programme for next 45 days and authorized the Secretary-General to establish (alternative) sites for the delivery of humanitarian supplies and equipment.

UNSC 1454 (December 2002): implemented revisions to the Goods Review List.

UNSC 1447 (December 2002): extended the Oil-for-Food Programme by 6 months, called for the council to review the goods review list within one month and asked the Secretary General to produce a report on the adequacy of Iraq's distribution chains.

UNSC 1443 (November 25, 2002): extended the Oil-for-Food Programme by 9 days only due to disagreements over the Goods Review List.

Significant United Nations Resolutions Leading Up to the War of 2003:

UNSC 1441 (November 8, 2002): stated that Iraq "has been and remains in material breach of its obligations" under previous resolutions, and it demanded that "Iraq cooperate immediately, unconditionally, and actively with UNMOVIC and IAEA"; called for the immediate and complete disarmament of Iraq and its prohibited weapons; called for full access by UNMOVIC and the IAEA to Iraqi facilities, individuals, means of transportation, and documents; and stated that the Security Council has repeatedly warned Iraq and that it will face serious consequences as a result of its continued violations of its obligations.

Note: Earlier drafts of this resolution are as follows: the U.S./U.K. drafts of October 2, 2002, October 25, 2002 and November 5, 2002; the Russian draft and the French draft of October 23, 2002.

UNSCR 1284 (December 17, 1999): created the United Nations Monitoring, Verification and Inspections Commission (UNMOVIC) to replace previous weapons inspection team (UNSCOM); demanded that Iraq allow UNMOVIC "immediate, unconditional and unrestricted access" to Iraqi officials and facilities; required Iraq to fulfill its commitment to return Gulf War prisoners; and called on Iraq to distribute humanitarian goods and medical supplies to its people and address the needs of vulnerable Iraqis without discrimination.

UNSCR 1205 (November 5, 1998): condemned the decision by Iraq of 31 October 1998 to cease cooperation with U.N. inspectors as "a flagrant violation" of UNSCR 687 and other resolutions and required Iraq to provide "immediate, complete and unconditional cooperation" with U.N. and IAEA inspectors.

UNSCR 1194 (September 9, 1998): condemned the decision by Iraq of 5 August 1998 to suspend cooperation with U.N. and IAEA inspectors, which constitutes "a totally unacceptable contravention" of its obligations under UNSCR 687, 707, 715, 1060, 1115, and 1154; and required Iraq to cooperate fully with U.N. and IAEA weapons inspectors, and allow immediate, unconditional and unrestricted access.

UNSCR 1154 (March 2, 1998): required Iraq to cooperate fully with U.N. and IAEA weapons inspectors and allow immediate, unconditional and unrestricted access, and noted that any violation would have the "severest consequences for Iraq".

UNSCR 1137 (November 12, 1997): condemned the continued violations by Iraq of previous U.N. resolutions, including its "implicit threat to the safety of" aircraft operated by U.N. inspectors and warned against any tampering with U.N. inspector monitoring equipment; reaffirmed Iraq's responsibility to ensure the safety of U.N. inspectors; and required Iraq to cooperate fully with U.N. weapons inspectors and allow immediate, unconditional and unrestricted access.

UNSCR 1134 (October 23, 1997): condemned repeated refusal of Iraqi authorities to allow access" to U.N. inspectors, which constitutes a "flagrant violation" of UNSCR 687, 707, 715, and 1060; required Iraq to cooperate fully with U.N. weapons inspectors and allow immediate, unconditional and unrestricted access; and required Iraq to give immediate, unconditional and unrestricted access to Iraqi officials whom U.N. inspectors want to interview.

UNSCR 1115 (June 21, 1997): condemned repeated refusal of Iraqi authorities to allow access to U.N. inspectors, which constitutes a "clear and flagrant violation" of UNSCR 687, 707, 715, and 1060; required Iraq to cooperate fully with U.N. weapons inspectors and allow immediate, unconditional and unrestricted access; and required Iraq to give immediate, unconditional and unrestricted access to Iraqi officials whom U.N. inspectors want to interview.

UNSCR 1060 (June 12, 1996): deplored Iraq's refusal to allow access to U.N. inspectors and Iraq's "clear violations" of previous U.N. resolutions; and required Iraq to cooperate fully with U.N. weapons inspectors and allow immediate, unconditional and unrestricted access.

UNSCR 1051 (March 27, 1996): required Iraq to report shipments of dual-use items related to weapons of mass destruction to the U.N. and IAEA and required Iraq to cooperate fully with U.N. and IAEA inspectors and allow immediate, unconditional and unrestricted access.

UNSCR 949 (October 15, 1994): condemned Iraq's recent military deployments toward Kuwait; required Iraq not to utilize its military or other forces in a hostile manner to threaten its neighbors or U.N. operations in Iraq and required Iraq to cooperate fully with U.N. weapons inspectors; forbade Iraq to enhance its military capability in southern Iraq.

UNSCR 715 (October 11, 1991): required Iraq to cooperate fully with U.N. and IAEA inspectors.

UNSCR 707 (August 15, 1991): condemned Iraq's "serious violation" of UNSCR 687; further condemned Iraq's noncompliance with IAEA and its obligations under the Nuclear Non-Proliferation Treaty; required Iraq to halt nuclear activities of all kinds until the Security Council deemed Iraq in full compliance; required Iraq to make a full, final and complete disclosure of all aspects of its weapons of mass destruction and missile programs; required Iraq to allow U.N. and IAEA inspectors immediate, unconditional and unrestricted access; required Iraq to cease attempts to conceal or move weapons of mass destruction, and related materials and facilities; required Iraq to allow U.N. and IAEA inspectors to conduct inspection flights throughout Iraq; and required Iraq to provide transportation, medical and logistical support for U.N. and IAEA inspectors.

UNSCR 688 (April 5, 1991): condemned repression of the Iraqi civilian population, the consequences of which threatened international peace and security; required Iraq to immediately end repression of its civilian population; and required Iraq to allow immediate access to international humanitarian organizations to those in need of assistance.

UNSCR 687 (April 3, 1991): required Iraq to "unconditionally accept" the destruction, removal or rendering harmless "under international supervision" of all "chemical and biological weapons and all stocks of agents and all related subsystems and components and all research, development, support and manufacturing facilities"; required Iraq to "unconditionally agree not to acquire or develop nuclear weapons or nuclear-weapons-usable material" or any research, development or manufacturing facilities; required Iraq to "unconditionally accept" the destruction, removal or rendering harmless "under international supervision" of all "ballistic missiles with a range greater than 150 KM and related major parts and repair and production facilities"; forbade Iraq to "use, develop, construct or acquire" any weapons of mass destruction; required Iraq to reaffirm its obligations under the Nuclear Non-Proliferation Treaty; created the United Nations Special Commission (UNSCOM) to verify the elimination of Iraq's chemical and biological weapons programs and mandated that the International Atomic Energy Agency (IAEA) verify elimination of Iraq's nuclear weapons program; required Iraq to declare fully its weapons of mass destruction programs; forbade Iraq to commit or support terrorism, or allow terrorist organizations to operate in Iraq; and required Iraq to cooperate in accounting for the missing and dead Kuwaitis and others; required Iraq to return Kuwaiti property seized during the Gulf War.

UNSCR 686 (March 2, 1991): required Iraq to release prisoners detained during the Gulf War; required Iraq to return Kuwaiti property seized during the Gulf War; and required Iraq to accept liability under international law for damages from its illegal invasion of Kuwait.

UNSCR 678 (November 29, 1990): required Iraq to comply fully with UNSCR 660 (regarding Iraq's illegal invasion of Kuwait) "and all subsequent relevant resolutions" and authorized U.N. Member States "to use all necessary means to uphold and implement resolution 660 and all subsequent relevant resolutions and to restore international peace and security in the area".

Significant United Nations Security Council Resolutions Related to the U.N. Oil-for-Food Programme

Resolution 1483 (22 May 2003): lifted civilian sanctions, provided for termination of the Oil-for-Food Programme within six months and transferred responsibility for the administration of any remaining activity to The Authority representing the occupying powers.

Resolution 1476 (24 April 2003): extended the provisions contained in paragraph 4 of resolution 1472 (2003) until 3 June 2003 and noted that these provisions may be subject to further renewal by the Council.

Resolution 1472 (28 March 2003): adopted unanimously by the Security Council on 28 March to adjust the Oil-for-Food Programme and give the Secretary-General authority for a period of 45 days to facilitate the delivery and receipt of goods contracted by the Government of Iraq for the humanitarian needs of its people.

Resolution 1454 (30 December 2002): introduced changes to the list of goods subject to review and approval by the 661 Committee under the United Nations Oil-for-Food Programme (the changes to the goods review list (GRL) also required a thorough review of the List and its procedures, both 90 days after the commencement of phase XIII of the program, 5 December 2002, and prior to the end of its defined 180-day period, 3 June 2003).

Resolution 1447 (4 December 2002): renewed the Oil-for-Food Programme for another 180 days until 3 June 2003 (phase XIII).

Resolution 1443 (25 November 2002): extended phase XII for another 9 days until 4 December 2002.

Resolution 1409 (14 May 2002): introduced the Goods Review List (GRL) and a new set of procedures for the processing of contracts for humanitarian supplies and equipment (this marked the second most significant change in the program after resolution 1284 (1999)) and extended the program for another 180 days (phase XII), effective 30 May 2002 - this phase ended on 25 November 2002.

Resolution 1382 (29 November 2001): renewed the Oil-for-Food Programme for another 180 days until 29 May 2002 (phase XI).

Resolution 1360 (3 July 2001): renewed the Oil-for-Food Programme for another 150 days until 30 November 2001 (phase X).

Resolution 1352 (1 June 2001): extended the terms of resolution 1330 (2000), or phase IX, for another 30 days.

Resolution 1330 (5 December 2000): extended the program for additional 180 days (phase IX).

Resolution 1302 (8 June 2000): renewed the Oil-for-Food Programme for another 180 days until 5 December 2000 (phase VIII).

Resolution 1293 (31 March 2000): increased oil spare parts allocation from $300 million to $600 million under phases VI and VII.

Resolution 1284 (17 December 1999): stressed the importance of a comprehensive approach to the full implementation of all relevant Security Council resolutions regarding Iraq and the need for Iraqi compliance with these resolutions and established, as a subsidiary body of the Council, the United Nations Monitoring, Verification and Inspection Commission (UNMOVIC), which replaced the Special Commission.

Resolution 1281 (10 December 1999): renewed the Oil-for-Food Programme for a further six months (phase VII).

Resolution 1280 (3 December 1999): extended phase VI of the Oil-for-Food Programme for one week, until 11 December 1999.

Resolution 1275 (19 November 1999): extended phase VI of the Oil-for-Food Programme for two weeks, until 4 December 1999.

Resolution 1266 (4 October 1999): permitted Iraq to export an additional amount of $3.04 billion of oil in phase VI to make up for the deficit in revenue in phases IV and V.

Resolution 1242 (21 May 1999): renewed the Oil-for-Food Programme for a further six months.

Resolution 1210 (24 November 1998): renewed the Oil-for-Food Programme for a further six months from 26 November at the higher levels established by resolution 1153 and including additional oil spare parts.

Resolution 1175 (19 June 1998): authorized Iraq to buy $300 million worth of oil spare parts in order to reach the ceiling of $5.256 billion.

Resolution 1158 (25 March 1998): permitted Iraq to export additional oil in the 90 days from 5 March, 1998 to compensate for delayed resumption of oil production and reduced oil prices.

Resolution 1153 (20 February 1998): allowed the export of $5.256 billion of Iraqi oil.

Resolution 1143 (4 December 1997): extended the Oil-for-Food Programme for another 180 days

Resolution 1129 (12 September 1997): decided that the provisions of resolution 1111 (1997) should remain in force, but authorizes special provisions to allow Iraq to sell petroleum in a more favorable time frame.

Resolution 1111 (4 June 1997): extended the term of SCR 986 (1995) another 180 days.

Resolution 1051 (27 March 1996): established the export/import monitoring system for Iraq.

Resolution 986 (14 April 1995): enabled Iraq to sell up to $1 billion of oil every 90 days and to use the proceeds for humanitarian supplies to the country; and set terms of reference for the Oil-for-Food Programme.

Resolution 778 (2 October 1992): authorized transferring back money produced by any Iraqi oil transaction on or after 6 Aug 90 and which had been deposited into the Escrow account, to the states or accounts concerned for so long as the oil exports took place or until sanctions were lifted.

Resolution 712 (19 September 1991): confirmed the sum of $1.6 billion to be raised by the sale of Iraqi oil in a six-month period to fund an Oil-for-Food Programme.

Resolution 706 (15 August 1991): set outs a mechanism for an Oil-for-Food Programme and authorized an escrow account to be established by the Secretary-General.

Resolution 687 (3 April 1991): set terms for a cease-fire, maintained the terms of the embargo.

Resolution 661 (6 August 1990): imposed comprehensive economic sanctions on Iraq exempting food and medicine and established the 661 Committee to oversee implementation of the sanctions.[1]

---

[1] United Nations Data, Office of the Iraq Oil-for-Food Programme (2003) and US Department of State (2003).

III. The Iraqi Resource Base

An Overview of the Iraqi Economy

Macroeconomic Overview

Iraq's economy has been severely damaged over the past 25 years, by war, mismanagement, corruption and the U.N. sanctions. A summary of key economic indicators over the past 5 years as well as a forecast for 2003 is shown in Table III-1.[1] The change of political regime in 2003 marks the beginning of radical economic changes that should unleash the considerable economic potential locked up in Iraq's oil and gas reserves, in its agricultural land, and in its relatively well-educated and long-repressed people.

Iraq's economy has long been dominated by the oil sector, which has traditionally provided about 95 percent of the foreign exchange earnings.[2]

---

[1] The composition of nominal GDP is estimated in accordance with the notes in Appendix III.1.

[2] U.S. Central Intelligence Agency (2002), p. 4.

Table III-1
Key Economic Indicators: Iraq 1998-2003

Key Macroeconomic Indicators	Units	1998	1999	2000	2001	2002	2003E
Real GDP (2000 Prices)	$'s US billions	18.7	24.2	31.8	27.2	27.6	23.7
Growth Rate (%)	percent	-	29.1%	31.4%	-14.5%	1.6%	-14.3%
Private Consumption Spending	$'s US billions	8.8	9.2	11.6	11.9	12.2	16.0
Government (G&S) Expenditures	$'s US billions	3.7	3.8	4.8	4.9	5.1	6.5
Gross Private Investment	$'s US billions	4.5	4.7	6.0	6.1	6.3	4.9
Exports of Goods and Services	$'s US billions	5.5	12.8	20.6	15.9	16.4	10.7
Imports of Goods and Services	$'s US billions	4.4	6.9	11.2	11.0	11.3	13.0
Nominal GDP	$'s US billions	18.1	23.7	31.8	27.8	28.6	25.1
Nominal GDP Growth Rate	percent	-	31%	34%	-13%	3%	-12%
Nominal GDP Per Capita	$'s US/person	846	1,077	1,400	1,194	1,191	1,015
Private Consumption Per Capita	$'s US/person	411	419	510	509	508	648
Population	millions	21.4	22.0	22.7	23.3	24.0	24.7

Source: CountryWatch (2003c).

The country's petroleum resource base is truly impressive: proven oil reserves of 112 billion barrels[3] and possible additional oil reserves of 100 billion barrels. Of 73 discovered oil fields, however, only 15 have been developed as a result of the political and military tumult of the past 20 years.[4] In addition to these huge oil reserves, Iraq has 110 trillion cubic feet of proven gas reserves with probable reserves of 150 trillion cubic feet.[5]

The potential in the petroleum sector is significant in Iraq. Only about 20 percent of the country's discovered fields have been developed and modern 3-D seismic techniques have not been widely applied.[6] If political stability can be attained and the politics of oil production within the Organization of Petroleum Exporting Countries (OPEC) can be managed, there is little doubt that the country's output of oil could expand dramatically over the next decade.

In the 1980s, as a result of financial problems caused by massive defense expenditures and damage to Iraq's oil export facilities during the eight-year war with Iran, Iraq is estimated to have suffered estimated economic losses of at least $100 billion.[7] After the end of the war with Iran in 1988, oil exports gradually

---

[3] U.S. Department of Energy (2003a), p. 1.

[4] U.S. Department of Energy (2003a), p. 2.

[5] *Ibid*, p 8.

[6] *Ibid*, p 2.

[7] *Ibid*, p. 4.

increased with the construction of new pipelines and restoration of damaged facilities.[8] Iraq's attack on Kuwait in August 1990 and the subsequent international economic sanctions imposed after 1991 drastically reduced economic activity and increased international oil prices.[9]

The government's policies of supporting large military and internal security forces and allocating resources to key supporters of the regime, exacerbated shortages and resulted in widespread malnutrition, health care deficiencies, and a collapse of the education system during the 1990s and first years of the new millennium.[10] OPEC estimated that real GDP in Iraq in 2002 was about one third of its 1990 level.[11]

The U.N. Oil-for-Food Programme, established in April 1995, improved economic conditions by allowing Iraq to export oil in exchange for food, medicine and other humanitarian goods. Seventy two percent of the earnings of the program went to fund the country's humanitarian needs and twenty five percent went to the Compensation Commission, which pays claims arising from Iraq's 1990 invasion of Kuwait. The remainder went to pay the

---

[8] *Ibid*, p. 4-5.

[9] *Ibid*, p 5.

[10] For example, teacher salaries in Iraq went from $500 - $1,000 per month in 1990 to $5 - $10 per month in 2003. United Nations (May 2003).

[11] OPEC Annual Statistical Bulletin (2001), p. 3.

costs of the U.N. Monitoring, Verification and Inspection Commission and U.N. operational costs. [12]

Iraq's external debt, including potential reparations claims from the first Gulf War, has been estimated to be between $300 to $400 billion.[13] With export revenues running at about $16 billion in 2002, obviously, there is no feasible way that Iraq's creditors can be fully repaid.

With Saddam Hussein gone, however, and with the security situation stabilized, there is the potential for very rapid economic growth driven by development of the country's oil and gas reserves, its modest agricultural potential, and the newly liberated efforts of its relatively well-educated populace.

Recent Economic Performance

Continued high oil prices and increased oil production in 2000, 2001, and 2002 combined with a more favorably run U.N. Oil-for-Food Programme to increase badly needed food and medical supplies to the Iraqi populace. GDP, as measured in U.S. dollars, was up 31 percent in 1999, driven by fast-rising oil output and rising prices.[14] Oil production leveled off during 2000 as technical problems and infrastructure constraints combined to

---

[12] United Nations (2003a).

[13] The Center for Strategic and International Studies (2003), p. 1, puts the estimate at $383 billion.

[14] See Table III-1.

stop growth in the oil sector, but GDP still expanded at an estimated 34 percent, as world oil prices increased by over 60 percent.[15] Problems in the oil sector continued and intensified in 2001 and 2002, to the extent that GDP is estimated to have contracted by 13 percent in 2001[16] and stagnated in 2002. In 2003, the severe disruption to the economy and commerce associated with the war to remove Saddam Hussein's regime from power is projected to result in a 16 percent decline in GDP in 2003.[17]

Notwithstanding the significant increases in Iraqi GDP since the institution of the U.N. Oil-for-Food Programme in 1995, the vast majority of the Iraqi population during that time was surviving at the subsistence level. Economic opportunities were substantially limited by the sanctions, and most Iraqis did not share in the bounty brought in by higher oil prices. High levels of inflation have persisted since 1995 with domestic inflation rates ranging between 15 and 30 percent between 1999 and 2001.[18] With U.N. sanctions lifted, there is potential for Iraqis to work, save and invest freely. Given the natural resources of the country, the historical technical competence of its civil service, relatively good infrastructure and regionally high education levels in the workforce, Iraq has all it needs to be a regional economic power-

---

[15] U.S. Department of Energy (2003c), p. 121.

[16] Central Intelligence Agency (2003).

[17] See Table III-1.

[18] CountryWatch (2003c).

except political stability and the rule of law, conditions that are required to turn potential into reality.

Aside from oil revenue, Saddam Hussein's government had very little capacity to collect tax revenue from its beleaguered citizens. The scarcity of data published by the Hussein regime makes it difficult to determine the impact of government policy on the fiscal situation in Iraq, as the tax collection system was not functional and details of recent budgets in Iraq are not available. To complicate matters further, any reports in Iraq dinars would be suspect as the official exchange rate of 0.311 Iraqi dinars (ID) per U.S. dollar in 2002 was significantly overvalued. The actual market rate averaged ID 3,250 per U.S. dollar in 2002.[19]

Official exports exceeded imports in Iraq by $5 billion in 2002 and net exports were down sharply from the surplus registered in 2000 when oil production and prices peaked.[20]

---

[19] OPEC (2002).
[20] Table III-1.

The Structure of the Economy

An estimate of the structure of the Iraqi economy is developed here which has been pieced together from a variety of sources to provide a crude estimate of the workings of the economy. One of the major tasks of the new administration in post-war Iraq will be to begin to initiate a national economic statistical program that will enable management of the economy to be based on more accurate information.

The basic structure of the Iraqi economy is detailed in the inter-industry matrix of the economy shown in Table III-2. Model documentation is described in Appendix III.1 to this chapter. The input-output matrix describes our forecast for economic activity for 2004, the first full year after the war in 2003, based on our planning assumptions described below.

The key characteristic of the economy as shown in Table III-2 is the dominance of the economy by the petroleum sector. Table III-3 shows the estimates of value added by economic sector.

Table III-2
Input-Output Matrix for Iraq - 2004
($US Millions)

Intermediate Product Sales to Each Economic Sector

Final Demands from Each Sector

Sectors	O&G	Ser	Agr	Man	Pow	T&T	Total Sales	C	G	I	X	M	Final Demand	Total Demand
Oil & Gas (O&G)	404	215	0	150	1,279	87	2,134	2,126	207	0	15,543	0	17,876	20,011
Services (Ser)	51	1,061	48	96	276	221	1,753	5,786	3,865	1,975	1,000	2,023	10,603	14,378
Agriculture (Agr)	0	0	125	158	92	0	375	6,298	404	0	0	6,000	702	7,077
Manufacturing (Man)	77	701	107	325	92	564	1,866	3,554	855	5,136	0	8,411	1,134	11,411
Power (Pow)	31	494	22	38	63	152	799	1,596	97	0	0	0	1,693	2,492
Tele/Transport (T & T)	39	618	24	41	92	195	1,008	3,523	1,867	790	0	2,852	3,329	7,189
Total Purchases	602	3,089	326	806	1,893	1,219	7,935	22,883	7,296	7,901	16,543	19,285	35,338	62,558
Labor Services	243	6,950	564	1,316	120	2,183	11,375							
Capital Services	19,166	2,317	188	878	479	936	23,963							
Value Added	19,409	9,267	751	2,194	599	3,119	35,338							
Total Production	20,011	12,355	1,077	3,000	2,492	4,337	43,273							
Imports	0	2,023	6,000	8,411	0	2,852	19,285							
Total Supply	20,011	14,378	7,077	11,411	2,492	7,189	62,558							

Sources: See Appendix III-1
Abbreviations:
C: Private Consumption Spending
G: Government Spending
I: Investment Spending
X: Exports
M: Imports

Table III-3
GDP by Sector of Origin - 2004
($US Billions)

	Final Demand	Imports	GDP	GDP%
Oil&Gas	17.9	0.0	17.9	50.6%
Services	12.6	2.0	10.6	30.0%
Agriculture	6.7	6.0	0.7	2.0%
Manufacturing	9.5	8.4	1.1	3.2%
Power	1.7	0.0	1.7	4.8%
Telecom/Transport	6.2	2.9	3.3	9.4%
Total	54.6	19.3	35.3	100.0%

Source: Table III-2

Another important aspect of the economy detailed in the structure shown is the composition of final demand. Table III-4 shows our forecast of the composition of final demand of the Iraqi economy in 2004. A key point to note here is that with a population of 25 million,[21] a consumption level of $23 billion implies an annual per capita living standard of about $900; substantially less than the standard of living of other oil rich nations in the region[22] and a level substantially less than the potential of the economy if the resource base were to be properly managed.

A second point to note concerning the composition of final demand is that the ratio of imports to GDP is approximately 55

---

[21] U.S. Census Bureau (2003).

[22] See Table IV-2.

Table III-4
GDP By Final Demand Component - 2004
($US Billions)

	GDP	GDP%
Consumption	22.9	64.8%
Investment	7.3	20.6%
Government	7.9	22.4%
Exports	16.5	46.8%
Imports	19.3	54.6%
Total	35.3	100.0%

Source: Table III-2

percent. The Iraqi economy is significantly import and export dependent; this observation once again illustrates the importance of the petroleum sector in the Iraqi economy.

The Hydrocarbon Sector

The hydrocarbon sector in Iraq is estimated in 2004 to contribute about 50 percent of Iraqi GDP. A key element in rebuilding the Iraqi economy will be to use Iraq's hydrocarbon wealth to finance a set of future investments designed to expand and diversify the economy. With proved reserves of 112 billion barrels of oil and 110 trillion cubic feet of natural gas, Iraq has one of the largest hydrocarbon resource bases in the world and this represents over 10 percent of the world's known oil reserves, more oil reserves than any other country except for Saudi

Arabia[23] and Canada.[24] Given its large resource to population ratio, the ability of Iraq to export these resources and generate a substantial export income will be key to Iraqi economic development. Table III-5 shows the primary oil producing fields in Iraq and their associated oil reserves.

Figure III-1 shows the history of oil production in Iraq and as the data indicates, the industry has operated in an irregular and inconsistent manner over the past 40 years. The key point to note is that the fortunes of the petroleum industry in Iraq have fluctuated directly with the political climate. Over the past 40 years there have been three major military conflicts in Iraq, each resulting in a rapid escalation, then de-escalation of petroleum production capacity.

The first conflict in 1980 was the Iraq-Iran War. The timing of this war was after the first two OPEC oil shocks when oil production capacity in Iraq was at its peak. During 1979, Iraq produced 3.5 million barrels per day, an annual level that would not be seen again for the rest of the century.

---

[23] U.S. Department of Energy (2003d).

[24] U.S. Department of Energy (2003e).

**Table III-5
Iraqi Proven Oil Reserves By Field
(Billions of Barrels)**

Field	Proved Reserves
Majnoon	21.0
West Qurna	13.2
East Bagdad	11.0
Kirkuk	10.0
Rumaila	10.0
Bin Umar	6.0
Ratawi	3.1
Halfaya	3.6
Sadaam	3.0
Nassiriya	2.3
Suba-Luhais	2.2
Tuba	1.5
Khurmala	1.0
Gharaf	1.1
Rafidain	0.7
Amara	0.5
Sub-Total	90.1
Other	22.0
Total	112.0

Source: US Dept of Energy (2003a)

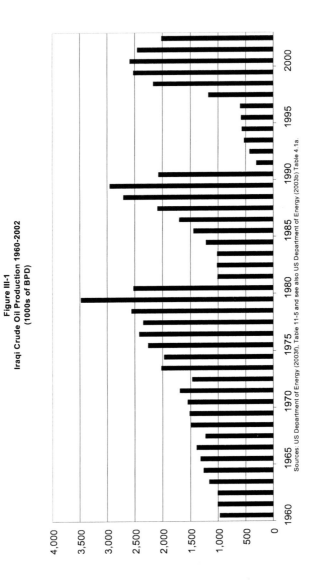

Figure III-1
Iraqi Crude Oil Production 1960-2002
(1000s of BPD)

Sources: US Department of Energy (2003f), Table 11-5 and see also US Department of Energy (2003b) Table 4.1a

The second conflict was the Gulf War in 1990. After repairing the initial damage to the oil fields resulting from the Iran-Iraq War, the Iraqi petroleum sector was again approaching production of 3 million barrels per day when the invasion of Kuwait was initiated. Once again the military conflict resulted in significant damage to both Kuwaiti and Iraqi oil fields after U.S. led Coalition Forces routed Iraqi forces. This time, production of oil in Iraq was reduced to levels less than .5 billion barrels per day, levels not experienced in Iraq since the 1950s.

Oil production fell to about .3 million barrels per day after the Gulf War because Iraq could not export oil under the U.N. sanctions.[25] In April of 1995, however, production of oil under U.N. Resolution 986 became subject to the jurisdiction of the United Nations under the Oil-for-Food Programme.[26] After 1996, oil production rose sharply reaching a peak of 2.5 million barrels per day in 2000. The continued effect of U.N. sanctions however and pressure by the U.S. on dealing with Iraq began to effect Iraqi oil production capacity and in 2002, the year prior to the War of 2003, oil production in Iraq had slipped to 2.0 million barrels per day.[27]

In April 2003, oil production in Iraq essentially shut down at the start of hostilities in the War of 2003. While many had expected

---

[25] Department of Energy (2003a), p. 3.

[26] *Ibid.*

[27] *Ibid.*

that the Hussein regime would sabotage the oil fields as a result of a coalition attack, and it was reported that in fact Saddam Hussein had given the order to sabotage the oil wells at Rumaila, only 10 of the 1,000 wells in the large oil field were set on fire. By the end of April all fires had been extinguished and production resumed.[28]

Initial expectations are that oil production in Iraq can be brought back on line quickly. It was reported that the Rumaila field could be back on line with its capacity of 1.1 million barrels of oil per day by mid-year. Because the damage to the petroleum infrastructure during the War of 2003 was light it is expected that other oil reservoirs could also be brought back on line later in the year so that oil production would be averaging 1.5 million barrels per day in 2003 by the end of the year.[29]

Iraq's existing petroleum infrastructure, however, uses antiquated techniques. The technology employed was forced upon very capable Iraqi petroleum engineers because of the scarcity of funds and the lack of technology transfer resulting from the misadventures of the Hussein regime.

---

[28] Associated Press (2003b).
[29] Bonionvevo (2003).

Using Iraq's pre-war oil-management techniques to squeeze more oil out of their existing wells could damage these reservoirs and make them less productive in the future.[30]

In our projections, we have assumed that $1 billion of repair work is done on existing capacity to bring the most efficient wells back on line by the end of 2003.[31] We assume this will result in a production level of 1.5 million barrels per day at the end of 2003, which will decline at an estimated 7 percent per year. Actual and projected levels of oil production for 2003 are shown in Table III-6. In 2004, a new production program funded at $4 billion will target the most efficient incremental new fields to generate a steady stream of production using the most efficient new technologies to yield 1.5 million barrels per day over a 7-year production plateau. One-half of this level, or .75 million barrels per day, should be realized in 2004 so that total productivity from existing and new development is estimated to be 2.24 million barrels per day in day in 2004. The complete plan for the Iraqi National Oil Company (INOC) is described in Chapter IV and the detailed production estimates and assumptions are given in Appendix IV.1.

For the future, Iraq's oil potential remains huge. Of 2,000 wells drilled to date, an estimated 1,500 – 1,700 are producing oil at

---

[30] U.S. Department of Energy (2003a), p.3.
[31] Bonionvevo (2003).

very low production costs.[32] Less than one-half of the country's currently proven reserves have been developed. Assuming the coalition can establish security in the country, repair of existing facilities and new investment and exploration can almost surely expand Iraq's production of oil substantially.

Table III-6
Iraqi Oil Production in 2003
(1000s of Barrels/Day)

Month	Production
Jan	2,555
Feb	2,490
Mar	1,373
Apr	53
May	290
Jun	450
Jul	1,000
Aug	1,000
Sep	1,250
Oct	1,250
Nov	1,500
Dec	1,500

Sources:
US Department of Energy (2003a);
US Department of Energy (2003h);
Bonionvevo (2003).

---

[32] U.S. Department of Energy (2003a), p. 2.

A comment should be made on the natural gas potential of Iraq. As noted above, Iraq has substantial reserves of natural gas. This is a significant resource and can replace domestic oil consumption within Iraq and be exported via pipelines and liquefaction facilities. The gas sector is less well developed and less financially liquid than the oil sector. Consequently the natural gas sector should remain a secondary focus to oil.[33] Within the initial planning horizon, however, much of the oil production that will take place has associated natural gas as a joint product. It is likely therefore that some initial investment in natural gas related infrastructure would need to be planned. The issue of the combined development of the oil and natural gas sector will be further discussed in the context of an economic plan for the petroleum sector in Chapter IV and Appendix IV.3.

The Services Sector

The service sector is estimated to contribute about 30 percent of Iraqi GDP.[34] The services provided by government employees and the military are assumed to be a large percentage of this total as an estimated 2 million civil servants, pensioners and military personnel derive their livelihood from the public sector.[35] In

---

[33] This was also the conclusion of the Council on Foreign Relations – Baker Institute report (2002).

[34] See Table III-3.

[35] National Public Radio (2003).

addition to government bureaucrats, the government sector in Iraq also includes health care services, education, waste disposal and the provision of water supplies. With their dependents, this implies that one in three Iraqis are dependent on income from services in the public sector.

Private sector services are also important in a vibrant and growing market based economy that includes banking, insurance, retail operations, wholesale trades and other financial services. These services have been somewhat repressed in the autocratic and arbitrarily run economic system under the regime of Saddam Hussein, but will end up playing a major role in the more vibrant market place in a reconstructed Iraq.

Estimates of government spending in the pre-war years are shown in Table III-7 along with the size of the Iraqi armed forces. The level of the armed forces is an obvious major determinant of the Iraqi government budget.

Table III-7
Government Spending Indicators in Iraq

	1997	1998	1999	2000	2001
Government Spending ($'s US billions)	3.004	3.242	3.102	3.754	3.884
Armed Forces ($'s US billions)	1.277	1.266	1.449	1.572	1.501
Armed Forces (000's)	383	429	429	429	429
Reservists (000's)	650	650	650	650	650

Sources: Institute for Strategic Studies (1999, 2000, 2001, 2002, 2003) and CountryWatch (2003c).

In Chapter IV, we develop a rationalized government budget for Iraq. The size of the budget will be determined by the need for government services and by expected revenues generated by the petroleum sector and other sources. Key issues in determining the size of the government budget include rearmament, healthcare, education, and the length of time necessary to phase out subsidies for food and essential public services, including electricity and power.

The Agricultural Sector

The agricultural sector is estimated to contribute about 2 percent of Iraqi GDP.[36] The main agricultural crops produced are shown in Tables III-8 and III-9, which provide U.N. Food and Agricultural Organization (FAO) estimates for the Iraqi economy from 1997 to 2002.

The performance of the agricultural sector under the Hussein regime has been dismal. Figure III-2 charts the production of barley, rice and wheat production over the past twenty years. As the data shows, crop production experienced some growth in the 1980s but has been in a tailspin ever since the Gulf War in 1990.

---

[36] See Table III-3.

Table III-8
Key Economic Sectors in Iraq
Agriculture/Food: Production of Primary Crops
(Metric Tons)

Product	1997	1998	1999	2000	2001	2002
Barley	778,000	859,000	500,000	400,000	500,000	500,000
Maize	121,000	133,000	115,000	53,000	50,000	60,000
Potatoes	580,000	650,000	730,000	545,000	623,000	625,000
Rice, Paddy	244,000	300,000	180,000	60,000	90,000	90,000
Soybeans	1,750	1,780	1,650	1,600	1,650	1,650
Sugar Beets	7,800	7,850	7,500	7,500	7,500	7,500
Sugar Cane	70,000	71,000	68,000	65,000	65,000	65,000
Wheat	1,063,000	1,130,000	800,000	384,000	650,000	800,000

Sources: Food and Agricultural Organization of the United Nations (2003)

Table III-9
Key Economic Sectors in Iraq
Area of Primary Crops Under Cultivation
(Hectares Cultivated)

Cultivated Area	1997	1998	1999	2000	2001	2002
Barley	1,173,000	1,213,000	1,220,000	1,110,000	1,205,000	1,200,000
Maize	61,000	61,000	60,000	60,000	50,000	50,000
Potatoes	35,000	40,000	44,250	38,750	38,000	38,500
Rice, Paddy	121,000	128,000	130,000	60,000	100,000	100,000
Soybeans	1,250	1,250	1,250	1,200	1,250	1,250
Sugar Beets	320	330	335	330	330	330
Sugar Cane	3,050	3,150	3,200	3,000	3,000	3,000
Wheat	1,405,000	1,400,000	1,300,000	1,200,000	1,220,000	1,200,000

Sources: Food and Agricultural Organization of the United Nations (2003)

The overall production levels of the three crops in 2002 were less than 50 percent of the overall production levels in 1990. The decline in production has been the result of reduced cultivation, lower overall productivity per acre, and in the past several years, drought, and conflict over water rights with Turkey.

Figure III-3 shows the area under cultivation for each of the three main cereal crops. As the data shows, the area under cultivation has been significantly reduced since the Gulf War. Area reductions have been most likely due to the military hostilities associated with the Gulf War, variations in water availability, and limited availability of funds for inputs and capital equipment due to the U.N. sanctions.

Figure III-4 shows output per hectare for barley, rice and wheat. Once again the data shows significant reductions in crop yields for the three crops since 1990. This decline in productivity is most likely the result of a lack of funds as a result of the U.N. sanctions. The sanctions led to reduced fertilizer availability and a shortage of seeds, spare parts and capital equipment utilized in the agricultural sector.

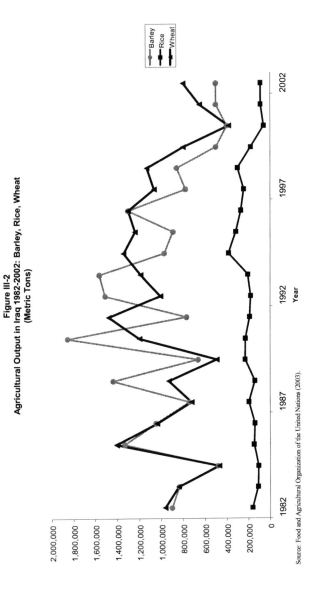

Figure III-2
Agricultural Output in Iraq 1982-2002: Barley, Rice, Wheat
(Metric Tons)

Source: Food and Agricultural Organization of the United Nations (2003).

With a resumption of funds from oil exports and other economic activity, the agricultural sector in Iraq should be able to rebound nicely. With proper funding, Iraqi agricultural production should be able to reach 1990 levels within a few years, depending on the availability of water. The growth in agricultural production will enable Iraq to reduce its dependence on imported food, which should be a priority for the new government.

The agricultural sector should be able to thrive in a dynamic and open market economy in Iraq. While it is doubtful that Iraq will be able to raise sufficient food to feed 100 percent of its swelling population over the next ten years, it is reasonable to assume that the output of the agricultural sector could be quadrupled – thereby reducing the volume of required agricultural imports. In Chapter IV we examine the potential of the economy, including the agricultural sector, to grow at rates designed to improve Iraq's self sufficiency with the help of petroleum revenues.

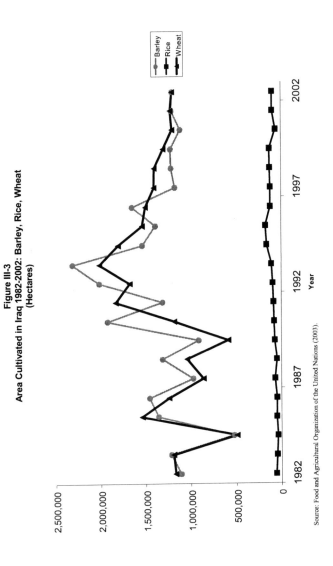

Figure III-3
Area Cultivated in Iraq 1982-2002: Barley, Rice, Wheat
(Hectares)

Source: Food and Agricultural Organization of the United Nations (2003).

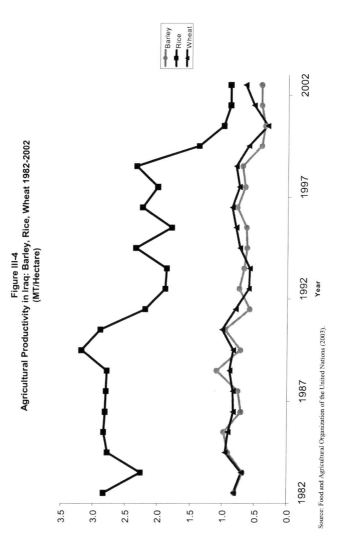

Figure III-4
Agricultural Productivity in Iraq: Barley, Rice, Wheat 1982-2002
(MT/Hectare)

Source: Food and Agricultural Organization of the United Nations (2003).

The Manufacturing Sector

The manufacturing sector is estimated to contribute about 3 percent of Iraqi GDP.[37] The manufacturing sector has been crippled by a combination of war, the government's focus on the military sector, and the dominance of the petroleum industry. As a result of sanctions and the highly speculative political situation in Iraq, very little national or foreign investment has taken place in the Iraqi economy, other than in the petroleum sector. The major industries include petroleum refining, chemicals, and food processing.

The largest manufacturing investment is petroleum refining. The nameplate capacity of Iraq is just over 600,000 barrels per day, but as of January 2003, the U.S. Department of Energy reported an effective capacity of 417,000 barrels per day. It is likely that a significant portion of that capacity was knocked out of service during the War of 2003 or as a result of the looting and sabotage which followed the war.[38] One priority, in the transition administration, will be to develop a program to repair the refineries that can efficiently produce refined petroleum products. These products are mainly used for Iraqi domestic consumption.

---

[37] See Table III-3.

[38] U.S. Department of Energy (2003a), p. 8.

A manufacturing industry in Iraq with significant future potential is the chemical industry. Because of the concern of the U.S. over weapons of mass destruction and in particular chemical weapons, the chemical industry in Iraq was a primary target of Coalition Forces in the War of 2003. While chemical weapons are certainly a concern, the potential for Iraq to exploit its rich hydrocarbon base with a vibrant petrochemical industry is significant. Like many of the neighboring Gulf States, Iraq will have a significant opportunity to vertically integrate production in its petroleum sector and produce value added chemical products for export or for domestic consumption such as fertilizer.

Other manufacturing industries in Iraq include food processing, cement production, and steel production. These industries have been stagnant in the past several years, no doubt as the lack of foreign exchange has crippled their ability to expand. Data on production in these sectors where data is available is shown in Table III-10.

Iraq is estimated to have approximately 100 state enterprises, including those in textiles, food, construction, chemicals, pharmaceuticals and engineering. The director general of the ministry of industry and mining resources has said that there are 52 companies and 186 companies under consideration (for privatization).[39]

---

[39] Agence France-Presse (2003d).

Table III-10
Iraqi Manufacturing
Production From Key Industries

Product		1997	1998	1999	2000	2001
Refined Petroleum	(BBLs/Day 1000s)	445	459	443	493	532
Food Processing						
Beer	(MT)	68,250	68,250	68,250	68,250	68,250
Veg. Oil and Fat	(MT)	2,000	2,000	1,800	1,800	1,800
Wine	(MT)	23,358	24,234	23,186	22,056	22,972
Cement	(MT 1000s)	1,598	2,000	2,000	2,000	2,000
Raw Steel	(MT 1000s)	300	200	800	200	NA

Sources: US Geological Survey (2003), US Department of Energy (2003c) and the Food and Agricultural Organization of the United Nations (2003).

These enterprises have either been directly controlled by the government or via entities that are associated with the state. In the case of the food processing industry, government control and subsidies have been substantive. The significant number of state enterprises is largely a legacy of the socialist Ba'athist paradigm, as has been discussed earlier in Chapter 1. Such state enterprises were affected by corruption and cronyism within the Ba'ath regime.

The Electric Power Sector

The electric power sector in Iraq is estimated to contribute about 5 percent of Iraqi GDP. The electric power sector in both the Gulf War and the War of 2003 was severely damaged. In the Gulf War over 85 percent of the national power grid and 20 power stations were destroyed bringing the total electric power capacity in the country down from 9,000 megawatts in December of 1990 to 340 megawatts by March of 1991.[40]

In the intervening years the power sector was brought back up to an estimated 4,300 megawatts mainly through the reconstruction of the Baiiji and Mosul thermal plants and the Saddam Hussein hydroelectric power station.[41] Notwithstanding this development, a U.N. study estimated the shortage of electric power capacity in

---

[40] U.S. Department of Energy (2003a), p. 9.

[41] *Ibid.*

August of 2000 at 1,800 megawatts;[42] this power capacity level suggests an extremely low level of electrification for a country of more than 24 million people.[43] The latest data on the electric capacity of the Iraqi economy just prior to the War of 2003 is shown in Table III-11.

In the War of 2003, a similar amount of destruction is estimated to have occurred with the entire power grid shut down in Baghdad for the last phases of Operation Iraqi Freedom. In May of 2003 the Wall Street Journal reported that the capacity of the electric system had been reduced to 2,100 megawatts from a level of 5,500 megawatts in the summer of 2002 and that the major grid system in Iraq had severe damage to 26 major transmission towers as a result of bombing runs.[44]

One of the most urgent requirements in the transitional period will be to increase basic human services including electric power. At roughly $500 per kilowatt, our plan increases the available power capacity by a little more than 80 percent over the next five years.

---

[42] *Ibid.*

[43] For comparison as of January 1, 2001 the U.S. had 813,000 megawatts (MW) installed for a population of 282.3 million people, or almost 2,900 MW per million persons compared with 4,300 MW for 24.7 million people or 174 MW per million persons in Iraq. U.S. Department of Energy (2003f) and U.S. Census Bureau (2003). Iraqi data from Table III-1 and Table III-11.

[44] Dohram (2003).

Table III-11
Key Economic Sectors in Iraq
Energy: Electric Power Sector Data

		1997	1998	1999	2000	2001
Production						
Thermal	Billion of kwh	27.241	27.979	27.372	31.141	35.429
Hydro	Billion of kwh	0.575	0.587	0.599	0.605	0.58
Total	Billion of kwh	27.816	28.566	27.971	31.746	36.009
Consumption	Billion of kwh	25.869	26.566	26.013	29.524	33.488
Effective Capacity	Megawatts	4,000	4,300	4,300	4,300	4,300
Installed Capacity	Megawatts	9,500	9,500	9,500	9,500	9,500

Source: US Department of Energy, Energy Information Administration (2003)

The Telecom/Transport Sector

The telecom/transport sector in Iraq is estimated to contribute almost 10 percent of Iraqi GDP. As with the power sector, telecommunications and transportation are key sectors in getting the economy moving again and will have a high priority in the competition for funds to get the country back on an acceptable development trajectory.

In the area of telecommunications, lack of data prevents a meaningful analysis of what has transpired in the past 5 years. There were an estimated 675,000 main telephone lines in Iraq in 2001[45] and a very limited cellular phone network in the northern part of the country.[46] Since then, there has been some war damage to the system of landlines and cellular towers. The telecom infrastructure was a key target in the initial phases of the war as the coalition attempted to destroy the ability of the Hussein government to communicate with troops in the field.

The transportation infrastructure in Iraq includes 45,000 kilometers of roads, 2,300 kilometers of railway, 1,000 kilometers of inland waterway, 5,200 kilometers of petroleum pipelines, 1,300 kilometers of gas pipelines, 77 airports with paved runways, and the 3 major ports of Umm Qasr, Khwar az

---

[45] ITU (2003).
[46] U.S. Central Intelligence Agency (2003).

Zubayr, and Al Basrah.[47] There will have been varying amounts of damage to this infrastructure, during the War of 2003, which will need to get put back in service as an initial priority. A key focus here will be to ensure the infrastructure for the transportation of crude oil and petroleum products is quickly repaired. Table III-12 indicates the systemic decline in the tanker tonnage that occurred over the past 5 years as Iraq accommodated the U.N. sanctions on oil exports. This is indicative of the transportation infrastructure requirements that must be addressed as the nation rebuilds.

---

[47] U.S. Central Intelligence Agency (2003), p. 7.

Table III-12
Key Economic Sectors in Iraq
Telecom/Transport Sectors

		1997	1998	1999	2000	2001
Telecom Sector						
Main Lines	1,000's	651	650	675	675	675
Transport Sector						
Tanker Fleet	Ships	17	16	9	9	9
Tanker Fleet	DWT mm*	1.5	1.4	0.5	0.5	0.5

Sources: US Central Intelligence Agency (2003), OPEC (2001) and ITU (2003).

* millions of deadweight tons - deadweight tons are a measure expressed in metric tons (1,000 kg) or long tons (1,016 kg) of a ship's carrying capacity, including bunker oil, fresh water, crew and provisions.

Appendix III.1: Notes on the Economic Model

About the models

We used two primary models to analyze the Iraqi economy. The first is the standard CountryWatch Forecast model that we use with the CountryWatch Forecast product and the second is a custom input-output model for Iraq.

The standard CountryWatch model utilizes a simple Keynesian macroeconomic framework that has been adapted to an open economy.[48] The model consists of three major sections: a nominal income model, a real income model, and related special calculations. Each model comes with an excel file where an interactive panel allows the user to vary the parameters to explore the sensitivity of the assumptions and to create custom forecasts.

The second model is an input-output model.[49] We chose to use this type of model because it is extremely useful in exploring the various interdependencies and opportunity costs associated with the production process. The model has an intermediate uses section that accounts for all of the production inputs that get consumed in producing other products. For example, to produce

---

[48] Theoretical background on the CountryWatch Forecast model can be found at this URL: http://www.countrywatch.com/forecast/methodology.pdf

[49] For a classical view of input-output theory see Chenery (1967).

another megawatt of electricity would require the use of more fuel inputs. The model forces these inputs to be accounted for.

We also tied this basic input-output approach to an expanded economic model that also forced any new production to be driven by increased investment. This allowed us to explore the level of investment required in the economy and compare it with the level of resources expected to be available through national savings. We then constrained the projected level of growth accordingly. The free market should drive the actual growth this country will experience, but this type of investment analysis is designed to give public planners a better sense of the level of public investment required to support the needs of the private sector.

Economic Data on Iraq

Estimating the size and structure of the Iraqi economy is difficult because there is very little reliable public macroeconomic information that was released by the Iraqi government in recent years. The last Iraqi government macroeconomic statistics available for review, for example, were from the 1976 – 1980 Annual Economic Plan.[50] The fluctuating value of the Iraqi dinar also makes any analysis based on dinar denominated data from the earlier plans difficult to interpret. The Iraqi dinar has moved from a range of 3,350 dinars/U.S. dollars in the first quarter of

---

[50] Alnasrawi (1994).

2003 to 850 dinars/U.S. dollars a few months later in May and then upwards to 1,400 dinars/U.S. dollars the next month.

As a result of the lack of good data, we have resorted to making what we believe are reasonable assumptions on the Iraqi economy based on the best data available to the Authors. We've done this by estimating the market value of production in key economic sectors in Iraq, for example estimating the market value of agricultural production using production data from the United Nations. We have also estimated numbers that are not available by resorting to comparisons with economies that are similar to Iraq or from industries in other countries that are similar to those industries that are being studied in Iraq.

The Iraqi currency is not currently convertible. The availability of foreign currency in Iraq is a function of the anticipated inflow of petrodollars and the injection of dollars from United States aid and local troop support expenditures. While we have estimated conversion rates between the Iraqi dinar and the dollar, we have chosen to conduct the GDP analysis in dollars. We have elected to use a current market price approach in dollars as opposed to a purchasing power parity approach to estimate GDP in order to better model the nominal impacts of various levels of oil and gas sales on the Iraqi economy.[51]

Export Assumptions

Our analysis essentially starts with oil exports, which are fairly easily estimated given an assumed world price for oil and a reasonable projection of oil production in Iraq.[52] We estimate, based on our oil production plan, that oil production in Iraq will result in total oil and gas revenues of about $20 billion of which about $15.5 billion is exported. Control of the revenues from this production is assumed to be in the hands of the government – at least at the outset of this development process.

These export estimates are then supplemented with our assumptions on international aid contributions and the infusion of funds from local expenditures by Coalition Forces to result in a total level of exports of goods and services and other foreign exchange capital inflows for 2004 of about $16.5 billion.

---

[51] U.S. Central Intelligence Agency (2003). For comparative purposes, the CIA suggests that the size of the Iraqi economy on a purchase power parity basis was about $59 billion in 2001.

[52] See Appendix IV.2 for a detailed analysis of oil production and cost assumptions.

Given our assumptions on the amount of foreign exchange allocated to settle foreign claims against Iraq of $1.9 billion in 2004, we project that Iraqi imports will be about $19.3 billion for 2004. These funds are used as shown in Table A III-1, which shows the actual types of imported goods that will be needed in the economy to achieve the investment program in Chapter IV. Most of the imports utilized in the oil and gas sector and the power sector will be capital goods items with transportation services required to move these capital goods to the required site and some construction services required to install them at the required location.

Table A III-1
Projected Iraqi Imports in 2004
(by type of product - billions of $s US)

	Consumption Imports (G & C)	Investment Imports	Total Imports
Oil & Gas (O&G)	0.0	0.0	0.0
Services (Ser)	0.5	1.5	2.0
Agriculture (Agr)	6.0	0.0	6.0
Manufacturing (Man)	4.5	3.9	8.4
Power (Pow)	0.0	0.0	0.0
Tele/Transport (T & T)	2.3	0.6	2.9
Total Purchases	13.3	6.0	19.3

Source: CountryWatch Forecast Estimates

Imports of Consumer Goods

The documentation from the United Nations' Oil-for-Food Programme[53] is particularly useful in providing a specific sense of the value and the composition of items that the previous government was importing. In particular, the annual Iraq agricultural import allowance was typically about $2.5 billion per year to allow a daily food ration of 2,472 kilocalories per person per day[54]. This program fed an estimated 16 million Iraqis.[55] Our assumptions allow for the continuation of the food ration program at a level of $2.6 billion. The Coalition Forces and Iraqi citizens purchasing food on the open market are estimated to consume about $3.4 billion of imported food.

We assume that about $7.3 billion of foreign manufactured goods, transportation requirements and general services will be imported into this economy in 2004.

Investment Spending

Our plan, more fully described in Chapter IV, targets $6 billion of government investment spending in 2004 for key investments. These funds are focused in the sectors shown in Table A III–2.

---

[53] United Nations Data, Office of the Iraq Oil-for-Food Programme (2003).

[54] *Ibid.*

[55] *Ibid.*

The oil and gas capital spending is targeted to grow Iraqi oil production from an average of 1.5 million barrels per day in 2003 to over 5 million barrels per day by 2010. This will require an investment of $4 billion dollars in 2004. These assumptions are more fully described in Chapter IV.

Table A III-2
Iraqi Government Fixed Investments
(by sector in 2004)

	%	Investment (billions of $s)
Oil & Gas	67%	4.0
Services	17%	1.0
Agriculture	3%	0.2
Manufacturing	0%	0.0
Power	13%	0.8
Telecom/Transport	0%	0.0
Total Investments	100%	6.0

Source: CountryWatch Forecast Estimates

The agricultural level of investment shown above is designed to move this sector in a positive direction to increase the output and to lower the level of annual food imports required in Iraq.

The power sector investment of $800 million in 2004 should allow for an additional 400 megawatts (MW) of power generation assets along with all requisite power system distribution modifications and some war repairs to accommodate

225

this additional load.[56] This 400 MW is roughly 22 percent of the 1,800 MW currently needed in Iraq as estimated by the United States Department of Energy.[57]

Economic Structure

Our input-output analysis utilizes a six-sector model that highlights the most important development sectors. The domestic economy (excluding oil and gas) is dwarfed by the export economy, and the size of these sectors is outlined in the body of Chapter III. All GDP and sector size numbers shown in this analysis are in millions of current U.S. dollars unless otherwise indicated.

The size of the domestic agricultural sector was estimated from the United Nations FAO Statistical (FAOSTAT) database utilizing a list of agricultural crops and meat products produced in Iraq and evaluated at world market prices for 2002. [58]

The oil and gas sector size was based upon a production level of 2.24 million barrels a day at an average oil price of $24.48 per barrel (includes intermediate uses).

---

[56] Pacific Gas and Electric (2003). This level of investment was determined from a study of the ratio of power generation to distribution costs from a CountryWatch analysis of Pacific Gas and Electric's Annual Report for 2002.

[57] U.S. Department of Energy (2003a).

[58] Food and Agricultural Organization of the United Nations (2003).

The manufacturing sector was estimated at about $3 billion a year with just over 60 percent of the output of this sector absorbed by intermediate uses to support other sectors as inputs.

The power sector was estimated at a capacity of 4,300 MW running at a 90 percent base load with an 8,000 BTU/kWh[59] heat rate.

Transportation and communications were estimated at 10 percent of the costs involved in all domestic production for agriculture, oil and gas production, and manufacturing (to include intermediate uses) as well as 10 percent of all of the costs involved in imported goods.

The services sector was estimated using fixed percentages shown below of various transactions.

Retail services, as shown in Table A III–3, were assumed to be a 35 percent markup on the value of the domestic consumption of agriculture, oil and gas, and manufacturing sector.

Wholesale services were estimated as shown in Table A III-3 as 10 percent of the intermediate consumption of agriculture, oil and gas and manufacturing sector.

---

[59] British thermal units and kilowatts per hour.

Residential rental income was assumed as 15 percent of all wage income. Assuming a 20-year housing life and an expected 10 percent return for capital in this sector yielded a very rough estimate of 7.5 percent of all wage income as the annual construction rate.

Commercial construction used a similar methodology with commercial rental income estimated at 10 percent of all domestic transactions (including intermediate uses) of all sectors excluding oil and gas. A 10 percent return was utilized and a 10 year depreciation life to obtain the net estimate for the annual commercial construction budget.

Table A III-3
Description of Iraqi Services in 2004
(billions of $US)

Sector	Value
Retail Services	4.2
Wholesale Services	0.4
Construction Services	0.0
Residential	0.7
Commercial	1.2
Major Investment Projects	1.2
Financial and Banking Services	0.8
Government Services	3.9
Total Service Sector	12.4

Source: CountryWatch Forecast Estimates

25 percent of major investment projects in the oil and gas sector and power sector were assumed to consist of construction services.

Financial and banking services were assumed to require a fixed percentage of the value added from the oil and gas sector and the same services were assumed in the retail sector.

Government services are identified in the proposed government budget.

Production Functions and Coefficients

The agricultural and manufacturing production functions were derived from a four-sector United Nations Industrial Development Organization (UNIDO) World model (1977)[60] for the Middle East. For the hydrocarbon and power sectors, CountryWatch derived the production functions used in the model through an analysis of these sectors.

The production function for the oil and gas sector was assumed to follow the operating cost structure used in the model of the INOC based on DOE estimates of capacity addition costs in the Persian Gulf with a development cost of $.47 per barrel of reserves developed and a lifting cost of $1.12 per barrel of oil produced.[61]

---

[60] International Center for Industrial Studies. 1977.

[61] U.S. Department of Energy (2003f).

The power sector production function was calculated based upon estimated power generation costs and implied distribution costs from an analysis of electric power production, transmission, and distribution costs from the latest published reports of Pacific Gas and Electric.[62]

Transportation and services output estimates were based on CountryWatch estimates of the demand for these services from the other sectors and import volumes as described above.

Final Demand Estimate Sources

The sector that is best documented in the Iraqi economy is the petroleum sector. Both OPEC[63] and the U.S. Department of Energy[64] provide detailed information for this sector. Since it is the largest sector of the Iraqi economy and oil is fungible, it provides a strong point of departure for an economic estimate for Iraq.

The second sector, which is modestly well documented, is the power sector. Once again, the U.S. Department of Energy

---

[62] Pacific Gas and Electric (2003).

[63] OPEC (2001).

[64] U.S. Department of Energy (2003a).

provides some basic information on the status and capability of the Iraqi electricity industry.[65]

A third sector which is modestly well documented, but small, is the agricultural sector. The Food and Agricultural Organization of the United Nations[66] provides some information on the volume of arable land and the crops produced on this land.

Information on the manufacturing and the transportation & communications sectors of the economy is fairly sketchy and a reasonable amount of estimating was done based upon known, but dated, information on the relative size of these sectors after taking into account years of neglect during the Saddam Hussein era. In his major review of the economy of Iraq,[67] Alnasrawi reported that the manufacturing sector was about 12 percent of the economy in 1988 and the transportation & communications sector was estimated to be about 7 percent of the economy in 1988.[68]

The services sector includes both private and public services. The private services include banking and finance, construction, wholesale and retail operations. The public services included government administration, education, military, police, water,

---

[65] U.S. Department of Energy (2003a).

[66] Food and Agricultural Organization of the United Nations (2003).

[67] Alnasrawi (1994).

[68] *Ibid.*

fire, public health and de-mining. Of these services, the size of the military and the government work force was estimated from various sources, to include, various editions of *The Military Balance*[69], and crude numerical estimates from media sources.

Services were estimated to be about 46 percent of the economy in 1988 (includes construction, trade and other activities) and have been estimated to be as large as 80 percent in 1993 while Iraq was subject to a significantly constraining oil embargo.[70] Since our model looks at all private and public services, this number is going to be a large percentage of the current economy.

Capital, Material Resources and Labor Inputs

The model uses a linear production function. Factor inputs as a ratio of value added will generally vary significantly depending upon the relevant sector. The capital and natural resource factor inputs as a percentage of value added were a little less than 99 percent for oil and gas (5 percent physical capital and 94 percent from natural resources), 80 percent for power, 40 percent for manufacturing, 30 percent for transportation, 25 percent for agriculture, and 25 percent for services. The share of labor services in each sector are the complement of this or a little more than 1 percent for oil and gas, 20 percent for power, 60 percent for manufacturing, 70 percent for transportation, 75 percent for

---

[69] The International Institute for Strategic Studies (2003).

[70] Alnasrawi (1994).

agriculture and 75 percent for services. Across the entire economy, the input of services from physical capital and labor were 33 percent of value added from capital and 67 percent from labor services.

The rental return on capital was assumed to be 22 percent, which included an assumption of 10 percent depreciation[71], a real return on capital of 10 percent, and an allowance for inflation of 2 percent. This rental return on capital was also used to estimate the initial stock of capital required to support the national production level outlined in this forecast. The quality of this initial stock of capital is a major uncertainty in the model and a reconstruction fund was budgeted to reinvest heavily in this capital stock.[72]

For the power sector, a comparative industry analysis was used to estimate the breakdown between labor and capital costs. The value of the residual capital in this sector was estimated at $5.6 billion suggesting an annualized capital rental rate of 10 percent or $560 million. Labor was based on an estimated labor force of about 24,000 employees; this allows for about four times as many laborers (at relatively modest wage rates) as would be required in a typical power company in a developed country.[73]

---

[71] Assumes a 10 year useful life for capital equipment.

[72] See Table V-3 for details on the proposed reconstruction fund.

[73] See Appendix V.2 and Table B V-1 for a summary of the overall estimated employment picture for Iraq.

IV. The Iraqi Reconstruction Plan

Introduction

There is an urgent need for the United States to develop and communicate to the international community a comprehensive plan for reconstruction in Iraq. The lack of such a plan will sow the seeds of discontent not only in the Iraqi people, but also in the global community at large, particularly among Arab nations.

Achieving the objective of a truly democratic and capitalist society in Iraq, which is integrated into world markets, will not be easily accomplished. Consequently, our goal is simply to delineate the major economic and political structures that will be required in order to achieve this objective while leaving prescriptive details for future consideration.

Certainly, we might have tried to customize these prescriptions to accommodate the rich tapestry of legal, cultural and historical precedents throughout the various regions and echelons of society in Iraq. We, however, deliberately choose not to do so.

First, Iraqis might appreciate the fact that more than any foreign entity, they are much more qualified to identify the specific nuances of their government, associated economic system, and their framework of jurisprudence.

Second, we wanted to focus this plan solely on its structural elements; we do not see an obvious governmental prototype in the historical context of Iraq, nor among the other various Middle Eastern oil rich countries for Iraq to emulate. Consequently, we have borrowed liberally from the United States' system of government, not because this approach is necessarily superior to that found in any other liberal democracy, but because of Iraq's cultural and regional diversity. Such diversity and pluralism would seem to lend itself to a federal system.

There is an historic opportunity to develop governing structures and systems that will set the nation state of Iraq on a rapidly growing and positive trajectory. Iraq's natural resource endowment offers a potential development advantage for the future, but it simultaneously offers a trove of spoils to be high-jacked by corrupt leadership, via an insufficiently developed institutional system.

Thus, with considerable hope for a revitalized Iraq, we put forward this potential reconstruction plan. We understand that it is based upon an evolving capitalist economy and a democratic political paradigm, and we assume that others may well envision a different path and conceptualization for Iraq.

Security Development Plan

This plan describes a security structure that should enable Iraq to reduce and greatly minimize the level of threat from guerilla forces and terrorist activities.

A qualifier to this structure is that this plan ought not to be so harsh or alienating in its execution that it will damage the long-term prospects for peace and economic development in Iraq. The health, lives, property, and beliefs – particularly the religious beliefs - of ordinary Iraqis need to be respected as much as possible by Coalition Forces and follow-on Iraqi forces. These security efforts should endeavor to employ a "soft touch" in these operations.

Efforts to clear unexploded ordinance, restore basic utility services, and to achieve small economic gains for ordinary Iraqi citizens will help the Coalition Forces win the battle for the popular support of the Iraqi people.

Security Principles

The security of the Iraqi people during the transitional administration is critical to the success of the reconstruction plan.

Key principals of security in the transitional administration will include the following nine (9) points:

1. The Ba'athist Party is to be disbanded.

2. Former members of the Ba'athist Party identified by the transition administration are required to turn themselves in to Coalition Forces or they will be apprehended.

3. All Iraqi citizens will be issued photo identity cards with identity numbers. These cards, during the pre-constitutional period, shall be carried at all time for security purposes. These cards shall also entitle those of voting age, over 18, to sign petitions endorsing political parties for the constitutional convention, to receive ration allocations, and to participate in the distribution of benefits from the INOC.

4. Strict gun control will apply during the transitional period. All weapons in Iraq outside of Coalition Force control and outside the control of the reconstituted Iraqi military and national police will be registered and turned into Coalition Forces, with the exception of small arms that can be retained after being registered.

5. Laws in Iraq will be governed by Coalition Provisional Authority Regulation 1 which states that Iraqi law in effect as of April 16, 2003 applies in Iraq unless the existing law prevents the

Administrator from carrying out his obligations under U.N. Resolution 1483. U.S. forces in Iraq come under the jurisdiction of the U.S. Uniform Code of Military Justice (UCMJ).

6. Coalition forces will maintain a significant presence on the streets of major population centers in Iraq and along critical supply corridors for electric power, communications, oil pipelines, refining, and port facilities.

7. Military personnel are authorized to use deadly force to protect themselves, Iraqi citizens, and key logistical installations.

8. A new Iraqi military force and national police force will be constituted and trained by Coalition Forces.

9. The new Iraqi military force and national police force will be organized and trained to take over from Coalition Forces no later than July 15, 2005.

Coalition Forces

The security of the transitional administration will require a large coalition force for a period of at least two years. The size of the Coalition Forces will be nearly 200,000 troops including army, navy and air force elements. The military commander in the country will be responsible for implementing the security development plan and will report through the military chain of command to the United States Secretary of Defense. The

Secretary of Defense with the advice and counsel of his military joint staff will have overall responsibility for the implementation and execution of the security development plan.

Defeat the Ba'athist Government

The threat of sporadic violence by the remnants of the Ba'athist government needs to be eliminated. The necessary approach is to continue to apprehend key members of the former government of Saddam Hussein prosecute them as appropriate for war crime trials in Iraqi courts and under Iraqi law. In particular, Saddam Hussein, if he is still alive, must be apprehended; if he is not alive, evidence of his demise should be located and then shared with the Iraqi people. In addition, security operations need to be conducted by Coalition Forces to search for and capture unregistered weapons and to apprehend key leaders of the former Ba'athist government that do not voluntarily surrender.

Enforce Law and Order

Coalition forces will conduct security patrols in major population centers and along key logistical installations to safeguard Iraqi citizens and key logistical facilities. The use of deadly force will be authorized under specified rules of engagement. Joint patrols with Iraq's new police force and Army should be quickly expanded over time. These Iraqi forces are particularly important for security operations since they speak the local language, understand local customs, and will be seen as a sense of pride for ordinary Iraqis.

Train a New Iraqi Military

The size and composition of a new Iraqi military and National Police Force is discussed further below. A key mission of the transitional Coalition Forces, supported by the military schools and training commands principally of the United States Army, will be to train Iraqi forces to be prepared by June 30, 2005 to assume the security mission under the newly implemented Iraqi Constitution. This is a critical task that must be managed well for which the track record on previous efforts is unsatisfactory. Considering difficulties in establishing indigenous forces in Bosnia, Kosovo, and Afghanistan, an intensive effort must be made to ensure success in Iraq.

Political Development Plan

Democratic Federal Republic

The framework for a new government of Iraq will be built upon the principles of a democratic federal republic where each individual is guaranteed the right to freely elect their leadership and personal freedoms of free speech, the right of free assembly, the right to a free press, the right to own private property, the right to travel freely within the country and freedom of religion. A bill of rights will prohibit illegal search and seizure and protect against illegal detention with a right of *habeus corpus*.

Governing Council

To begin the process of moving toward self-rule, the Administrator will constitute a Governing Council of 25 Iraqis representing the primary political power groups in Iraq. The Governing Council will begin to develop the procedure for devising a new Iraqi constitution consistent with the principles enumerated above.

Constitutional Convention

The rights of the Iraqi people in a Democratic Federal Republic will be enumerated in a new constitution in Iraq developed with the help of the Governing Council and the Administrator during a constitutional convention. The constitutional convention will be held in Baghdad and will commence in November of 2003. The convention will have a timetable of six months, or until May of 2004 to complete the constitution. The transition authorities will outline procedures to ensure that political parties in good standing in Iraq shall be represented at the convention and that their relative importance in determining the new constitution is adequately reflected in coming to a consensus. Political parties in good standing shall include all political groups in Iraq, excluding current and former members of the Ba'ath Party, that register with the occupying authorities, and show a minimum of 10,000 signatures on petitions indicating exclusive support of the signatories for that party in the constitutional process. Signatories on petitions must include their identification number.

The Governing Council shall be a consultative body to the Administrator in helping to govern the country during the interim period prior to the completion of the constitution and the election of a new President of Iraq. In addition, additional executive authority will be phased in for the Governing Council over time. The provisional Governing Council will also help the Administrator shape a consensus on the elements of the draft constitution. The Administrator, however, shall arbitrate all disputes among political parties in good standing in determining and approving the final provisions of the draft constitution. The draft constitution for the initial meeting of the constitutional convention shall include the rights enumerated in the preceding paragraphs.

The constitutional convention shall meet and vote on the new draft constitution. Each political party in good standing will be able to cast votes amounting to the number of exclusive certified signatures that each party is able to secure and to present to the Administrator by November of 2003.

Once the constitution is approved, the Administrator will remain in power until a new government is elected. Elections will be scheduled for November of 2004. However, even during this period before the establishment of a new government, the Administrator will phase-in executive power in certain areas to the Governing Council.

The Federal Government

The constitution will provide for a federal government consisting of an executive branch, a legislative branch, and a judicial branch. The head of state will be the president of Iraq who will be elected in a national election to be held every four years in November, starting in 2004. Inauguration will occur in the January following the election. While the form of government reflects that of the United States more than the mixed presidential-parliamentary systems of Turkey and Egypt, the republican style of government is not new to the Middle East. Moreover, it presents a form of government that can effectively manage the different regional and sectarian constituencies of the country. The overriding principle will be that of a secular federal-style government which recognizes Iraq's pluralism.

The Executive Branch of Government.

The President will run the executive branch of government. The Vice President will assist the President in running the federal government and will govern in the case of death or mental incapacity of the President. The executive branch will consist of 8 ministries and the President of Iraq will have a cabinet of 8 ministers that report in directly to the President.[1] These will include:

---

[1] We have proposed 8 ministries. While there are certainly other functions which the government must handle we have chosen to focus on what we

The *Defense Minister* will have responsibility for the national security of Iraq. The federal budget will allocate sufficient funds to reconstitute the Iraqi armed forces into an Army, Navy, and Air Force at a force level of 240,000 active duty personnel and 240,000 reserve personnel. Consistent with the principle of civilian control of the military, the Defense Ministry will be a civilian.

The *Foreign Minister* will have the responsibility of normalizing Iraq's relations with the international community through a corps of Ambassadors, and responsibility for Iraqi relations with the United Nations. The federal budget will allocate sufficient resources for embassies at the United Nations and in key countries.

The *Finance Minister* will have responsibility for operating the treasury of the government of Iraq, for collecting taxes and preparation of the annual government budget and macroeconomic operating plan in coordination with the other Ministers.

The *Justice Minister* will have responsibility for the enforcement of the laws enacted by the legislature under the provisions of the Constitution. The justice minister will act as a prosecutor on

---

believe are the most important. The budget shown in Table IV-1 provides for a 10 percent contingency to be used by the President for such other functions.

behalf of the government and will be responsible for the internal security of the country through a Federal Bureau of Investigation, the senior law enforcement agency in Iraq.

The *Energy Minister* will have responsibility for oversight of the Iraqi National Oil Company (INOC). The Energy minister will review and report to the President on the operations of the INOC and will also coordinate with the Minister of Finance on securing capital for the reconstruction of the petroleum sector.

The *Education Minister* will have responsibility for the operational development of the public education system in Iraq, including K-12 schools and the state universities. The federal budget shall provide adequate resources to ensure the availability of educational capacity for 100 percent of the school age children for a K-12 education, and the capacity for 30 percent of the university age students to attend public schools.

The *Health Minister* will have responsibility for providing for an initial public health care system in Iraq and for maintaining national hospitals. This ministry will also have responsibility for promoting the development of a private health care system in Iraq.

The *Agriculture Minister* will have responsibility for promoting the development of the agricultural sector in Iraq and administering the food ration program. The major responsibility of this ministry will be to develop a program for food security and self-sufficiency in Iraq.

The Regional Governments

The constitution of Iraq will provide that regions of Iraq will be governed by 18 or more regional provincial governments, each with a regional governor. The regions will have the right to enact local regulations that do not conflict with the constitution.

The 18 provinces (muhafazat, singular - muhafazah) are: Al Anbar, Al Basrah, Al Muthanna, Al Qadisiyah, An Najaf, Arbil, As Sulaymaniyah, At Ta'mim, Babil, Baghdad, Dahuk, Dhi Qar, Diyala, Karbala', Maysan, Ninawa, Salah ad Din, Wasit .

The regional governments shall have responsibility for organizing a regional police force that shall work with the federal armed forces to maintain law and order in Iraq. The federal forces will only be called in after a request of the regional governor to the President of Iraq in case of an emergency.

The regional governor shall also have responsibility for developing and training a local fire force and for working with the Minister of Justice on developing local correctional facilities to handle regional level criminal and civil offenses.

An initial budget for each province is developed later in this Chapter.

The New Iraqi Armed Forces

The government of Iraq shall have a military force to defend the country from the threat of foreign military aggression and to provide for domestic security when provincial forces need to be augmented. Federal troops could also be employed, even after the establishment of the local forces, to ensure domestic security in the case of an emergency as declared by the regional governor and with the consent of the President of Iraq.

While the United States and Coalition Forces would guarantee Iraqi security over a two-year period, effective June 30, 2005, Iraq will need to provide for its own national and domestic security. The Government of Iraq would be offered a non-aggression treaty by the coalition governments, which would provide for the stationing of one brigade of Coalition Forces in Iraq and the use by coalition air elements of Iraqi air bases. A status of forces agreement will be signed with the new Iraqi government after the elections; Coalition Forces will arrange for appropriate compensation for the use of Iraqi land and port facilities. In addition, the Iraqi government will be offered a full bi-lateral military partnership with the United States so that Iraqi military forces can participate in joint exercises with United States military forces and also allow Iraqi officers to be educated in U.S. military schools. In addition, Iraq's military forces should be an integral part of the existing Gulf security agreements with the United States and its allies.

The size of the Iraqi army is dictated by the national security requirements of Iraq. The armed forces are envisioned in our plan to have 4 full army divisions, a small air force, and a small navy. Given Iraq's previous military history, in particular with Iran, the force would deploy one division in the east along the Iranian border, one division in the west along the Syrian border, one division along the Turkish border in the north and one division around Baghdad. In general, the force will need to be highly mobile because of the large size of the country. The air force would be centrally located around Baghdad and the navy would operate out of Umm Qasr.

In support of the regular forces, there would be an equal complement of reserve forces. The reserves would drill once per month and would be headquartered in the same areas as the regular forces to accommodate training and support.

The military hardware associated with the new Iraqi military will be a significant capital item. While there is a significant amount of useable military hardware left over from the Saddam Hussein regime in reasonable condition, there will be a need for modernization of the Iraqi military. Based on a review of other armed forces and budgetary considerations, the initial force structure would, in addition to equipment left over from the previous government (which needs to be inventoried and retrofitted), add 150 tanks, 200 armored personnel carries, 10 helicopters, 20 fighter aircraft, 1 warship and 2 support ships. This equipment list includes less than 50 percent of the typical capital equipment allocation of comparable military forces, but with the continued presence of Coalition Forces, the useable equipment from the previous regime and with appropriate security treaties with Coalition Forces, this force structure should be more than adequate to provide for national security.

The Government Civil Service

As in most governments, the civil service bureaucracy that supports the government on a day in and day out basis maintains the continuity of the government. There is surprisingly little turn over after elections in most bureaucracies of most nations.

This plan allows for the government to be elected by a fixed date, but the clear expectation is that the development of the bureaucracy should be well on its way at that point with considerable urgency. It is not only appropriate that the Administrator undertake these activities, but absolutely essential. Since the Administrator has the responsibility to run the government prior to the elections, his team, with whatever input is provided by the Governing Council, needs to ensure that the governmental backbone is functional. To further complicate the difficulty of this task, these bureaucracies operate at all levels of government - national, regional, and local.

Table IV-1 outlines the specifics of our plan in the form of an operating budget for the government of Iraq. As the data indicates, this plan envisions employing a government of over 760,000 employees. This plan, if executed quickly and expeditiously, would have a profound effect on the revitalization of Iraqi government services. As we outline below, our plan is to fund these efforts with income earned from oil exports.

The Government Budget

Funding levels for the budget for 2004 are given in Table IV-1. The budget includes an operating budget as well as subsidies for the food ration program and for state water and power companies. Detailed budget data for each major organizational element is given in Appendix IV.1. The largest expenditure items include the armed forces, education, healthcare, and expenditures for provincial governments.

Table IV-1
Government Budget and Employment

Government Agency	Employment (Persons)	Budget (millions of $s)
Office of the President	49	7
Legislature	1,165	226
Judiciary	4,186	210
Defense Ministry	33	3
Armed Forces	480,844	2,354
Ministry of Justice	3,689	182
Foreign Ministry	750	62
Finance Ministry	663	38
Energy Minstry	45	5
Education Ministry	165,320	1,561
Health Ministry	48,989	660
Agriculture Ministry	25,045	332
Provincial Governments	31,539	991
Sub-Total	762,316	6,632
Contingency	0	663
Total Operations	762,316	7,296
Transfers		
Food Rations		2,600
Water, Power		1,600
Capital Costs		
Armed Forces		1,000
Public Works		1,000
Compensation Claims		1,900
Total Budget	**762,316**	**15,396**

As noted above, the armed forces budget is driven by the national security requirements of the new Iraqi state. There is a particular concern about relations with Iran and in any event the area is beset with political uncertainty with continued hostile relations between former Ba'athist elements and the new regime. As noted above, the budget developed here envisions a military force of 4 regular army divisions and 4 reserve divisions, 1 air force squadron and a small navy. This force would cost approximately $2.4 billion per year, but it would provide for both domestic and international security and would employ either full time or part time approximately 480,000 Iraqi citizens.

In the educational arena the budget provides for the revitalization of the public education system. Funds are provided for K-12 and university activities including funding for major universities and K-12 schools. The plan calls for over 6,500 university teaching positions to be filled as well as 130,000 K-12 teaching positions. The initial goal will be to provide for the availability of education through the K-12 level and if qualified for a university education. The education budget would cost an estimated $1.6 billion per year. It would enable the youth of Iraq to resume their education, gaining needed skills for their employment in the new Iraqi economy, and keeping them productively employed. It would also give meaningful employment to 165,000 Iraqi citizens in the educational sector.

In the healthcare sector, the budget provides for a minimal public health system including 9,000 doctors and 27,000 nurses to provide care at 7 major hospitals and 240 clinics. The government would also aggressively encourage the development of a private health care sector.

The judiciary budget provides for staffing of the court system in Iraq including the supreme court, the appeals courts, and the provincial court system. The judiciary budget also includes provisions for the court clerk system, which will be critical for adjudicating the claims concerning property rights, which is further discussed below. This system must tie culturally to a long pre-Hussein judicial history.

The budget for the Ministry of Agriculture includes funds for administering the food ration program, including fund for 25,000 ration agents that would be responsible for administering the post-war ration program.

The provincial budgets include funds for local governance. Financing should be sufficient to allow for a clear sharing of power between the federal, regional and local governments. The provincial budgets provide for police, fire and administration of the provincial prison system. The budget calls for the creation of a police force with over 18,000 national policemen, which will work with the armed forces to provide for local security as well as 9,000 fire fighters to provide for local fire fighting capability.

The two wage subsidy programs include the food ration program at $2.6 billion in 2004 and the power and water subsidies at $1.6 billion dollars in 2004. These subsidies will be phased out by 2010 as the economic program increases Iraqi GDP.

Economic Development Plan

Overriding Principles

The recent course of history tells us that there is no substitute for a market-oriented economy. The failure of central planning and state run industries, in general, is well documented with both the Russian and Chinese examples. Even so, a transition to a more market based system can be difficult and problematic; recent Russian efforts to privatize prized sectors of the Russian economy under Boris Yeltsin frequently resulted in concentrated ownership of these resources by a few well-positioned Russians. The central principle of the reconstruction should therefore be a rapid, but deliberate, move toward a market-oriented economy with emphasis on those industries in which Iraq has a competitive advantage. Given the natural resource position of the country, this will naturally and rightly start with a focus on the petroleum sector.

A smoothly functioning market oriented economy, however, will not simply materialize out of the chaos of the War of 2003 and years of autocratic rule under the Saddam Hussein regime in Iraq.

Some key foundations need to be laid and some initial guidance needs to be provided. The key foundations include the political development plan as well as the institutional development plan and international financial plan discussed below. Finally, a macroeconomic plan is needed with public investment targets for each sector to jump-start the development of a smoothly functioning market.

The overall macroeconomic goals of the Economic Development Plan are to raise the standard of living of the Iraqi population and to do so in a climate of relative domestic price stability while, at the same time, maintaining a stable and convertible Iraqi dinar.

The standard of living in Iraq for the ordinary citizen has deteriorated significantly during the last 10 years of the Hussein regime. As shown in Table IV-2 the level of GDP per capita in Iraq, ranks at the bottom of the chart compared with the other neighboring Middle Eastern members of OPEC. Consequently, the challenge in improving the living standard in Iraq is going to be formidable. With Iraq's enormous hydrocarbon resource base, however there is a reasonable opportunity to make a substantial improvement in that standard in a short period of time.

Table IV-2
Comparative GDP Per Capita
Middle Eastern OPEC Nations 2001
(US Dollars)

Country	GDP Per Capita
Qatar	$27,853
UAE	$20,576
Kuwait	$14,420
Saudi Arabia	$8,962
Iran	$1,767
Iraq	$1,194

Sources: OPEC (2001), Table III-1.

Price stability is a key economic objective. A well-planned monetary policy, coordinated by the Finance Ministry and the Central Bank, is essential to avoid the run-away inflation experienced in many post-war economies. The essential requirement here is to make sure that the government budget is adequately supported by either domestic taxation or foreign aid. This eliminates the necessity of the government resorting to inflationary finance by issuing domestic currency to fund a large portion of the budget deficit.

A stable, convertible currency is also critical. Lack of a free market in foreign exchange brings on a number of problems, including black markets and parallel rates structures, with the ultimate effect being the creation of significant pricing distortions with associated major misallocation of resources.

The Institutional Foundations

The institutional development plan will clearly articulate programs by the reconstruction authorities and the new government for establishing a going forward set of institutions and policies concerning property rights, taxation, monetary policy, and international trade.

Property Rights Plan

The plan for property rights is critical to the operation of a free market economy. The cornerstone of property rights lies in the constitution and the sections in the constitution for establishing and protecting these rights.

The most difficult issues will involve a transition from what was experienced in the past to the new regime. The fundamental principle here should be the right to own property and a set of institutions for recording and documenting property records and a legal framework to adjudicating property disputes.

A critical issue surrounding property rights that needs to be resolved quickly is the ownership of mineral rights and in particular the ownership of the hydrocarbon wealth in Iraq. Before any international private capital can flow to the country these rights must be defined. The Russian oil sector was held up for many years by an unclear definition of these rights.

The key components of the *Property Rights Plan* include:

1. The establishment of the principle of private property ownership in the newly created constitution.

2. The re-codification of Iraqi civil law procedure in accordance with the constitution

3. The reinstitution of a viable criminal and civil court system for implementing the constitutional principles of private property ownership.

4. The establishment at an appropriate local level, under the supervision of the local judicial authority, of a Property Registry; common records system for recording property ownership.

5. A mandatory property recording and claims period where all Iraqi citizens who own property, as well as the Government of Iraq, register with the newly created Property Registry to record their property ownership.

6. Disputes arising during the mandatory registration period will be resolved by the judicial authority supervising the Property Registry which during the mandatory registration period will

have authority as outlined in Coalition Provisional Authority Regulation 1.

The starting point in asserting ownership will be based on the prevailing laws and customs at the time of the War of 2003, except that mineral rights in Iraq, with respect to oil and gas reserves, shall revert to the new Government of Iraq effective June 30, 2003 and shall be owned by a newly created Iraqi National Oil Company (INOC). Compensation claims for those oil and natural gas mineral rights not formerly owned by the Saddam Hussein regime will be adjudicated by the courts supervising the Property Registry.

The Taxation Plan

As Iraq evolves into a modern state, public spending should be financed with an efficient and equitable taxation system. The plan will specify the initial programs and tax rates for income taxes, sales taxes, property taxes, severance taxes, and customs duties. The initial tax rates were selected pragmatically to reflect rates reasonably in line with taxation norms in the United States and Europe. Based on our calculations, this tax regime should provide sufficient revenue to meet the funding requirements of the new government. Adjustments to these rates are expected to ensure that they meet the goals described below.

The new taxation system must be designed to be easy to administer and understand. An oppressive and cumbersome tax system would be an obstacle to stability and would be counterproductive. The combination of taxes must also be sufficient to finance the initial public spending plan.

The key components of the *Taxation Plan* include:

1. The creation of a Finance Ministry with the responsibility for administering the national taxation system. The Finance Ministry would have representatives at the local level co-located with the Property Registry to facilitate the creation of a fiscal system.

2. The institution of a simple flat rate income tax system with two rates on personal income: 5 percent for incomes below $1,000 and 15 percent for incomes in excess of $1,000. The tax rate on corporations and proprietorships would be 15 percent. Depreciation allowances would be allowed as deductions based on a 5-year useful life for all capital expenditures. The tax would be due and payable on income earned in any calendar year by April of the following year. Corporations would be required to collect withholdings on wage earners and remit them to the Finance Ministry with each pay period as well as to issue wage and earnings statements by January of the year following. The tax would be payable in person, by mail, or over the Internet using a charge card. Income tax forms would be promulgated and available at the Finance Ministry office co-located with the Property Registry.

3. The institution of a national value added sales tax of 5 percent. The sales tax would be collected by merchants and forwarded monthly to the Finance Ministry with a national sales tax form promulgated by the Finance Ministry. The tax would be collected on all sales but taxes paid on inter-industry purchases would be netted against amounts collected and remitted to the Finance Ministry at each stage in the production process to result in a value added sales tax.

4. The institution of a property tax of .5 percent on the value of real tangible property. This tax would require an appraisal of real tangible property by the Property Registry as of January 1st each year. The appraisal would be completed by June of each year based on the market value of property each year as of January 1st. Property owners would be notified of the appraised value of their property within 30 days following the appraisal deadline of June of each year and would have an opportunity to appeal the appraisal until November at which time final appraisal values would be set. Property taxes on final appraised value would be due and payable based on the June appraisal by January of the following year.

5. The institution of a severance tax on all oil and natural gas production from Iraqi oil and gas reserves. The severance tax will be initially set at 5 percent of the value of production. The tax would be remitted by the INOC to the Finance Ministry based on production records of the INOC.

6. The institution of a 5 percent import tariff on all goods entering Iraq. Corporations using imported goods for intermediate goods would be allowed to expense the import tariff against their corporate income taxes.

Monetary Policy Plan

Another critical element of the institutional plan is the monetary plan. In order to move forward with a market oriented approach to reconstructing the Iraqi economy and the Iraqi financial markets a plan to oversee the currency of Iraq and Iraqi monetary policy will be urgently required.

The central issue here will be the nature of the monetary system and the institutions under which Iraq will conduct its monetary and foreign exchange policy. The issue is both economic and political and there are different approaches as discussed above.

The key components of the *Monetary Plan* include:

1. The creation of a new Central Bank of Iraq that is independent of fiscal policy of the government and led by a Governor of the Bank. The Governor of the Bank shall have responsibility for the stability of the new Iraqi dinar and maintaining the rate of exchange of the dinar against other foreign currencies including the U.S. dollar and the euro.

2. The Central Bank of Iraq will have the responsibility of conducting a currency conversion of old Iraqi dinars for New Iraqi dinars.

3. The Central Bank will issue new banking regulations stipulating the rules under which the commercial banks in Iraq must operate including required reserve deposits and the methods and discount rates at which the Central Bank of Iraq will lend to the commercial banks.

4. The Central Bank will maintain a floating exchange rate designed to keep the new dinar a freely convertible currency against the U.S. dollar.

5. The Central Bank shall utilize a monetary policy designed to maintain price stability. Table V-1 outlines a monetary expansion plan based on a relatively fixed ratio of the money supply in Iraq to the nominal GDP expressed in dollars. This money supply should allow for a supply of dinars to meet transaction demands and which will maintain a relatively stable domestic price level and exchange rate with the dollar.

6. The Central Bank shall be independent of the Finance Ministry and the Governor of the Central Bank shall be appointed by the President and impeachable by the legislature for high crimes and misdemeanors.

The International Trade Plan

As noted above, the overriding principle to be followed in the reconstruction of the economic system in Iraq will be to allow market forces to guide the flow of commerce and the allocation of resources. One of the implications of this principle in the area of international trade is to minimally interfere with the free flow of goods and capital into and out of Iraq while at the same time policing the borders for the flow of contraband and illegal migration.

The key components of the *International Trade Plan* include:

1. Except for items of contraband, including illegal narcotics, weapons and other goods determined by the new government to present a clear and present danger to law and order, goods shall be allowed to be freely exported and imported out of and into Iraq.

2. Foreign and domestic firms shall be allowed to make direct foreign investments and to freely import and export capital, intermediate, and final demand goods and services into and out of Iraq.

3. Foreign and domestic firms shall be allowed to fully repatriate profits into and out of Iraq.

4. All transfers of cash into and out of Iraq in denominations greater than $10,000 shall be reportable.

5. All citizens of Iraq shall be free to maintain both foreign and domestic bank accounts. Foreign bank accounts shall be reportable when filing income taxes.

The International Finance Plan

The International Finance plan details the resolution of three critical issues facing the new government of Iraq that will initially need to be resolved in order to clarify the status of the new government in the international financial community. These issues include the resolutions of claims against the government of Iraq by the international financial community including the international banking system, the resolution of the principles surrounding existing and new hydrocarbon contracts, and the resolution of the issue of U.N. sanctions and the Oil-for-Food Programme.

The International Claims Plan

With an estimated $380 billion in foreign claims, there is no way that the new Iraqi government can repay all the existing claims outstanding and provide for a rising standard of living for the people of Iraq. If the total amount claimed were repaid over a 20 year period, with interest accumulating at 10 percent on the unpaid balance, the annual claim service amount would be $56 billion, an amount in excess of the current estimate of the Iraqi GDP! In essence, the Saddam Hussein regime essentially bankrupted the Iraqi economy.

In our reconstruction plan, a process is advocated in which major claims against the Government of Iraq are not repaid in full. Instead, those with claims are to be reimbursed using a compensation fund. This formula is predicated on the notion that the claims burden on Iraq is so great that repaying all claims in full would be unduly burdensome and onerous.[2] A large portion of the claims against the Government of Iraq is derived from war claims and reparations resulting from the war with Iran in the 1980s and the invasion of Kuwait in 1990. The possibility that these claims – mostly to other Middle Eastern countries – would ever be repaid in full has always been small. The rest of the claims are derived from countries such as France and Russia.

Since the United States is not seeking repayment for the estimated $150 billion spent on the war in Iraq and the subsequent occupation[3], some suggest that other countries should also extend this measure of goodwill and relinquish their claims. There are already reports that Russia is considering such a move.[4] Certainly, some critics of this position have said that the United States' actions in Iraq were not legal and as such, these estimated

---

[2] Wall Street Journal (2003a).

[3] Fram (2003) and further discussed on page 343.

[4] Friedman (2003).

war and occupation costs could not be regarded as a valid claim in the first place. The opposite perspective, however, is that the United States could also claim this $150 billion themselves and then, when it received its pro rata share of claim payments, it could turn these funds back over to Iraq. This approach would effectively dilute the existing claims collection process and achieve a measure of debt relief for Iraq in the process.

While there may be validity in either of the two aforementioned positions, the fact remains that debt forgiveness is not a new concept. Cuba's debt was cancelled back in 1898, and both debt forgiveness and rescheduling have been advocated for several developing countries around the world.[5] In the case of Cuba, it was believed that the island needed to have the opportunity for a new future following colonialism. In the case of several developing countries, it has become abundantly clear that without debt relief, their economies would be trapped in the throes of ruin for several decades to come with no hope of recovery.

Certainly it is true that the reconstruction plan ultimately offers dividends to the Iraqi people. As such, it may call into question the notion that claims repayment would be impossible to be realized. Still, even with the provisions of dividends for the Iraqi people, the Iraqi economy will still be significantly disadvantaged in comparison to other surrounding countries. For

---

[5] Hindawi and Thomson (2003) and Wall Street Journal (2003).

example, as noted in Table IV-2, Iraq's GDP per capita in 2001 was $1,194 as compared with Qatar at $27,853, the United Arab Emirates at $20,567, and Kuwait at $14,420. Even in a post-Saddam Hussein Iraq, the projection for Iraq in the next five years suggests that Iraq's GDP per capita in 2008 would be $2,557, as seen in Table V-1. Clearly, this improved GDP per capita for Iraq is still far less substantial than that in most of the other surrounding oil-rich countries. In this way, even if the dividend provision for the Iraqi people were not included, repayment of claims within this context would be far too exacting. As such, it would cripple Iraq's efforts at reconstruction and development.

Philosophically, the question must be asked as to whether or not it would be fair for the new Iraq to pay the claims arising from actions of the Hussein regime of the past. Of course, taking on debts from the past is normative practice. Russia, for example, took on repayment of the Soviet Union's $80 billion debt.[6] Iraq's situation might be distinguished in some measure. Principally, repaying all of these claims, plus interest, would require almost all of Iraq's oil resources over the course of the next twenty years. Russia's $80 billion debt is far less than the total claims against Iraq, which is variously estimated at between $300 billion and $400 billion.[7]

---

[6] Hindawi and Thomson (2003).

[7] *Ibid.*

Repayment of such a claim would also prevent investment and funding for most of Iraq's infrastructure. Excluding the possibility of external grants, this scenario would guarantee that Iraqis would suffer economically for the next two decades, seeing few tangible improvements in their daily life. The internal economic challenges in such an untenable situation might also fuel popular resentment and give rise to political instability; political instability could have dire consequences for the economic well being of Iraq and the rest of the world.

There is also a case to be made that Iraq's debt is illegitimate in the first place and as such, it should be dismissed. "Odious debt" is understood as (1) debt money used by a regime without a popular mandate; and (2) debt money used in ways that does not benefit the citizenry. If creditors knowingly financed activities such as corruption, human rights violations, as well as geopolitical assault and invasion, then these activities by a regime without popular backing would, essentially invalidate these particular claims for repayment. Based on these parameters, some of the debt portion of the claims might well be considered "odious debt" and consequently, debt relief would be the most ethical outcome.[8]

---

[8] Oxfam Policy Papers (2003).

Our plan requires that the new Iraqi government adopt a program of reasonable compensation for these claims that sets aside some percentage of the existing GDP as a stream of income that is allocated to service all claims for a specified period of time.

The key components of the International Claim Plan are as follows:

1. The provisions of U.N. Resolution 1483, Paragraph 21 and U.N. Resolution 687 will be changed in a new U.N. resolution as follows. Ten (10) percent of the net operating cash flow of the INOC will be set aside for a period of 20 years to settle all existing claims against the Government of Iraq as of the existing claim declaration date of October 31, 2003. This amount of revenue will be defined as the Claim Service Limit and is equal to an estimated $132 billion over this 20-year period.

2. All persons with a claim against the government of Iraq must file a claim declaration as of October 31, 2003.

3. A claims tribunal consisting of a committee of the members of the new Iraqi provisional Governing Council and headed by the provisional Minister of Finance shall prioritize claims and allocate a percentage of the Claim Service Limit against each claim. The Administrator will have final adjudication authority in the event of disputes and beginning at the end of each calendar

quarter in 2004, the transitional government shall begin to make payments based on quarterly receipts from the INOC.

4. The initial percentages of the Claim Service Limit based on the current estimate of the claims outstanding by CSIS shall be:

International Debt	*$127 billion*	*33% of the Claim Service Limit*
Contracts	*$57 billion*	*15% of the Claim Service Limit*
Gulf War Claims	*$199 billion*	*52% of the Claim Service Limit*

Each claimant in the above classes shall be assigned a percentage of the appropriate Claim Service Limit as a settlement of the outstanding claim. In addition, any outstanding claims by Iraqi citizens for pension entitlements will also be included in this mix of claims and valued as determined by the claims tribunal.

5. The new Iraqi government shall issue a Claim Service Limit Note against the claims. The Claim Service Limit Note shall be based on the estimate of the current level of the INOC operating cash flow as developed in the Oil and Gas Sector Plan below.

6. The notes will be guaranteed by the new government of Iraq and shall be freely tradable allowing immediate liquidity on each claim. No additional interest will accrue on these claims.

The Role of International Oil Companies

The development of the hydrocarbon sector in Iraq is critical to the success of future economic development in Iraq. The key to success in developing the hydrocarbon wealth of Iraq will be to mobilize sufficient capital and expertise to fully develop the petroleum and natural gas resources of the country as well as to utilize the best available technology in developing the new Iraqi oil fields. As noted later in this Chapter, the estimate of the capital required to revitalize the hydrocarbon sector over the next 10 years is $21 billion.

International oil companies will be asked to work with the INOC to develop the new fields on a contract basis. International oil companies that participate in this redevelopment program shall receive concessions which shall entitle them to have their expenses reimbursed and will allow them to lift at market prices oil produced from the fields they develop for their own refining operations. Furthermore, international oil companies that participate in the development program will have a right of first offer to develop the gas reserves that are associated with the field that they develop. These reserves will be developed using the production sharing agreement methodology outlined in paragraph 6 below. The government of Iraq will offer to purchase the gas so developed to offset internal oil consumption at Iraqi power plants. This consumption would amount to the equivalent of over 40 million barrels of oil per year, which at current market prices would amount to a revenue stream of over $1 billion per year. Participating international oil companies will be entitled to sell the remaining gas into the gas market in Iraq at market prices or to liquefy the gas and to sell it into the international liquefied natural gas market. As an additional incentive, the INOC shall develop a schedule for the development of non-associated gas reserves and participating international oil companies shall have the right of first offer to develop such reserves under production sharing agreements with the INOC.

The fundamental principles of the oil sector development program shall be as follows:

1. The new government of Iraq shall target the amount of $21 billion over the next 10 years for the re-development of the Iraqi oil fields

2. The estimated sources of capital for the initial development of the hydrocarbon sector will be:

U.S./U.K. Loan $ 4 billion 19 percent
INOC Cash Flow $17 billon 81 percent

3. The allocation of resources shall be 100 percent to the development of oil reserves. Gas reserves can be developed by foreign oil companies as described above. Initial associated gas reserves shall be developed under concessions as described above which compensate international oil companies for participation in the oil development program. Non-associated gas reserves shall be developed as described above under production sharing agreements.

4.The Iraqi Foreign Ministry will request International loans from the United States/United Kingdom. The Finance Ministry will negotiate these loans and INOC securities shall be used as collateral.

5. The Iraqi Finance Ministry shall authorize the INOC to retain up to $17 billion of internally generated funds up through 2012 to finance the development of the Iraqi oil fields.

6. Production Sharing Agreements ("PSA") shall be used to finance the development of associated and non-associated gas reserves. The PSA's shall be administered by the INOC. The INOC shall develop a standard methodology for awarding PSA's for the development of the Iraqi gas resources. The awards shall be made in a competitive bidding process with rights of first offer to those international oil companies participating with the INOC in the oil re-development program. The ultimate criteria for awarding contracts to develop gas reserves will be the capability and financial strength of the companies involved and, the rate of return criteria on investment required over a 20-year concession period to extract the natural gas resources.

Typically the PSA will split the gas produced between the government and the energy company, so that the gas allocated to the concessionaire at market prices will be sufficient to repay the capital invested and yield a target rate of return. Under current market conditions, given the risks involved in Iraq, the rate of return would be in the 15-25 percent range, but the return must be sufficient to attract the capital given the risks involved in this type of development. A reasonable mid-point, for planning purposes, would be a 20 percent un-levered return on equity. This would be the return offered on a right-of-first-offer basis for the development of the Iraqi gas fields.

The PSA would allow the concessionaire 75 percent of the cash flow from the proceeds and the government 25 percent until the target return of 20 percent is attained. In the year after the target return was attained, the proceeds of the development would be divided 50/50 between the concessionaire and the government.

Appendix IV.2 shows a standard term sheet for a gas development PSA and a sample pro-forma. This would be utilized by the INOC in negotiating production sharing agreements.

7. The Finance Minister and the Energy Minister will prepare The Hydrocarbon Development Plan in conjunction with the Foreign Minister and the INOC. The Finance Minister shall have responsibility for developing a coordinated macroeconomic plan to integrate each of the components of the Hydrocarbon development plan in with the overall economic program.

The Transition of the U.N. Food for Peace Program

The U.N. sanctions formerly existing against the government of Iraq were lifted under U.N. Resolution 1483 and the resumption of oil exports in the post sanction era began on June 22, 2003 as Iraq exported 8 million barrels of oil from storage at Ceyhan and 2 million barrels from oil stored at Mina al-Bakr on July 1, 2003.[9]

U.N. Resolution 1483 also phased out, over a six-month period, the U.N. Food for Peace Program and put the responsibility for future food aid into the hands of the Administrator. The Administrator will assume responsibility for this program in November 2003. Revenues from crude oil production and sales in Iraq are assumed henceforth to accrue to the INOC to be used, under the supervision of the Administrator, for the benefit of the new Government of Iraq.

The new budget provides funds for a distribution mechanism for channeling food provided under this agreement to the normal recipients of food rations in Iraq under the budget for the Minister of Agriculture. An allowance for managing and running this program has been included in the budget for the Agricultural Ministry.

---

[9] U.S. Department of Energy, Energy Information Administration (2003h).

Privatization of State Owned Companies

Iraq's public enterprises, with the exception of the Iraqi National Oil Company, are considered non-strategic and should be privatized. Each enterprise should be individually analyzed to determine its viability. If a minor investment will likely increase the value of these enterprises more than the value of the enterprise in its current state plus the investment, then the government should temporarily provide a subsidy. If additional investment is not warranted or unnecessary, then the enterprise should be privatized as soon as conditions permit.

The objective is to energize these enterprises so that they can compete within the marketplace or at least get these employees into an international company that can utilize their services. As has been the case in former communist states such as Poland, the movement away from state-controlled enterprises and industries, should be done in a systematic – and not a rushed -- fashion. The contingency component of the budget should be used to provide any required subsidies for these companies prior to their sale. Proceeds from any privatization sales should be allocated back to the contingency part of the budget.

Iraq and OPEC

Iraq has been a member of the Organization of Petroleum Exporting Countries (OPEC) since the inception of OPEC. OPEC is the worldwide oil cartel that meets regularly to fix the price of oil, presumably to benefit all of its members, by a system of quotas that typically are designed to adjust global world oil output so that the target price can be maintained. OPEC typically administers these quotas and gives each of the member nations a production quota. The quota sometimes implies that nations in OPEC such as Iraq must withhold potential production from the market.

There are two good reasons why Iraq should not feel compelled to follow an OPEC quota over the next several years. First, the country needs to generate oil revenues to rebuild, and second the world oil price is at a high level. The world prices for oil and gas are at their highest levels in the past 10 years and Iraq, even producing at its maximum sustainable capacity, should not have a significant impact on world oil prices in the near term. In fact, world demand for oil is expected to increase from 77 mmb/d[10] in 2000 to 89 mmb/d in the year 2010 – about 1.5 percent a year.[11]

We therefore propose that Iraq withdraw from OPEC as a member, but continue to communicate and coordinate information on production and pricing with the cartel.

---

[10] million barrels of oil per day

[11] O'Neil (1999), p. 2.

The Role of Multinational Companies

It is not clear when the classic entrepreneurial spirit of the Iraqi people will emerge to achieve the broad economic development objectives described in the next section on Sector Development Plans. While the Arab markets have thrived for over a thousand years, there are indicators that the previous administration's public sector dominance has produced a population with a reliance on welfare payments and state control. It is also not clear how much of the older population retained entrepreneurial skill sets, but for a majority of the population, there is no memory of the economy prior to Saddam Hussein. As noted earlier, more than 50 percent of the population is under the age of 20 and Saddam Hussein's government had been in power for more than 20 years, with the past 12 years characterized by considerable hardship and stagnation.

Recent development experience in Eastern Europe and the former Soviet Union suggests that entrepreneurial skills cannot be arbitrarily presumed in developing economies with a long history of rigid command economies.

However, what is likely, is that assuming (1) hostilities settle down and that a reasonable level of personal safety can be attained in Iraq and (2) a reasonable long term economic outlook for Iraq develops in the international community, then multinational companies will be motivated to go to Iraq to sign contracts and hire Iraqi nationals as their in-country agents or employees. This type of employment opportunity will provide considerably more structure for the typical Iraqi and would also serve as a learning vehicle for managing business requirements.

In addition, the influx of foreign business travelers will create a demand for greater support services for hotels, restaurants, and transportation. These business people will expend considerable resources putting private capital in place for their facilities. These investment funds, in essence, provide an economic multiplier for the development spending outlined in this plan. The first McDonalds or Wal-Mart will be a telling indicator of substantial improvement in the Iraqi economy.

This international investment wave will be a large part of the capital needed to grow the Iraqi economy faster than the rate described in this plan. However, it is clearly a function of the perceived investment risk, and this is a byproduct of the immediate political and security environment and inferred long-term outlook for the health of the Iraqi economy.

Sector Development Plans

Development Overview

The economy of Iraq will be driven over the next several years by the oil sector. As noted above, the vehicle for developing the oil sector is the Iraqi National Oil Company (INOC) that should, as discussed below, provide most, if not all, of the initial cash flow to jump-start the post-war development of Iraq. The INOC, however, is a state owned enterprise that will pay taxes to the Iraqi treasury as well as a dividend. The cash from the oil sector along with other smaller sources of cash derived from the taxation plan will, therefore, initially provide for the burst of investment spending to drive economic growth in Iraq.

While the long run goal of this development plan is to privatize the INOC, the plan assumes that it would be in the national interest in the short run to delay INOC privatization for a period of 6 years from 2004; this delay allows for transitional issues to be resolved and allows the government spending program to receive an interim dividend from the INOC. A privatization would therefore be planned for 2010. This will enable the INOC to get organized under the joint supervision of the provisional Iraqi administration and the coalition transition authority and to focus on getting increased oil production and oil exports reestablished. With a new reserve development program fully established and oil production growing, the INOC will be an immensely valuable enterprise and one that will have a market capitalization more readily discernable by market participants.

It is important that the citizens of Iraq, the eventual initial owners of the INOC shares, be given time to enable their appreciation of the reasonable market value of their individual shares. This delay in privatization will allow time for this education process and will reduce the risk of short run profiteering by speculators trading in INOC shares.

The initial public investment program in our plan was developed to accomplish several objectives:

1. To rapidly increase oil production to finance Iraqi growth

2. To increase domestic living standards at a rapid rate - 10 percent per year

3. To finance growth without major dependency on foreign resources

4. To enable the new Iraqi government to be self-sustaining

The investment program to accomplish these objectives is described in Table IV-3 for each of the major productive sectors.

Table IV-3
Investment Program in Iraq 2004-2008
(By Sector - $US Billions)

Sector	2004	2005	2006	2007	2008
Oil & Gas (O&G)	4.0	2.3	2.0	2.0	2.0
Services (Ser)	2.9	1.8	2.3	2.7	3.0
Agriculture (Agr)	0.2	0.2	0.2	0.3	0.3
Manufacturing (Man)	0.0	1.0	1.1	1.3	1.5
Power (Pow)	0.8	0.6	0.7	0.8	0.9
Tele/Transport (T & T)	0.0	1.5	1.4	1.6	1.8
Total Purchases	7.9	7.3	7.8	8.7	9.6

Sources: Appendix III-1, CountryWatch (2003c).

A detailed description of the strategy for each of the major productive sectors in the economy is outlined below as well as the plan to public finance these invest targets as well as current government spending. The overall results of the plan in terms of economic growth and the standard of living in Iraq is reviewed in Chapter V.

The Oil & Gas sector

The oil and gas reserves of Iraq are truly a national treasure. Properly developed and distributed they can raise the standard of living and wealth of the Iraqi people in a very short period of time to a level comparable with other nations in the Middle East and the developed countries of Western Europe and the United States.

The most critical element in the reconstruction plan in Iraq is the method and timing of the development of Iraqi oil reserves. As noted in Chapter III, Iraq has 112 billion barrels of oil reserves, second only to Saudi Arabia in terms of conventional worldwide oil reserves.

Earlier in this chapter we developed the concept of creating an Iraqi National Oil Company as the entity initially responsible for the stewardship of Iraqi oil reserves. In the remaining portions of this section we develop a strategic plan for the INOC and layout a scenario for the production of oil in Iraq and the resulting cash flows in the oil sector and the resulting revenue base to the government.

While economic data on Iraq is sketchy, the United States Department of Energy in 1996 published a study on capacity additions in OPEC countries that included an analysis of typical large Iraqi oil fields.[12] The main source of this data was from an oil field program, Estimator, developed by Petroconsultants. The oil field data on Iraq for large fields with high production rates was averaged to develop a set of base data to run projections in this analysis. The complete set of projections and assumptions are shown in Appendix IV.2. The remaining paragraphs in this section summarize the results of the planning program.

---

[12] U.S. Department of Energy, Energy Information Administration (1996).

The strategic plan for INOC assumes a focused emphasis on development of the existing proved reserves in Iraq over a twenty (20) year period. The development costs to bring production on line are estimated to start at $.47 per barrel of reserves developed and grow at 5 percent per year. The entire reserve base of the country is reviewed to determine the most efficient sequence of development and initially a capital spending plan totaling $21 billion over 10 years is projected to be allocated for oil field development.

The initial capital spending of $7 billion over the next three years (2003-2005) is projected to get Iraqi oil production quickly to a level of 3 million barrels per day. The ten-year target is for production to reach just over 6.5 million barrels per day. The ten-year plan for oil production is shown in figure IV-1. The cumulative capital spending requirement for the first 10 years of the oil field development program is $21 billion.

The revenue generated from oil production will depend on the world price of crude oil. Crude oil prices in June 2003 were in the $24 per barrel range with Kirkuk 36° crude setting the Iraq benchmark at $23.94 per barrel on 6 June 2003.[13]

---

[13] U.S. Department of Energy (2003g).

The future value of crude oil prices is highly speculative but we have assumed here a constant real price at $24 per barrel with a nominal price increase of 2 percent. With this price forecast, oil prices range between $24 and $28 per barrel over the next 10 years as shown in Figure IV-2. Projected oil production for Iraq in 2003 is shown in Table III-6.

The production and pricing assumptions lead to the revenue projections for oil revenues of $5.5 billion in 2003 increasing to $29.4 billion by 2005 and $69.1 billion by 2012.

The details of these projections and the impact of this revenue stream on INOC is shown in Table IV-4 which gives a 10 year pro-forma income statement and cash flow forecast for the company. If INOC were able to execute the plan proposed, it would quickly become one of the world's largest corporations with a market value as shown in Table IV-5 in the $1 trillion range within 10 years.

The value to the Iraqi population is significant. If the ownership of the INOC were distributed via a "spin out" to the population of Iraq, there would be an immediate and substantial increase in their wealth. For a family of four, the value of INOC securities by 2010 would range from $120,000 to $240,000 per family.

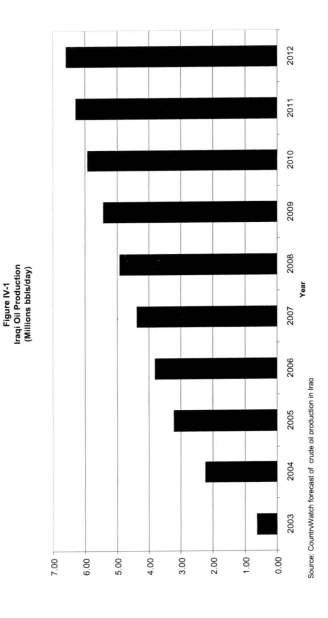

Figure IV-1
Iraqi Oil Production
(Millions bbls/day)

Source: CountryWatch forecast of crude oil production in Iraq

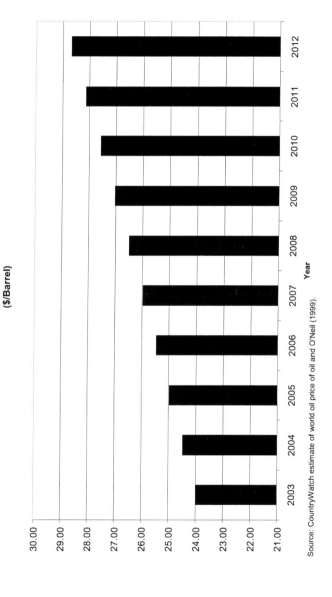

Figure IV-2
World Oil Price 2003-2012
($/Barrel)

Source: CountryWatch estimate of world oil price of oil and O'Neil (1999).

One factor left out of these calculations is the issue of associated gas. Much of the Iraqi oil that will be produced has significant amounts of associated gas that will also be produced with the crude oil and must be either flared, re-injected, or collected and consumed in some fashion. The working assumption, in these estimates, is that the gas is either flared or captured by participating international oil companies and sold into the power sector.

In our projections, this revenue item is not captured in the INOC income statement and is considered an upside to our forecast. The estimated amount of associated gas is quite significant as shown in Table IV-6 and Figure IV-3, totaling over 2 trillion cubic feet per year by 2005. The amount of associated gas available should provide a large incentive to international oil companies to participate in the oil re-development program.

Table IV-4
Iraqi National Oil Company
Income Statement 2003-2012
(US$ Billions)

	2003	2004	2005	2006	2007	2008	2009	2010	2011	2012
Income Statement										
Operating Revenues	5.5	20.0	29.4	35.5	41.5	47.6	53.6	59.6	64.6	69.1
Operating Expenses	0.3	1.1	1.7	2.0	2.4	2.7	3.0	3.4	3.7	3.9
EBITDA	5.2	18.9	27.7	33.5	39.2	44.9	50.6	56.3	60.9	65.2
Depreciation	2.2	3.0	3.4	3.8	4.2	2.4	2.0	2.0	2.0	2.0
Taxes										
Compensation	0.3	1.9	2.8	3.3	3.9	4.5	5.1	5.6	6.1	6.5
Severance Tax	0.0	0.9	1.4	1.7	2.0	2.2	2.5	2.8	3.0	3.3
Income Tax	0.0	2.0	3.0	3.7	4.4	5.4	6.1	6.9	7.5	8.0
Total Taxes	0.3	4.8	7.2	8.7	10.2	12.1	13.7	15.3	16.6	17.8
Net Income	2.7	11.1	17.1	20.9	24.7	30.4	34.8	38.9	42.3	45.4
Cash Flow Statement										
Net Income	2.7	11.1	17.1	20.9	24.7	30.4	34.8	38.9	42.3	45.4
Depreciation	2.2	3.0	3.4	3.8	4.2	2.4	2.0	2.0	2.0	2.0
Capital Spending	-1.0	-4.0	-2.0	-2.0	-2.0	-2.0	-2.0	-2.0	-2.0	-2.0
Net Cash Flow	3.9	10.1	18.5	22.7	26.9	30.8	34.8	38.9	42.3	45.4

Source: See Appendix IV.1

Table IV-5
INOC Net Income and Market Capitalization 2003-2012

	2003	2004	2005	2006	2007	2008	2009	2010	2011	2012
Net Income ($ Billions)	2.7	11.1	17.1	20.9	24.7	30.4	34.8	38.9	42.3	45.4
Market Value ($ Billions)										
Multiple										
20	55	222	343	419	495	608	697	779	847	908
30	82	333	514	628	742	911	1,045	1,168	1,270	1,361
40	110	443	686	838	989	1,215	1,393	1,558	1,693	1,815
Market Value Per Capita ($1000s)										
Population (Millions)	24.7	25.3	26.0	26.7	27.5	28.2	29.0	29.7	30.4	31.1
Growth Rate (%)	2.7%	2.7%	2.7%	2.7%	2.7%	2.7%	2.7%	2.7%	2.2%	2.2%
Multiple										
20	2.2	9.0	13.9	17.0	20.0	24.6	28.2	31.6	34.3	36.8
30	3.3	13.5	20.8	25.5	30.1	36.9	42.3	47.3	51.4	55.2
40	4.4	18.0	27.8	33.9	40.1	49.2	56.5	63.1	68.6	73.5

Source: See Text

One key factor in getting the plan underway would be the initial financing of $4 billion of capital needed for the 2004 development plan. While there are a number of options for the INOC in this regard, the simplest and least costly of these options, as well as one which would have substantial positive political implications for the United States and United Kingdom coalition would be to have the United States and United Kingdom governments provide the INOC with $4 billion of working capital in the form of short term loans. As the financial projections show, the equity value of INOC would be able to guarantee the loan and the funds would jumpstart the key component of the Iraqi recovery.

Another key issue to discuss with respect to the oil and gas sector is the impact of INOC revenues on the government. Including INOC taxes and a dividend of 95 percent of the net cash generated by INOC to the government, the net revenues to the government in 2004 are $14.4 billion. By 2005 the net revenues would be $24.80 billion. These estimates and the general public finance situation in Iraq over the next ten years are further discussed in Chapter V.

Table IV-6
Associated Natural Gas Production in Iraq

Year	2003	2004	2005	2006	2007	2008	2009	2010	2011	2012
Oil Production (mm barrels/day)	0.63	2.24	3.23	3.82	4.38	4.92	5.43	5.93	6.29	6.60
Gas Oil Ratio (scf/barrel)	1,500	1,500	1,500	1,500	1,500	1,500	1,500	1,500	1,500	1,500
Gas Production (bcf/day)	0.9	3.4	4.8	5.7	6.6	7.4	8.2	8.9	9.4	9.9
Gas Production (tcf/year)	0.3	1.2	1.8	2.1	2.4	2.7	3.0	3.2	3.4	3.6
Oil Offset (mm barrels/day)	0.2	0.6	0.8	1.0	1.1	1.3	1.4	1.5	1.6	1.7

Source: See Text and Appendix IV-2

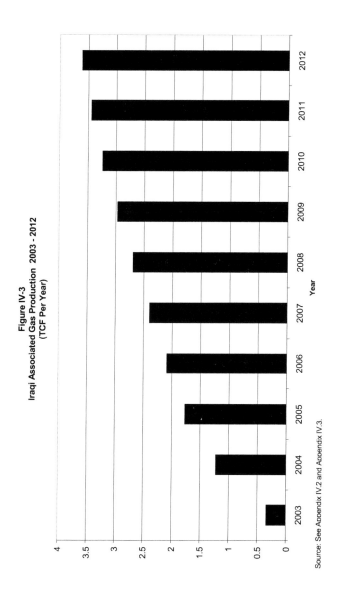

Figure IV-3
Iraqi Associated Gas Production 2003 - 2012
(TCF Per Year)

Source: See Appendix IV.2 and Appendix IV.3.

In the next section, we further discuss the budget for the new government of Iraq. The estimate of government spending, discussed below, is in the range of $7.3 billion. Given the projections of government revenue shown here, except for 2003, the taxes collected through severance taxes and income taxes from INOC would be sufficient to finance the government by the year 2010 without reliance on the dividend. At this point, it would be appropriate to "spin out" INOC to the Iraqi population either directly or in the form of a trust.

The Service Sector

The service sector in Iraq includes the government sector and the non-public services such as retail trade, banking, and insurance. In this section, our focus will be on the government sector and the rationalization of the government budget. Market forces will drive the non-public service sector; we give a total estimate of the service sector value added elsewhere in this discussion.

The public sector has traditionally been an important source of employment and income in Iraq. In this plan, the public sector has a significant initial role in providing the basic services of government, including police, national security, fire, education, and healthcare in addition to the normal legislative and judicial services typically provided by government. The direct impact of the budget is shown in Table IV-1.

The Agricultural Sector

There is significant potential, with proper funding, to substantially increase output in the agricultural sector and to move Iraq efficiently along a path toward food self-sufficiency. An illustration of this is shown in Table IV-7 where the annual ration requirements for two of the major food staples in Iraq, rice and wheat, are shown relative to current production levels and in relation to maximum production levels in Iraq over the last twenty years.

Table IV-7
Food Self Sufficiency Requirements in Iraq

Item	Annual Ration (MT)	Current Production (MT)	%	Peak Production (MT)	%
Rice	864,000	90,000	10.4%	383,000.0	44.3%
Wheat	2,304,000	800,000	34.7%	1,476,400.0	64.1%

Source: United Nations Data, Office of the Food-for-Oil Programme (2003)

As the data indicates, current agricultural production levels in Iraq meet only 10.4 percent of the rice ration requirement and 34.7 percent of the wheat ration requirement. If the agricultural sector were producing at the maximum production levels sustained over the past 20 years, however, the percentages would increase to 44.3 percent for rice and 64.1 percent for wheat.

The level of crop production and the specific crops produced will depend on market forces interacting with the natural competitive advantages of Iraqi land and the availability of water. The water supply in Iraq will depend seasonally on rainfall but also on the amount of water being diverted to uses in the upstream watersheds of the Tigris and Euphrates rivers in Turkey.

It makes sense as an initial goal to promote increased food self-sufficiency in Iraq both for security purposes as well as to reduce imports of food and therefore free up foreign exchange to be used for other purposes. Later in this chapter we propose a development-planning scenario in which the agricultural sector growth rates increase Iraqi self-sufficiency over a ten-year planning horizon.

The Electric Power Sector

One of the most critical sectors in the reconstruction effort is the power sector. While only making up 4.0 percent of Iraqi GDP, the electric power sector is a critical element in making the entire reconstruction program work. This is because there are no practical short run substitutes for electricity in most every production process.

As noted earlier the effective capacity of the Iraqi grid as the War of 2003 began was 4,300 megawatts. New oil or natural gas fired electric capacity should cost an estimated $500,000 per megawatt and each megawatt hour of electrical generation requires about 1 barrel of oil or the natural gas equivalent. Assuming Iraq's power capacity was at about 8,000 MW at the end of five years, the annual oil consumption to run the power stations would total around 265,000 barrels of oil per day[14] (about 50 percent of the current internal requirement for oil), or roughly .56 trillion cubic feet of natural gas a year. Once Iraq's associated natural gas is harnessed, it could meet all of the projected domestic power requirements for the foreseeable future.[15]

A critical point to note is that restoring electric power not only depends on having electric power generation capacity in place, but also having the electric distribution lines repaired in order to move energy to the locations where power is required. In the early days of the reconstruction effort, many of the problems associated with restoring power appeared to be caused by looters disrupting power lines and taking the copper or aluminum conductors down, re-melting metal into ingots and selling the bars into the Iranian market. This is a security issue and putting a reconstituted government and military in place will help prevent the looting. An additional $2 billion in capital over the next 5 years would be allocated to repair and improve the distribution infrastructure.

---

[14] Assumes that one barrel of oil is equivalent to 5.8 million BTU's and the generating heat rate is about 8,000 BTU's/kWh with a 90% capacity factor.

[15] See Figure IV-3 for a natural gas production estimate.

The electric power sector is the current responsibility of the Ministry of Energy, but is one of the public companies that would be a good candidate for privatization. This will require that the prices of electric power become economically distributed and that all customers pay a market price for power. The proceeds from such a privatization would also be used to defray the capital costs for other public sector purposes.

The Telecom/Transport Sector

The telecom sector in Iraq is, like the power sector, a critical element in rebuilding the Iraqi economy. The system as noted earlier consists of a landline network and a mobile phone network.

The landline network was significantly degraded in the War of 2003. The command and control facilities are high on the initial target list in a military campaign in order to deny the enemy the ability to communicate with troop commanders. Rebuilding the landline network commenced after the cessation of hostilities but progress has been slow.

In June 2003, the Administrator made a decision to issue a tender for the creation of a mobile phone network that would cover the entire country. The existing infrastructure in mobile phones included an MCI network that covered 10,000 lines used for United States forces and humanitarian organizations and a network by MCT of Kuwait that principally covers the city of Al Basrah.[16]

There is widespread interest in the new mobile phone tender in that it could become a permanent license in future Iraqi infrastructure. Key steps in order to get the tender launched will be getting the property rights mechanisms outlined earlier in this chapter underway.

The transportation infrastructure of Iraq was also degraded during the War of 2003. The BBC, in a story on March 27, 2003 reported that the U.S. Agency for International Development (USAID) had prepared initial plans for the reconstruction of critical transportation infrastructure. Subsequently, contracts have been awarded to private sector firms, including a major contract to Bechtel Corporation of the U.S., to commence work on the rehabilitation of the Iraqi transportation infrastructure. The total estimated cost for this initial repair work to be funded by USAID is $1 billion. This would also include funds for the electric power sector, the water sector, and for agricultural irrigation projects.[17]

---

[16] Reuters (2003b).
[17] BBC News (2003k).

In the area of ports and shipping, the reconstruction work will involve dredging and getting up to 12 shipping berths in the port of Umm Qasr ready to handle up to 50,000 ton ships.[18]

In the airport sector, the USAID reconstruction effort will be aimed at repairing runways and terminal facilities that can be used to open up Iraq to international and domestic air traffic within 12 months from the cessation of hostilities. In particular, the two major international airports at Baghdad and Al Basrah are critical to be opened during this time. Several major commercial international airlines, including Northwest Airlines, have already filed applications with the Transition Authority to begin serving the Iraqi market.[19]

Roads and railways are also dealt with in the reconstruction contract. In particular, bridges over roads and rail lines are to be inspected and repaired.

The Manufacturing Sector

The element of the manufacturing sector, which will be a critical reconstruction activity, is the restoration of the petroleum refinery capacity in Iraq. This is critical in order to meet the domestic requirement of Iraq for gasoline and other refined products.

---

[18] *Ibid.*

[19] USA Today (2003).

The future of the rest of the Iraqi manufacturing sector will depend on Iraq's comparative advantage in manufactured goods. Certainly the traditional sectors that have a competitive advantage for transportation reasons will grow in the new economy. Thus, industries such as cement and certain food processing activities such as beer production will continue to thrive due to their transportation cost advantage.

Iraq will also spawn new manufacturing sectors in areas where, due to transportation or because of the large amount of crude oil production, the country would have a competitive advantage over production elsewhere. One possibility here is petrochemicals. Given the local advantage of having the petroleum production in Iraq, the ability to process the crude without an added transport charge may give rise to a number of possible refining and chemical processes such as the production of liquefied petroleum gases and ethylene.

Communications Plan

The final element in the reconstruction plan for Iraq is the Communication Plan. The key elements of this plan are:

1. Communicate the Security Plan, the Political Development Plan, and the Economic Development plans to all stakeholders.

2. Highlight the targets and timetables assumed in the plan.

3. Highlight with special emphasis the key elements that are important to both the people of Iraq and the international community. In particular:

a. The timetable to achieve a democratically elected government.

b. The timetable for the withdrawal of Coalition Forces.

c. The timetable and value of the INOC spinout to the Iraqi people.

The Administrator should keep all stakeholders informed on progress in meeting the targets and timetables described in this plan. In addition, the Administrator must quickly bring to light the obstacles that arise to threaten the fulfillment of the plan and the actions that can be taken to keep the plan on target.

APPENDIX IV.1 Government Budget Detail

Key budget assumptions: General Assumptions[1]

1. Wage rates were assumed to be generally 10-25 percent of rates prevailing in the United States, depending on the particular job and skill sector.

2. Rents were based on assumptions on square footage required for each function and a net rental rate of $10 per sq foot.

3. Travel costs were based on travel, meals and lodging estimates comparable with international rates depending upon the job description.

4. Communication charges were based on usage and rate assumptions comparable with United States mobile phone networks in the United States.

5. Power assumptions were based on square footage data used to determine rentals and an estimate of 1 kWh/square foot per month with a $.10 per kWh delivered power price.

---

[1] All budget detail currency numbers are in thousands of US dollars.

6. Water rates were calculated based on an estimate of 52 gallons per person per day and a delivered water cost of $2 per 1,000 gallons.

7. Miscellaneous expenses were cost estimates based on requirements of the specified position.

8. A contingency of 10 percent was used to account for the costs and functions not specifically budgeted.

Key Budget Assumptions: Specific Budgets

1. Office of the President: The Presidential budget included significant wage and rental expense appropriate for his office.

2. Legislature: Same general assumptions on wages and rents as the Office of the President. Assumed 18 senators and 200 representatives in a bicameral legislature.

3. Judiciary: Same general assumptions on wages and rents as the Office of the President. Assumed a Supreme Court of 9 Justices and Provincial Supreme Courts with 5 Justices.

4. Defense Ministry: Defense Ministry includes a small civilian staff to oversee the Armed Forces.

5. Armed Forces: 240,000 regular troops and 240,000 reserves. This would amount to 4 army divisions of regulars and 4 army divisions of reserves at 50,000 troops (including the tail) per division. The air force is manned at 30,000 and the navy at 10,000. The wage rates were 20 percent of U.S. Armed Forces rates.

6. Ministry of Justice: Includes a department of justice with prosecutorial arm and an FBI, Secret Service and federal prison system.

7. The Foreign Ministry: Includes funding for 80 Ambassadors to serve in foreign posts plus a contingent for the United Nations.

8. The Finance Ministry: Provided with a financial administration group capable of handling the federal budget.

9. The Energy Ministry: Provided funds for government oversight of the Iraqi National Oil Company.

10. The Education Ministry: Provided funds for the K-12 system of public education in Iraq and the university system.

11. The Health Ministry: Provided funds to run the public health system.

12. The Agricultural Ministry: Provided funds to oversee the agricultural sector and also provided with funds to manage the food rationing program.

13. The Provisional Governments: Provided funds to run the local governments, including, justice officials, local police and fire.

Appendix A IV-1
New Iraqi Government Budget Detail
Office of the President Expenses

Office of the President	Personnel	Wages $	Rent $	Travel $	Commo $	Power $	Water $	Misc $	Total $
President	1	240	240	260	48	19	0	1,000	1,807
Vice President	1	180	120	260	48	10	0	500	1,118
Admin Assts	2	48	6	104	24	0	0	24	207
Special Asst	4	320	12	208	48	1	0	48	637
Ministry Coordination	8	288	24	416	96	2	0	96	922
Admin Assts	12	216	36	624	144	3	0	144	1,167
Legislative Liason	4	144	12	208	48	1	0	48	461
Capital Mgt	1	60	3	0	2	0	0	12	78
Utility Staff	4	48	12	0	10	1	0	48	119
Cleaning Staff	4	48	12	0	5	1	0	48	114
Housing Staff	4	48	12	0	5	1	0	48	114
Transportation Staff	4	48	12	208	48	1	0	48	365
Total	**49**	**1,688**	**501**	**2,288**	**526**	**40**	**2**	**2,064**	**7,109**

Appendix A IV-2
New Iraqi Government Budget Detail
Legislature Expenses

Legislature	Personnel	Wages $	Rent $	Travel $	Commo $	Power $	Water $	Misc $	Total $
Senators	18	2,160	540	936	864	43	1	18,000	22,544
Representatives	200	24,000	6,000	10,400	9,600	480	8	100,000	150,488
Admin Assts	218	3,924	654	0	2,616	52	8	2,616	9,871
Staff Asst	436	15,696	1,308	2,616	5,232	105	17	5,232	30,205
Capital Mgt	3	144	9	0	36	1	0	36	226
Utility Staff	36	1,296	108	0	86	9	1	432	1,932
Cleaning Staff	36	216	108	0	43	9	1	432	809
Transportation Staff	218	1,308	654	2,834	2,616	52	8	2,616	10,089
Total	1,165	48,744	9,381	16,786	21,094	750	44	129,364	226,163

Appendix A IV-3
New Iraqi Government Budget Detail
Judiciary Expenses

Judiciary	Personnel	Wages $	Rent $	Travel $	Commo $	Power $	Water $	Misc $	Total $
Supreme Court	9	1,080	270	468	432	22	0	9,000	11,272
Prov. Supr. Court	90	7,200	2,700	4,680	4,320	216	3	45,000	64,119
Prov. Courts	200	12,000	600	200	2,400	48	8	2,400	17,656
Admin Assts	299	7,176	897	0	718	72	11	3,588	12,462
Clerks	598	14,352	1,794	0	1,435	144	23	7,176	24,923
Court Mgt	299	7,176	897	0	718	72	11	3,588	12,462
Utility Staff	1,196	7,176	3,588	0	1,435	287	45	14,352	26,884
Cleaning Staff	1,196	7,176	3,588	0	1,435	287	45	14,352	26,884
Transportation Staff	299	1,794	897	3,887	3,588	72	11	3,588	13,837
Total	**4,186**	**65,130**	**15,231**	**9,235**	**16,481**	**1,218**	**159**	**103,044**	**210,498**

Appendix A IV-4
New Iraqi Government Budget Detail
Defense Ministry Expenses

Defense Ministry	Personnel	Wages $	Rent $	Travel $	Commo $	Power $	Water $	Misc $	Total $
Defense Minister	1	120	20	52	48	2	0	1,000	1,242
Secretary of Army	1	48	20	52	48	2	0	500	670
Secretary of Navy	1	48	2	52	48	0	0	12	162
Secretary of Air Force	1	48	2	52	48	0	0	12	162
Asst Secretaries	4	144	8	104	48	1	0	48	353
Admin Assts	8	48	16	0	19	2	0	96	181
Bldg Administrator	1	6	2	0	2	0	0	12	23
Utility Staff	4	24	8	0	5	1	0	48	86
Cleaning Staff	4	24	8	0	5	1	0	48	86
Transportation Staff	8	48	16	104	96	2	0	96	362
Total	**33**	**558**	**102**	**416**	**367**	**12**	**1**	**1,872**	**3,329**

Appendix A IV-5
New Iraqi Government Budget Detail
Armed Forces Expenses

Armed Forces	Personnel	Wages $	Rent $	Travel $	Commo $	Power $	Water $	Misc $	Total $
Active Forces	240,000	1,171,771	120,000	240,000	72,000	28,800	9,110	120,000	1,761,682
Reserve Forces	240,000	121,993	120,000	240,000	28,800	28,800	9,110	24,000	572,703
Bldg	4	144	8	0	10	1	0	48	211
Utility Staff	400	2,400	800	0	960	96	15	4,800	9,071
Cleaning Staff	400	2,400	800	0	480	96	15	4,800	8,591
Transportation Staff	40	240	80	520	480	10	2	480	1,811
Total	**480,844**	**1,298,948**	**241,688**	**480,520**	**102,730**	**57,803**	**18,253**	**154,128**	**2,354,069**

Appendix A IV-6
New Iraqi Government Budget Detail
Ministry of Justice Expenses

Ministry of Justice	Personnel	Wages $	Rent $	Travel $	Commo $	Power $	Water $	Misc $	Total $
Justice Minister	1	120	20	26	12	2	0	1,000	1,180
Federal Prosecutors	18	864	360	468	216	43	1	9,000	10,952
Asst Prosecutors	72	2,592	144	1,872	864	17	3	864	6,356
Admin Assts	91	1,092	182	0	218	22	3	1,092	2,610
Clerks	91	1,092	182	0	218	22	3	1,092	2,610
Director FBI	1	80	20	26	12	2	0	12	152
Provincial Deputies	18	1,080	360	468	216	43	1	216	2,384
Agents	72	1,296	144	1,872	864	17	3	864	5,060
Director Secret Ser.	1	48	20	26	12	2	0	12	120
Secret Service	508	6,096	1,016	13,208	6,096	122	19	6,096	32,653
Admin Assts	84	501	167	0	200	20	3	1,002	1,894
Wardens	19	684	380	114	228	46	1	228	1,680
Guards	1,900	22,800	38,000	0	4,560	4,560	72	22,800	92,792
Prison Untility	190	1,140	380	0	456	46	7	2,280	4,309
Prison Cleaning	190	1,140	380	0	228	46	7	2,280	4,081
Bldg Mgt	38	912	76	0	91	9	1	456	1,546
Utility Staff	152	912	304	0	365	36	6	1,824	3,447
Cleaning Staff	152	912	304	0	182	36	6	1,824	3,265
Transportation Staff	91	546	182	2,366	1,092	22	3	1,092	5,303
Total	**3,689**	**43,907**	**42,621**	**20,446**	**16,132**	**5,115**	**140**	**54,034**	**182,394**

Appendix A IV-7
New Iraqi Government Budget Detail
Foreign Ministry Expenses

Foreign Ministry	Personnel	Wages $	Rent $	Travel $	Commo $	Power $	Water $	Misc $	Total $
Foreign Minister	1	120	30	260	48	2	0	1,000	1,460
Deputy For. Min	1	80	30	260	48	2	0	500	920
Representitive to UN	1	80	30	260	48	2	0	500	920
Ambassadors	40	2,400	1,200	2,080	1,920	96	2	480	8,178
Counsel	80	3,840	240	4,160	3,840	19	3	960	13,062
Asst Ministers	4	192	12	208	192	1	0	48	653
Admin Assts	127	3,048	406	6,604	762	30	5	1,524	12,380
Bldg	41	2,460	123	0	492	10	2	492	3,578
Utility Staff	164	1,968	492	0	394	39	6	1,968	4,867
Cleaning Staff	164	1,968	492	0	197	39	6	1,968	4,670
Transportation Staff	127	1,524	381	6,604	1,524	30	5	1,524	11,592
Total	750	17,680	3,436	20,436	9,464	273	28	10,964	62,282

315

Appendix A IV-8
New Iraqi Government Budget Detail
Finance Ministry Expense

Finance Ministry	Personnel	Wages $	Rent $	Travel $	Commo $	Power $	Water $	Misc $	Total $
Finance Minister	1	120	20	260	48	2	0	1,000	1,450
Deputy Fin. Minister	1	80	20	260	48	2	0	500	910
Director Treasury	1	80	20	260	48	2	0	500	910
Director Revenue	1	80	20	26	48	2	0	12	188
Revenue Agents	180	8,640	360	4,680	2,160	43	7	2,160	18,050
Asst Directors	4	192	8	104	48	1	0	48	401
Admin Assts	188	2,256	376	0	451	45	7	2,256	5,392
Bldg	11	396	22	0	26	3	0	132	579
Utility Staff	44	264	88	0	106	11	2	528	998
Cleaning Staff	44	264	88	0	53	11	2	528	945
Transportation Staff	188	1,128	376	2,444	2,256	45	7	2,256	8,512
Total	663	13,500	1,398	8,034	5,292	168	25	9,920	38,337

Appendix A IV-9
New Iraqi Government Budget Detail
Energy Ministry Expenses

Energy Ministry	Personnel	Wages $	Rent $	Travel $	Commo $	Power $	Water $	Misc $	Total $
Energy Minister	1	120	20	260	48	2	0	1,000	1,450
Deputy Energy Min.	1	80	20	260	48	2	0	500	910
Director Planning	1	60	20	24	12	2	0	500	618
Director G&G	1	60	20	24	12	2	0	12	130
Analysts	4	96	8	96	48	1	0	48	297
Asst Directors	4	96	8	96	48	1	0	48	297
Admin Assts	12	144	24	0	29	3	0	144	344
Bldg	1	24	2	0	2	0	0	12	41
Utility Staff	4	24	8	0	10	1	0	48	91
Cleaning Staff	4	24	8	0	5	1	0	48	86
Transportation Staff	12	72	24	156	144	3	0	144	543
Total	**45**	**800**	**162**	**916**	**406**	**19**	**2**	**2,504**	**4,809**

Appendix A IV-10
New Iraqi Government Budget Detail
Education Ministry Expenses

Education Ministry	Personnel	Wages $	Rent $	Travel $	Commo $	Power $	Water $	Misc $	Total $
Education Minister	1	120	20	52	48	2	0	1,000	1,242
Deputy Educ. Min	1	48	20	52	48	2	0	500	670
Director Universities	1	24	2	1	1	0	0	500	528
Director K-12	1	24	2	1	1	0	0	1	28
Analysts	4	48	8	2	5	1	0	2	66
Asst Directors	4	48	8	2	5	1	0	2	66
Admin Assts	12	144	24	0	14	3	0	6	192
University Presidents	60	1,440	120	30	72	14	2	30	1,709
University Faculty	6,500	78,000	13,000	3,250	7,800	1,560	247	3,250	107,107
University Admin	240	1,440	480	120	288	58	9	120	2,515
Admin Assts	1,685	10,110	3,370	0	2,022	404	64	843	16,813
K-12 Superintendent	1,200	14,400	2,400	600	1,440	288	46	600	19,774
K-12 Faculty	130,000	780,000	260,000	6,500	31,200	31,200	4,935	65,000	1,178,835
Admin Assts	14,200	85,200	28,400	0	3,408	3,408	539	7,100	128,055
Bldg	1,261	7,566	2,522	0	303	303	48	631	11,372
Utility Staff	5,044	30,264	10,088	0	1,211	1,211	191	2,522	45,487
Cleaning Staff	5,044	30,264	10,088	0	1,211	1,211	191	2,522	45,487
Transportation Staff	62	372	124	31	15	15	2	31	590
Total	165,320	1,039,512	330,676	10,640	49,091	39,681	6,276	84,659	1,560,534

Appendix A IV-11
New Iraqi Government Budget Detail
Health Ministry Expenses

Health Ministry	Personnel	Wages $	Rent $	Travel $	Commo $	Power $	Water $	Misc $	Total $
Health Minister	1	120	20	52	48	2	0	1,000	1,242
Deputy Health Min.	1	80	20	52	48	2	0	500	702
Director Hospitals	1	24	2	1	1	0	0	500	528
Director Clinics	1	24	2	1	1	0	0	1	29
Analysts	4	48	8	2	5	1	0	4	68
Asst Directors	4	48	8	2	5	1	0	4	68
Admin Assts	12	144	24	6	14	3	0	12	204
Hospital Presidents	7	168	14	7	8	2	0	7	206
Medical Doctors	9,000	108,000	18,000	4,500	10,800	2,160	342	9,000	152,802
Nurses	27,000	162,000	54,000	13,500	32,400	6,480	1,025	27,000	296,405
Admin Assts	9,019	108,228	18,038	4,510	10,823	2,165	342	9,019	153,124
Clinic Directors	240	5,760	480	120	288	58	9	240	6,955
Clinic Staff	480	8,640	960	240	576	115	18	480	11,029
Admin Assts	240	2,880	480	0	288	58	9	240	3,955
Bldg	248	2,976	496	0	298	60	9	248	4,087
Utility Staff	992	5,952	1,984	0	1,190	238	38	992	10,394
Cleaning Staff	992	5,952	1,984	0	1,190	238	38	992	10,394
Transportation Staff	747	4,482	1,494	374	896	179	28	747	8,201
Total	48,989	415,526	98,014	23,365	58,880	11,762	1,860	50,986	660,393

Appendix A IV-12
New Iraqi Government Budget Detail
Agriculture Minister Expenses

Agriculture Ministry	Personnel	Wages $	Rent $	Travel $	Commo $	Power $	Water $	Misc $	Total $
Agriculture Minister	1	120	20	130	48	2	0	1,000	1,320
Deputy Agr. Min	1	80	20	52	24	2	0	500	678
Director Planning	1	80	20	12	12	2	0	500	626
Director Research	1	80	20	12	12	2	0	12	138
Analysts	4	96	8	24	24	1	0	48	201
Asst Directors	4	96	8	48	24	1	0	48	225
Admin Assts	12	288	24	0	29	3	0	144	488
Food Ration Agents	25,000	150,000	12,500	75,000	60,000	3,000	949	25,000	326,449
Bldg	1	36	2	52	2	0	0	12	105
Utility Staff	4	24	8	208	10	1	0	48	299
Cleaning Staff	4	24	8	208	5	1	0	48	294
Transportation Staff	12	72	24	624	144	3	0	144	1,011
Total	**25,045**	**150,996**	**12,662**	**76,370**	**60,334**	**3,019**	**951**	**27,504**	**331,836**

Appendix A IV-13
New Iraqi Government Budget Detail
Provincial Governments Expenses

Provincial Governments	Personnel	Wages $	Rent $	Travel $	Commo $	Power $	Water $	Misc $	Total $
Governors	18	1,440	360	432	216	43	1	18,000	20,492
Provincial Prosecutors	18	1,080	360	216	216	43	1	9,000	10,916
Asst Prosecutors	72	3,456	144	864	864	17	3	864	6,212
Admin Assts	108	1,296	216	0	259	26	4	1,296	3,097
Clerks	108	2,592	216	0	259	26	4	1,296	4,393
Chief of Police	18	864	360	216	216	43	1	216	1,916
Provincial Deputies	18	648	360	216	216	43	1	216	1,700
Police Officers	18,000	162,000	36,000	9,000	43,200	4,320	683	216,000	471,203
Fire Chief	18	864	360	108	216	43	1	216	1,808
Provincial Deputies	18	648	360	108	216	43	1	216	1,592
Firemen	6,000	54,000	12,000	3,000	14,400	1,440	228	72,000	157,068

Appendix A IV-14
New Iraqi Government Budget Detail
Provincial Governments Expenses

Provincial Governments (continued)	Personnel	Wages $	Rent $	Travel $	Commo $	Power $	Water $	Misc $	Total $
Governor Security	18	432	360	108	216	43	1	216	1,376
Security Police	180	4,320	360	1,080	2,160	43	7	2,160	10,130
Admin Assts	77	918	153	0	184	18	3	918	2,194
Wardens	18	648	360	18	216	43	1	216	1,502
Guards	1,800	16,200	36,000	0	4,320	4,320	68	21,600	82,508
Prison Untiltiy	180	1,080	360	0	432	43	7	2,160	4,082
Prison Cleaning	180	1,080	360	0	216	43	7	2,160	3,866
Bldg Mgt	38	456	76	0	91	9	1	456	1,090
Utility Staff	152	912	304	0	365	36	6	1,824	3,447
Cleaning Staff	152	912	304	0	182	36	6	1,824	3,265
Transportation Staff	4,348	26,088	8,696	56,524	52,176	1,044	165	52,176	196,869
Total Provincial Governm	**31,539**	**281,934**	**98,069**	**71,890**	**120,836**	**11,768**	**1,197**	**405,030**	**990,725**
Total Government	**762,316**	**3,378,923**	**853,941**	**741,342**	**461,632**	**131,709**	**28,938**	**1,036,073**	**6,632,558**

APPENDIX IV.2 INOC Planning Model

The Iraqi National Oil Company strategic planning model was based on the key assumptions shown in the following pages. The primary source of data on Iraqi oil and gas fields was the United States Department of Energy's Energy Information Administration.[2]

Other assumptions are detailed in the following tables.

---

[2] U.S. Department of Energy, Energy Information Administration (1996).

Appendix B IV-1
Iraqi National Oil Company Planning Model
Key Assumption Summary

Existing Oil Production Data

Average Year 2003 Effective Capacity, mm bbls/day	0.63
End of Year 2003 Effective Capacity, mm bbls/day	1.5
Production Decline Rate, %	7
Incremental Capital Costs, $mm	2

Incremental Oil Development

Capital Invest per bbl of Reserves, $/bbl	0.47
Peak Operating Expense, $/bbl	1.12
Peak Production, % of Field Size	6.33
Production Plateau, yr	7
Production Decline Rate, %	7
GOR, scf/bbl	1,500

Other Economic Data

Initial Oil Price ($/barrel)	24
Oil Price Growth Rate (%)	2.0%
INOC Company Overhead (% Revenues)	1.0%
Tax Depreciation (%)	20.0%
Compensation Claims Rate (% of EBITDA)	10.0%
Severance Tax Rate (% of EBITDA)	5.0%
Income Tax Rate (%)	15.0%
Dividend Payout Rate (%)	95.0%

Appendix B IV-2
Iraqi National Oil Company Planning Model
Reserve Position and Existing Productive Capacity

Program Year	1	2	3	4	5	6	7	8	9	10
Calendar Year	2003	2004	2005	2006	2007	2008	2009	2010	2011	2012
Reserve Position										
Proven Reserves (beginning of year)	112.00	111.77	110.95	109.78	108.38	106.78	104.99	103.00	100.84	98.54
Less: Production	0.23	0.82	1.18	1.39	1.60	1.80	1.98	2.16	2.30	2.41
Plus: Reserves Added	0.00	0.00	0.00	0.00	0.00	0.00	0.00	0.00	0.00	0.00
Proved Reserves (end of year)	111.77	110.95	109.78	108.38	106.78	104.99	103.00	100.84	98.54	96.13
Probable Reserves	100.00	100.00	100.00	100.00	100.00	100.00	100.00	100.00	100.00	100.00
Total Reserves	**211.77**	**210.95**	**209.78**	**208.38**	**206.78**	**204.99**	**203.00**	**200.84**	**198.54**	**196.13**
Existing Productive Capacity										
Production % of Initial Production		100.0%	93.0%	86.5%	80.4%	74.8%	69.6%	64.7%	60.2%	56.0%
Capital Spending Program ($billions)	1.00	0.00	0.00	0.00	0.00	0.00	0.00	0.00	0.00	0.00
Initial Year Production (millions of barrels/day)	0.6295	1.50	1.40	1.30	1.21	1.12	1.04	0.97	0.90	0.84

Appendix B IV-3
Iraqi National Oil Company Planning Model
New Productive Capacity

	1	2	3	4	5	6	7	8	9	10
Program Year										
Calendar Year	2003	2004	2005	2006	2007	2008	2009	2010	2011	2012
New Productive Capacity										
Production % of Initial Production	50.0%	100.0%	100.0%	100.0%	100.0%	100.0%	100.0%	93.0%	86.5%	80.4%
Capital Spending Program ($billions)	0.00	4.00	2.00	2.00	2.00	2.00	2.00	2.00	2.00	2.00
Capacity Addition Costs ($/bbl)	0.47	0.49	0.52	0.54	0.57	0.60	0.63	0.66	0.69	0.73
Capacity Addition Cost Growth (%)	5%	5%	5%	5%	5%	5%	5%	5%	5%	5%
Production Capacity Added (billions of barrels)	0.00	8.15	3.88	3.70	3.52	3.35	3.19	3.04	2.90	2.76
Initial Year Production (millions of barrels)	0.00	539.86	257.08	244.83	233.18	222.07	211.50	201.43	191.83	182.70
Initial Year Production (millions of barrels/day)	0.00	1.48	0.70	0.67	0.64	0.61	0.58	0.55	0.53	0.50
Production Profile Year 1	0.00	0.00	0.00	0.00	0.00	0.00	0.00	0.00	0.00	0.00
Production Profile Year 2		0.74	1.48	1.48	1.48	1.48	1.48	1.48	1.38	1.28
Production Profile Year 3			0.35	0.70	0.70	0.70	0.70	0.70	0.70	0.66
Production Profile Year 4				0.34	0.67	0.67	0.67	0.67	0.67	0.67
Production Profile Year 5					0.32	0.64	0.64	0.64	0.64	0.64
Production Profile Year 6						0.30	0.64	0.64	0.61	0.61
Production Profile Year 7							0.29	0.61	0.61	0.61
Production Profile Year 8								0.58	0.58	0.58
Production Profile Year 9									0.55	0.55
Production Profile Year 10									0.26	0.53
										0.25
Total Production (millions of barrels/day)	0.63	2.24	3.23	3.82	4.38	4.92	5.43	5.93	6.29	6.60
Cumulative Capital Invested ($ Billions)	1.00	5.00	7.00	9.00	11.00	13.00	15.00	17.00	19.00	21.00

Appendix B IV-4
Iraqi National Oil Company Planning Model
Income Statement

Program Year	1	2	3	4	5	6	7	8	9	10
Calendar Year	**2003**	**2004**	**2005**	**2006**	**2007**	**2008**	**2009**	**2010**	**2011**	**2012**
Income Statement										
Revenues										
Oil Price ($/barrel)	24.00	24.48	24.97	25.47	25.98	26.50	27.03	27.57	28.12	28.68
Growth Rate (%)	2%	2%	2%	2%	2%	2%	2%	2%	2%	2%
Production (millions of barrels/day)	0.63	2.24	3.23	3.82	4.38	4.92	5.43	5.93	6.29	6.60
Production (millions of barrels/year)	230	817	1178	1393	1599	1796	1984	2163	2298	2409
Total Operating Revenues ($ billions)	5.5	20.0	29.4	35.5	41.5	47.6	53.6	59.6	64.6	69.1
Operating Costs										
Operating Expenses ($/barrel)	1.12	1.15	1.17	1.19	1.22	1.24	1.26	1.29	1.32	1.34
Growth Rate	2%	2%	2%	2%	2%	2%	2%	2%	2%	2%
Operating Expenses ($ billions)	0.26	0.94	1.38	1.66	1.94	2.23	2.51	2.79	3.02	3.23
Overhead (Percent of Revenue)	0.01	0.01	0.01	0.01	0.01	0.01	0.01	0.01	0.01	0.01
Overhead ($ billions)	0.06	0.20	0.29	0.35	0.42	0.48	0.54	0.60	0.65	0.69
Total Operating Expenses ($ billions)	0.31	1.14	1.67	2.02	2.36	2.70	3.05	3.39	3.67	3.92
EBITDA ($ billions)	**5.20**	**18.87**	**27.73**	**33.46**	**39.17**	**44.88**	**50.57**	**56.26**	**60.94**	**65.16**

Appendix B IV-5
Iraqi National Oil Company Planning Model
Depreciation, Compensation Claims, and Taxes

Program Year	1	2	3	4	5	6	7	8	9	10
Calendar Year	2003	2004	2005	2006	2007	2008	2009	2010	2011	2012
Depreciation										
Gross Plant BOY	10.00	11.00	15.00	17.00	19.00	21.00	23.00	25.00	27.00	29.00
Capital Spending ($ billions)	1.00	4.00	2.00	2.00	2.00	2.00	2.00	2.00	2.00	2.00
Gross Plant EOY	11.00	15.00	17.00	19.00	21.00	23.00	25.00	27.00	29.00	31.00
Depreciation Rate	20%	20%	20%	20%	20%	20%	20%	20%	20%	20%
Depreciation ($ billions)	2.2	3	3.4	3.8	4.2	2.4	2	2	2	2
Compensation Claims										
Rate %	5.0%	10.0%	10.0%	10.0%	10.0%	10.0%	10.0%	10.0%	10.0%	10.0%
Amount ($ billions)	0.26	1.89	2.77	3.35	3.92	4.49	5.06	5.63	6.09	6.52
Severance Tax										
Rate %	0.0%	5.0%	5.0%	5.0%	5.0%	5.0%	5.0%	5.0%	5.0%	5.0%
Amount ($ billions)	0.00	0.94	1.39	1.67	1.96	2.24	2.53	2.81	3.05	3.26
EBT ($ billions)	2.74	13.04	20.17	24.64	29.10	35.74	40.98	45.82	49.80	53.39
Income Tax										
Rate %	0.0%	15.0%	15.0%	15.0%	15.0%	15.0%	15.0%	15.0%	15.0%	15.0%
Amount ($ billions)	0.00	1.96	3.03	3.70	4.36	5.36	6.15	6.87	7.47	8.01
Net Income	**2.74**	**11.09**	**17.15**	**20.95**	**24.73**	**30.38**	**34.84**	**38.94**	**42.33**	**45.38**

Appendix B IV-6
Iraqi National Oil Company Planning Model
Net Cash Flow and Uses of Net Cash Flow

Program Year	1	2	3	4	5	6	7	8	9	10
Calendar Year	2003	2004	2005	2006	2007	2008	2009	2010	2011	2012
Net Cash Flow										
Net Income	2.74	11.09	17.15	20.95	24.73	30.38	34.84	38.94	42.33	45.38
Depreciation	2.20	3.00	3.40	3.80	4.20	2.40	2.00	2.00	2.00	2.00
Capital Spending	-1.00	-4.00	-2.00	-2.00	-2.00	-2.00	-2.00	-2.00	-2.00	-2.00
Net Cash	3.94	10.09	18.55	22.75	26.93	30.78	34.84	38.94	42.33	45.38
Uses of Net Cash Flow										
Payout Rate	95%	95%	95%	95%	95%	95%	95%	95%	95%	95%
Dividend to Government	3.74	9.58	17.62	21.61	25.59	29.24	33.09	37.00	40.21	43.11
Increase in Cash	0.20	0.50	0.93	1.14	1.35	1.54	1.74	1.95	2.12	2.27
Uses of Cash	3.94	10.09	18.55	22.75	26.93	30.78	34.84	38.94	42.33	45.38
Cash Balance of INPC	0.20	0.70	1.63	2.77	4.11	5.65	7.39	9.34	11.46	13.73

APPENDIX IV.3 Typical PSA

Appendix C IV-1
Typical Production Sharing Agreement
Key Assumption Summary

Typical Production Sharing Agreement

Key Assumptions

Oil Development Expense	$billions	2
Reserves Developed	billion barrels	4.3
Gas Oil Ratio	scf/bbl	1,500
Associated Gas Reserves	TCF	6.4
Development Cost	$billions	0.25
Cost per mcf		$0.04
Peak Production	%of field size	6.33
Oil Price	$/barrel	24
Gas Price	$/mcf	4.14
Price Inflation	%	2.00
Operating Expenses	$/barrel	1.12
Operating Expenses	$/mcf	0.19
Depreciation	years	5
Compensation Tax		10.0%
Severance Tax		5.0%
Income Tax		15.0%
Sharing Ratio Before Flip		25.0%
Sharing Ratio After Flip		50.0%
Target IRR		20.0%
Discount Rate		10.0%

Appendix C IV-2
Typical Production Sharing Agreement
Decline Curve

Project Year	Percent
1	50.0%
2	100.0%
3	100.0%
4	100.0%
5	100.0%
6	100.0%
7	100.0%
8	93.0%
9	86.5%
10	80.4%
11	74.8%
12	69.6%
13	64.7%
14	60.2%
15	56.0%
16	52.0%
17	48.4%
18	45.0%
19	41.9%
20	38.9%

Appendix C IV-3
Typical Production Sharing Agreement
Project Net Income

Project Year Net Income	1	2	3	4	5	6	7	8	9	10
Revenues										
Production (Bcf/yr)	20	41	41	41	41	41	41	38	35	33
Price ($/mcf)	4.14	4.22	4.31	4.39	4.48	4.57	4.66	4.75	4.85	4.95
Gross Revenue ($mm)	84.1	171.5	175.0	178.5	182.0	185.7	189.4	179.6	170.4	161.7
Expenses										
Operating Costs per Mcf ($/mcf)	0.19	0.20	0.20	0.21	0.21	0.21	0.22	0.22	0.23	0.23
Operating Expenses ($mm)	3.9	8.0	8.2	8.4	8.5	8.7	8.9	8.4	8.0	7.6
Depreciation ($mm)	50	50	50	50	50	0	0	0	0	0
Compensation Tax ($mm)	8	17	17	18	18	19	19	18	17	16
Severance Tax ($mm)	4	9	9	9	9	9	9	9	9	8
Total Expenses ($mm)	67	84	84	85	86	37	37	35	34	32
Earnings Before Tax	18	88	91	93	96	149	152	144	137	130
Income Tax	3	13	14	14	14	22	23	22	21	19
Net Income	15	75	77	79	82	127	129	123	116	110

Appendix C IV-4
Typical Production Sharing Agreement
Project Returns

Project Year	1	2	3	4	5	6	7	8	9	10
Project Operating AT Cash										
Net Income ($mm)	15	75	77	79	82	127	129	123	116	110
Depreciation ($mm)	50	50	50	50	50	0	0	0	0	0
Net Cash Flow ($mm)	65	125	127	129	132	127	129	123	116	110
Sharing Arrangements										
Sharing Ratio	25.0%	25.0%	25.0%	25.0%	50.0%	50.0%	50.0%	50.0%	50.0%	50.0%
Cash to Government ($mm)	16	31	32	32	66	63	65	61	58	55
Cash to Oil Company ($mm)	49	93	95	97	66	63	65	61	58	55
Net Cash Flow ($mm)	65	125	127	129	132	127	129	123	116	110
Oil Company Return										
Oil Company Net Cash Flow ($mm)	-201	93	95	97	66	63	65	61	58	55
Oil Company IRR			-4%	20%	28%	33%	36%	38%	39%	40%

V. Conclusions

Security and Political Stability

In the aftermath of the War of 2003, the most pressing initial requirements for the reconstruction of Iraq are to maintain security of the country while completing the process of creating a new government. At the same time, and on a parallel path, it is critical to make progress on the political and economic front. In the short run it will be vitally important that the people of Iraq see a plan for their future that persuades them (1) the coalition occupation is for a finite term and that this presence is not simply a "toe-hold" of some type of re-colonization scheme (2) the rights of the larger minority groups, in particular the Kurds, will be protected during this government creation process and (3) most importantly, economic benefits will trickle down to the local level. These actions will ensure the legitimacy of the new government.

Making progress on both the political and economic front needs to be accompanied by a communications effort. This plan is noted in Chapter IV, and outlines the action plan with specific objectives and targets to get the new Iraq moving and to monitor progress against the key benchmarks described in the preceding chapters.

On the political front, the key point to emphasize is the movement to a new constitution, which provides for a democratically elected government and guarantees personal freedoms. One core objective here is to conduct a legitimate constitutional convention, and to draft a constitution with widespread Iraqi participation. At the same time, developing a legal framework for property rights and civil codes under which business in Iraq can be conducted is an absolute imperative.

Most importantly, the civil service administration must be put in place as soon as possible and the vast numbers of teachers, doctors, and career professionals need to be employed and paid. The suggested budget and structure shown in Appendix IV.1 offers a starting point for this analysis. This organization will report to the Administrator until elections are held. While the Iraqi oil sector can fund this bureaucracy over time, funds need to be advanced to allow this sector to get moving now. Additional Iraqi workers can be hired on a temporary basis to assist the Coalition Forces in their duties, to include security efforts, and to clean up the residue from the recent war. These latter funds should come from the Coalition Force budget. Iraqis performing these tasks are far more cost effective than Coalition Forces performing them and the work stimulus would go a long way toward getting the Iraqi economy moving.

On the economic front, the key goals are to: get oil production up to an average of 1.5 million barrels per day by the end of 2003; to increase agricultural production of key staple crops to a level where at least over 50 percent of local food requirements are met with Iraqi agricultural production; and to form a new interim government structure -- along the lines mentioned in the preceding chapter -- which can deal with the current problems of providing essential public services pending the formation of the new Iraqi government.

As these goals are being pursued, it will be critical that the U.S./U.K. coalition maintain law and order while the new national and local police forces are constituted and while a new Iraqi military is formed. To ensure political stability, while the new government and economic system is being created, will require Coalition Forces to remain in Iraq for a period of at least two years at a level of up to 200,000 troops. While this will be a sensitive political issue in the United States and United Kingdom, withdrawal of these forces without creating the preconditions for a lasting political and economic solution would be ill-advised and jeopardize the great expenditure of blood and treasury paid to date.

The Post-war U.N. Role

U.N. Resolution 1483 calls for the establishment of a Special Representative for Iraq whose responsibilities are to coordinate

U.N. humanitarian assistance in Iraq and to work with the Administrator to help bring a representative government to power in Iraq.[1] In addition, the Special Representative is tasked by Resolution 1483 to encourage international efforts to contribute to basic civilian administrative functions, rebuild the capability of the Iraqi civilian police force, and to promote legal and judicial reform.[2]

The Administrator should coordinate with the Special Representative to work out a plan to have multi-lateral funding to financially support the Iraq budget if necessary in these areas.

The Macroeconomic Outlook

Over the next decade, under the plan developed for the oil sector in Iraq, the net income of the INOC will increase from $2.7 billion in 2003 to $45.4 billion in 2012, a compound growth rate of over 30 percent per year. While there may be sectors in the Iraqi economy that do not grow as fast as the petroleum sector, we expect the entire economy will be boosted by the performance

---

[1] On the latter objective, Special Representative Sergio Viera de Mello has said that the United States has demonstrated a "lack of clarity" in regard to the development of the political process in Iraq; see BBC News (2003l) and BBC News (2003m).

[2] The possibility of a new U.N Resolution has been under discussion, primarily advocated by the United Kingdom. A new resolution would be aimed at getting other countries to join the peacekeeping efforts. The United States has said such a move is under discussion; see Dunphy (2003).

in the oil sector and the overall compound rate of nominal GDP growth over the next five years will be in excess of 20 percent per annum as indicated by the nominal GDP data shown in Table V-1.

In terms of the standard of living, within the next five years, Iraqi GDP per capita is expected to be in the range of $2,557 or more than twice the level in the pre-war economy, as illustrated in Table V-1. We estimate that this growth in GDP will increase employment, decrease unemployment, and increase wages significantly in Iraq over the next five years.[3] Not only will the standard of living be enhanced by the new economy in Iraq, but also the level of personal wealth for the average Iraqi will be increased significantly by the INOC spin off program discussed below. This benefit, if it can be adequately communicated to the Iraqi on the street, will also assist in achieving the political objectives of the reconstruction of Iraq.

Public Finance and the INOC Spinout

Tables V-2 and V-3 show a rough estimate of the public finance situation in Iraq over the next ten years based on data extracted from the INOC analysis in Chapter IV and an estimate of taxes generated by the non-petroleum sectors. The data provides a cash flow analysis of the public sector, and is broken down into uses of cash by the government and sources of cash.

---

[3] See Appendix V.2.

Table V-1
Key Economic Indicators: Iraq 2003-2008

Key Macroeconomic Indicators	Units	2003E	2004	2005	2006	2007	2008
Real GDP (2000 Prices)	$'s US billions	23.7	32.6	42.0	48.5	55.0	61.6
Growth Rate	percent	-14.3%	37.8%	28.9%	15.4%	13.4%	11.8%
Private Consumption Spending	$'s US billions	16.0	22.9	27.0	31.9	37.6	44.4
Government (G&S) Expenditures	$'s US billions	6.5	7.3	7.4	7.6	7.7	7.9
Gross Private Investment	$'s US billions	4.9	7.9	7.3	7.8	8.7	9.6
Exports of Goods and Services	$'s US billions	10.7	16.5	25.1	30.3	35.3	40.2
Imports of Goods and Services	$'s US billions	13.0	19.3	20.4	22.9	26.1	29.8
Nominal GDP	$'s US billions	25.1	35.3	46.4	54.7	63.3	72.2
Nominal GDP Growth Rate	percent	-12.3%	66.2%	31.4%	17.7%	15.7%	14.1%
Nominal GDP Per Capita	$'s US/person	1,015	1,393	1,781	2,042	2,301	2,557
Private Consumption Per Capita	$'s US/person	648	902	1,036	1,190	1,367	1,571
Population	millions	24.7	25.4	26.1	26.8	27.5	28.2
Money Supply (MS)	billions of $s US	1.9	2.9	3.8	4.5	5.3	6.0
Money Supply (MS)	trillions of dinars	2.9	4.4	5.7	6.8	7.9	9.0
Ratio of MS to Nominal GDP	percent	7.6%	8.2%	8.2%	8.2%	8.3%	8.3%

Source: CountryWatch (2003c).

Public consumption, capital spending by the government, and compensation payments discussed in Chapter IV are shown in the uses of funds analysis of Table V-2.

The sources of funds estimate, shown in Table V-3, includes the net cash flow from INOC, which goes to the government in the form of taxes. It also includes the distribution of the INOC dividend to the government. In addition, the estimate for sources of funds includes an estimate of taxes generated by non-oil sectors in the economy. We have been very conservative in other taxes. We have significantly discounted collections from income taxes (other than from INOC), sales taxes, property taxes, and import taxes because of the need to set up and properly administer these tax structures. The estimate begins at $500 million in 2003, and grows at 10% a year. As the projections show, the INOC dividend is critical to meeting the government budget for the next seven years. At that time, however, the taxes generated by the INOC and the non-oil sector should be sizeable enough to generate sufficient revenues to cover projected government expenditures without having to tap into the INOC dividend. In seven years, the new government should spin out the INOC to Iraqi citizens either directly, or in a trust, and give the people of Iraq ownership of the INOC and the INOC dividend stream.

Table V-2
Public Finance in Iraq - Uses of Funds 2003-2012
(US Dollars Billions)

Public Finance in Iraq	2003	2004	2005	2006	2007	2008	2009	2010	2011	2012
Uses of Funds										
Government Spending	5.3	7.3	7.4	7.6	7.7	7.9	8.1	8.2	8.4	8.5
Growth Rate	2.0%	2.0%	2.0%	2.0%	2.0%	2.0%	2.0%	2.0%	2.0%	2.0%
Food Ration Program	0.0	2.6	2.7	2.7	2.8	2.8	2.9	0.0	0.0	0.0
Growth Rate	2.0%	2.0%	2.0%	2.0%	2.0%	2.0%	2.0%	2.0%	2.0%	2.0%
Subsidies to Electricity, Water	1.2	1.6	1.8	1.8	1.6	1.4	0.8	0.0	0.0	0.0
Capital Costs	0.0	0.0	0.0	0.0	0.0	0.0	0.0	0.0	0.0	0.0
Armed Forces	0.3	1.0	1.0	1.0	1.0	1.0	1.0	1.0	1.0	1.0
Public works	1.0	1.0	1.0	1.0	1.0	1.0	1.0	1.0	1.0	1.0
Compensation Claims	0.0	1.9	2.8	3.3	3.9	4.5	5.1	5.6	6.1	6.5
Total Cash Required	7.7	15.4	16.7	17.4	18.1	18.6	18.8	15.8	16.5	17.1

Source: CountryWatch Forecast Estimates

Table V-3
Public Finance in Iraq - Sources of Funds 2003-2012
(US Dollars Billions)

Public Finance in Iraq	2003	2004	2005	2006	2007	2008	2009	2010	2011	2012
Sources of Funds										
Cash From INOC	0.3	1.9	2.8	3.3	3.9	4.5	5.1	5.6	6.1	6.5
Tax Receipts from INOC										
Compensation Tax	0.0	0.9	1.4	1.7	2.0	2.2	2.5	2.8	3.0	3.3
Severance Tax	0.0	2.0	3.0	3.7	4.4	5.4	6.1	6.9	7.5	8.0
Income Tax (INOC only)	0.3	4.8	7.2	8.7	10.2	12.1	13.7	15.3	16.6	17.8
Total Taxes from INOC	3.7	9.6	17.6	21.6	25.6	29.2	33.1	37.0	40.2	43.1
Other Taxes	0.5	0.6	0.6	0.7	0.7	0.8	0.9	1.0	1.1	1.2
Growth	0.1	0.1	0.1	0.1	0.1	0.1	0.1	0.1	0.1	0.1
U.N./U.S.	3.2	0.5	0.0	0.0	0.0	0.0	0.0	0.0	0.0	0.0
Total Cash Available	7.7	15.4	25.4	31.0	36.6	42.1	47.7	53.3	57.9	62.1
Net Deficit (-) or Surplus (+)	0.0	0.0	8.7	13.6	18.5	23.6	28.9	37.4	41.4	45.0
Reconstruction Fund	0.0	0.0	8.7	13.6	18.5	23.6	28.9	0.0	0.0	0.0
Cumulative Reconstruction Fund	0.0	0.0	8.7	22.3	40.8	64.4	93.3	0.0	0.0	0.0
Net Deficit Relative to Taxes*	-7.0	-10.1	-8.9	-8.0	-7.1	-5.7	-4.2	0.4	1.2	1.9
*Excludes Food Ration Program										

Source: See Appendix IV.2

The spinout would consist of an equal distribution of shares in the INOC to every Iraqi citizen in the country as of April 30, 2003 and to the children of those in the country as of the effective date either directly or in a trust. The spinout date would be set as of December 31, 2010. The shares would be non-transferable prior to the distribution date.

The financial effect of such a move would be to provide the people of Iraq the financial benefit of the INOC dividend stream within a reasonable period of time following the establishment of a functioning government. As noted earlier, the value of the spin out to an Iraqi family of four would be between $120,000 and $240,000 five years after the new government is inaugurated.

The political effect of such a program would be spectacular. It would mean that the current generation, which has suffered under the hands of the Saddam Hussein regime, would reap an immense benefit. It would provide the new government with a powerful tool to remind the population that while the former regime spent Iraq's enormous oil wealth on itself, the new regime would give the people the oil wealth in the form of share ownership of the INOC. This program should also have an enormous impact on the countries in the region, which might moderate the move toward radicalism.

These benefits should make the money spent on the war and the occupation a long-term justifiable investment.

The Cost of the War to the United States

The U.S. Defense Department estimated the cost to the United States of military operations in Iraq from January of 2003 through September of 2003 at $58 billion.[4] Secretary of Defense Rumsfeld reported to the U.S. Congress in July of 2003 and estimated that the incremental cost of the U.S. military forces remaining in Iraq after the completion of major combat operations was $3.9 billion per month and that expense would continue for the foreseeable future.[5]

In our reconstruction plan we have proposed that Iraq rearm and that U.S. forces, or their equivalent, remain in Iraq until June 30, 2005. At that time, the Iraqi national police and the Iraqi military would perform security operations in Iraq. If this plan were adopted then the ultimate cost of the war and occupation, as well as the initial funding for the Iraqi petroleum sector, would be in the neighborhood of $150 billion from January of 2003 through June of 2005. This estimate does not include expenses for military operations in Iraq that would have been incurred by the United States prior to January of 2003.

This cost is significant and controversial. In our plan, however, we outline a target and timetable for the cessation of U.S. military operations in Iraq, as well as a quantifiable cost.

---

[4] Fram (2003).

[5] The Wall Street Journal (2003b).

Furthermore, in our plan, other than the initial pump priming for the Iraqi petroleum sector, reconstruction in Iraq is self-funding.

Future Risks and Opportunities

The ability of Iraq to achieve political stability will only be possible with the cooperation of competing ethnic and religious factions in Iraq. The ability of Sunni and Shi'a Muslims and Kurds to work together in a coalition, as well as the ability of the Islamic and non-Islamic factions to work together, will be necessary to achieve a durable democracy. While this will be difficult to accomplish, all stakeholders in Iraq have a significant vested interest in making it happen. As we have noted in Chapter II, there are applicable models of democracy that take into consideration the diversity of a country's population in the context of a federal system.

Building a democracy in Iraq will not be an easy task. Iraq is blessed with tremendous hydrocarbon resources that give it a considerable development edge over other developing countries. As we have already discussed, democracy is enhanced in an environment of economic strength. However, the people of Iraq are not intimately familiar with the mechanics of democracy, given their particular history. To achieve economic integration with the rest of the world -- while building a democracy -- will be a tremendous challenge.

The development of Iraq's oil resource at a rate described in Chapter IV will also add needed supplies to a world oil market that in 2003 has tightened up due to increasing demand for oil and the political disturbances in Iraq and Venezuela. While Iraq has been a member of OPEC in the past, it needs to be made clear to the other OPEC members that Iraq intends to produce and sell oil into the market at the rate stipulated in the plan described herein until the country is back on a sound financial footing.

Finally, the Iraqi International Oil Company spinout can provide hope for a nation that has been betrayed by its former leadership and vilified by the world community. Within the current generation, there is the opportunity for the populace to accumulate wealth and move into a more normalized state of affairs.

A good thing can be achieved from what happened in Iraq in the spring of 2003. The tremendous cost in treasury and lives paid by the United States can achieve a significant national security benefit for current and future generations of Americans. Further, the Iraqi people, if our reconstruction program is successful, can thrive in a flourishing democracy where the great wealth of the country flows to the benefit of the people instead of a corrupt regime.

APPENDIX V.1 Input-Output Models 2005 - 2008

The input-output model described in Appendix III.1 was used to generate a five-year forecast for the Iraqi economy based upon the assumptions described in this chapter. The input-output matrix for 2004 is shown as Table III-2. The remaining four years of the forecast are shown in this Appendix.

The projected per capita consumption growth rate is the central model driver. See Appendix III.1 for detailed descriptions of how these models were generated.

Table A V-1
Input-Output Matrix for Iraq - 2005
($US Millions)

Sectors	O&G	Ser	Agr	Man	Pow	T&T	Total Sales	C	G	I	X	M	Final Demand	Total Demand
Oil & Gas (O&G)	593	230	0	173	1,483	109	2,588	2,509	212	0	24,096	0	26,816	29,404
Services (Ser)	75	1,137	55	110	319	278	1,975	6,827	3,942	1,837	1,000	2,346	11,260	15,581
Agriculture (Agr)	0	0	144	182	106	0	432	7,431	412	0	0	7,037	807	8,276
Manufacturing (Man)	114	751	123	373	106	709	2,176	4,194	872	4,776	0	8,568	1,274	12,018
Power (Pow)	46	529	25	43	73	191	906	1,883	99	0	0	0	1,983	2,889
Tele/Transport (T & T)	57	662	28	47	106	245	1,145	4,157	1,905	735	0	2,489	4,308	7,942
Total Purchases	885	3,309	375	927	2,194	1,532	9,222	27,002	7,442	7,348	25,096	20,439	46,448	76,109
Labor Services	342	7,445	648	1,514	139	2,745	12,832							
Capital Services	28,177	2,482	216	1,009	556	1,176	33,615							
Value Added	28,519	9,926	864	2,523	694	3,921	46,448							
Total Production	29,404	13,235	1,239	3,450	2,889	5,453	55,670							
Imports	0	2,346	7,037	8,568	0	2,489	20,439							
Total Supply	29,404	15,581	8,276	12,018	2,889	7,942	76,109							

Intermediate Product Sales to Each Economic Sector

Final Demands from Each Sector

Sources: See Appendix III-1

Abbreviations:
C: Private Consumption Spending
G: Government Spending
I: Investment Spending
X: Exports
M: Imports

Table A V-2
Input-Output Matrix for Iraq - 2006
($US Millions)

Sectors	O&G	Ser	Agr	Man	Pow	I&I	Total Sales	C	G	I	X	M	Final Demand	Total Demand
	Intermediate Product Sales to Each Economic Sector							Final Demands from Each Sector						
Oil & Gas (O&G)	716	255	0	198	1,720	127	3,016	2,960	216	0	29,283	0	32,459	35,475
Services (Ser)	91	1,260	64	126	371	325	2,236	8,056	4,021	1,959	1,000	2,605	12,430	17,271
Agriculture (Agr)	0	0	166	209	124	0	498	8,769	421	0	0	8,263	927	9,688
Manufacturing (Man)	137	832	141	429	124	829	2,492	4,949	889	5,092	0	9,455	1,475	13,423
Power (Pow)	55	587	28	50	84	223	1,027	2,222	101	0	0	0	2,324	3,351
Tele/Transport (T & T)	69	733	32	54	124	287	1,298	4,906	1,943	783	0	2,555	5,077	8,930
Total Purchases	1,067	3,667	431	1,066	2,545	1,791	10,567	31,862	7,590	7,834	30,283	22,879	54,692	88,138
Labor Services	418	8,250	745	1,741	161	3,208	14,523							
Capital Services	33,990	2,750	248	1,161	644	1,375	40,168							
Value Added	34,408	11,000	994	2,901	805	4,583	54,692							
Total Production	35,475	14,666	1,425	3,968	3,351	6,375	65,259							
Imports	0	2,605	8,263	9,455	0	2,555	22,879							
Total Supply	35,475	17,271	9,688	13,423	3,351	8,930	88,138							

Sources: See Appendix III-1
Abbreviations:
C: Private Consumption Spending
G: Government Spending
I: Investment Spending
X: Exports
M: Imports

Table A V-3
Input-Output Matrix for Iraq - 2007
($US Millions)

Sectors	O&G	Ser	Agr	Man	Pow	T&T	Total Sales	C	G	I	X	M	Final Demand	Total Demand
	Intermediate Product Sales to Each Economic Sector							Final Demands from Each Sector						
Oil & Gas (O&G)	838	284	0	228	1,997	148	3,495	3,493	220	0	34,325	0	38,038	41,533
Services (Ser)	106	1,406	73	145	430	376	2,537	9,506	4,101	2,170	1,000	2,943	13,835	19,315
Agriculture (Agr)	0	0	191	240	143	0	574	10,348	429	0	0	9,712	1,064	11,351
Manufacturing (Man)	160	929	162	494	143	959	2,848	5,840	907	5,642	0	10,675	1,714	15,237
Power (Pow)	64	655	33	57	98	258	1,165	2,622	103	0	0	0	2,726	3,891
Tele/Transport (T & T)	81	819	37	62	143	332	1,473	5,789	1,981	868	0	2,732	5,906	10,111
Total Purchases	1,250	4,093	496	1,226	2,955	2,074	12,093	37,598	7,742	8,680	35,325	26,062	63,283	101,438
Labor Services	486	9,209	857	2,002	187	3,714	16,456							
Capital Services	39,797	3,070	286	1,335	748	1,592	46,827							
Value Added	40,283	12,279	1,143	3,337	935	5,306	63,283							
Total Production	41,533	16,372	1,638	4,563	3,891	7,380	75,376							
Imports	0	2,943	9,712	10,675	0	2,732	26,062							
Total Supply	41,533	19,315	11,351	15,237	3,891	10,111	101,438							

Sources: See Appendix III-1

Abbreviations:
C: Private Consumption Spending
G: Government Spending
I: Investment Spending
X: Exports
M: Imports

Table A V-4
Input-Output Matrix for Iraq - 2008
($US Millions)

Intermediate Product Sales to Each Economic Sector | Final Demands from Each Sector

Sectors	O&G	Ser	Agr	Man	Pow	T&I	Total Sales	C	G	I	X	M	Final Demand	Total Demand
Oil & Gas (O&G)	960	318	0	262	2,320	169	4,029	4,122	225	0	39,203	0	43,549	47,578
Services (Ser)	122	1,573	84	167	500	431	2,877	11,217	4,183	2,389	1,000	3,353	15,436	21,666
Agriculture (Agr)	0	0	219	276	167	0	662	12,210	438	0	1	11,427	1,222	13,311
Manufacturing (Man)	184	1,039	187	568	167	1,099	3,243	6,891	925	6,212	0	12,024	2,004	17,271
Power (Pow)	74	733	38	66	113	296	1,319	3,094	105	0	0	0	3,200	4,519
Tele/Transport (T & T)	92	916	42	71	167	380	1,668	6,831	2,021	956	0	3,022	6,785	11,476
Total Purchases	1,431	4,578	570	1,410	3,432	2,375	13,797	44,365	7,897	9,556	40,204	29,826	72,197	115,820
Labor Services	547	10,301	986	2,302	217	4,255	18,608							
Capital Services	45,599	3,434	329	1,535	869	1,823	53,589							
Value Added	46,147	13,735	1,314	3,837	1,086	6,078	72,197							
Total Production	47,578	18,313	1,884	5,247	4,519	8,454	85,994							
Imports	0	3,353	11,427	12,024	0	3,022	29,826							
Total Supply	47,578	21,666	13,311	17,271	4,519	11,476	115,820							

Sources: See Appendix III-1

Abbreviations:
C: Private Consumption Spending
G: Government Spending
I: Investment Spending
X: Exports
M: Imports

APPENDIX V.2 Notes on Employment in Iraq

Table V-3 shows projected employment by sector for Iraq over the next five years.[1] The size of the available labor market was estimated at 63 percent of the population between the ages of 20 and 64.[2]

This analysis suggests that employment levels and wage rates will be improving over the next five years. The value of the INOC spin off, which has not been included in this wage rate analysis, will be a considerable contribution to the net worth of ordinary Iraqis.

---

[1] This analysis utilized the value added wage levels identified in the input-output matrices and then estimated wage rates for each sector. Average wage rates are expected to remain low by regional standards, though wages in the oil and gas and power sectors are expected to be higher than those in other sectors.

[2] This employment estimate utilized the official employment data for Turkey (a secular democracy with a predominately Muslim population adjacent to Iraq) for 2002 and adjusted it utilizing the estimated demographics for Iraq. Census (2003) and IFS (2003).

Table B V-1
Projected Employment in Iraq 2004 - 2008
(thousands of persons unless otherwise indicated)

Sector	2003	2004	2005	2006	2007
Oil & Gas (O&G)	24	33	38	42	45
Services (Ser)	3,475	3,545	3,741	3,978	4,237
Agriculture (Agr)	470	514	563	617	676
Manufacturing (Man)	658	721	789	865	947
Power (Pow)	24	26	29	32	36
Tele/Transport (T & T)	1,091	1,307	1,455	1,604	1,750
Total Employment	5,742	6,146	6,616	7,138	7,691
Labor Force	7,242	7,534	7,840	8,159	8,445
Employment	79%	82%	84%	87%	91%
Unemployment	21%	18%	16%	13%	9%
Average Wage Rate	$1,981	$2,088	$2,195	$2,305	$2,419

Sources: Appendix III-1, CountryWatch (2003c).

References

Acherio A., R. Chase and R. Cote. 1992. "Effect of the Gulf War on Infant and Child Mortality in Iraq", in *New England Journal of Medicine,* September Vol. 327 pp. 931-936.

Agence France-Presse. 2003a. "Russia Says U.N. Crucial In Iraq", April 11th.

Agence France-Presse. 2003b. "U.N. Must Play Central Role, Says Chirac", April 8th.

Agence France-Presse. 2003c. "U.S. Decided On Iraq War In December: Financial Times", May 26th.

Agence France-Presse. 2003d. "Privatization in Iraq Faces Long Road Ahead." August 3rd.

Aita, Judy. 2003. "Iraqi Governing Council Members Address U.N. For First Time", United States of America Embassy, July 22nd.

Alnasrawi, Abbas. 1994. *The Economy of Iraq: Oil, Wars, Destruction of Development and Prospects*, *1950-2010,* Greenwood Press. Westport, Connecticut, July.

American Friends Service Committee. 2000. "Resignation of Humanitarian Officials in Iraq Highlight Failures of the Sanctions Policy", February 18th.

Amnesty International. 2001. "Iraq Annual Report".

Appleby, Timothy. 2003. "Terrorism Experts Doubt bin Laden-Baghdad Link", *Globe and Mail,* February 6th.

Associated Press. 2003a. "U.S. Admits it's Facing Guerilla Warfare", July 7th.

Associated Press. 2003b. "U.S. Says all Oil Field Fires in Iraq Snuffed Out", April 15th.

Baldauf, Scott and Scott Stern. 2003. "How the United Nations Might Fit In Post-war Iraq", *Christian Science Monitor, April 23rd.*

Baruah, Amit. 2003. "No Troops For India Without Explicit U.N. Mandate", *The Hindu,* July 15th.

Basham, Patrick. 2003. "A Democratic Iraq? Don't Hold Your Breath", The Cato Institute, March 31st.

BBC News. 2003a. "Iraq's Most Wanted", July 22nd.

BBC News. 2003b. "Timeline: Iraq, A Chronology of Key Events", June 21st.

BBC News. 2003c. "Timeline: Niger Uranium Row", July 9th.

BBC News. 2003d. "Bush Sets Timetable On Iraq", March 17th.

BBC News. 2003e. "U.S. To Double Iraq Troops", March 28th.

BBC News. 2003f. "Blair Warns Of Difficult Days Ahead", March 24th.

BBC News. 2003g. "Paul Bremer: U.S. Tough Guy in Iraq", May 7th.

BBC News. 2003h. "Profile: John Abizaid", July 8th.

BBC News. 2003i. "Iraq Moves Towards Self-Rule", July 13th.

BBC News. 2003j. "CIA Takes Blame", July 12th.

BBC News. 2003k. "The Agenda for Rebuilding Iraq", March 27th.

BBC News. 2003l. "U.N.'s Iraq Envoy criticizes the U.S.", May 29th.

BBC News. 2003m. "U.N. Debates Democracy in Iraq", July 22nd.

BBC News. 2002. "Timeline: Iraq Weapons Inspections", November 18th.

Bonionvevo, Alexei. 2003. "Bremer Says Oil will Fund New Budget in Iraq", *Wall Street Journal*, July 9th, p. A4.

Bright, Martin, Ed Vulliamy and Peter Beaumont. 2003. "Revealed: U.S. Dirty Tricks To Win Vote On Iraq", *Observer,* March 2nd.

Brown, Anthony. 2001. "War in Afghanistan" *Observer,* November 18th.

CBS News. 2003a. "Face the Nation", March 16th.

CBS News. 2003b. "Point Man For Post-war Iraq", April 17th.

Center for Strategic and International Studies (CSIS). 2003. "A Wiser Peace: An Action Strategy for a Post-Conflict Iraq, Supplement I, Background Information on Iraq's Financial Obligations", Project Directors Frederick D. Burton and Bathsheba W. Crocker, January 23rd.

Chandrasekaran, Rajiv and Alan Sipress. 2003. "Clashes Continue Along Supply Lines; Airstrikes Hit Palace, Intelligence Complex", *Washington Post,* March 31st.

Chenery, Hollis B. and Paul G. Clark. 1967, 6th Edition. *Interindustry Economics.*John Wiley & Sons, London.

CNN News. 2003a. "U.K. To Send 26,000 Troops to Persian Gulf Region", January 20th.

CNN News. 2003b. "Moment of Truth for the World", Transcript of program available from CNN; program anchored by Paula Zahn.

CNN News. 2003c. "Blair: Iraq Weapons Threat Growing", January 14th.

Council on Foreign Relations – Baker Institute. 2002. "Guiding Principles of U.S. Post-Conflict Policy in Iraq", A report of an Independent Working Group cosponsored by the Council on Foreign Relations and the Jim A. Baker III Institute for Public Policy of Rice University.

CountryWatch. 2003a. *Country Review: Iraq.* Houston, Texas: http://www.countrywatch.com/cw_country.asp?vCOUNTRY=81

CountryWatch. 2003b. *Special Report: War in Iraq.* Houston, Texas: CountryWatch.com. http://www.countrywatch.com

CountryWatch. 2003c. *CountryWatch Forecast.* Houston: CountryWatch Press. http://www.countrywatch.com/forecast/

Curl, Joseph. 2002. "Iraq Report Cited By Bush Does Not Exist" in *The Washington Times,* September 27th.

de Soto, Hernando. 2000. *The Mystery of Capital: Why Capitalism Triumphs in the West and Fails Everywhere Else.* New York: Basic Books.

Dohram, David. 2003. "Pace of Iraq's Reconstruction Frustrates U.S.", *Wall Street Journal*, May 13th, p. A17.

Dunphy, Harry. 2003. "U.S. in Talks with Other Nations", *Associated Press*, July 16th.

Eland, Ivan. 2003. "Top 10 Reasons Not To Do Iraq", The Cato Institute.

Eland, Ivan. 2002. "President Bush's Case For Attack On Iraq Is Weak", The Cato Institute.

Energy Information Administration, U.S. Department of Energy. 2003. "Country Analysis Brief, Iraq." Washington, D.C.: GPO.

Entous, Adam. 2003. "U.S. Officials Play Down Iraq Reconstruction Needs" in *Reuters*, April 11th.

Fairness and Accuracy in Reporting. "New York Times, Networks Shun U.N. Spying Story", 2003, March 11th.

Firestone, David and Thom Shanker. 2003. "New Estimate of Iraq Costs Startles Some in Congress" in *New York Times,* July 11th.

Food and Agricultural Organization of the United Nations. 2003. United Nations. http://apps.fao.org/

Fram, Alan. 2003. "Post-war Iraq Likely to Cost More Than War", *Associated Press*, August 11th.

Friedman, Alan. 2003. "Russia Signals It May Ease Iraq's Debt", *The Wall Street Journal*, June 23rd, p. A3.

Friedman, Thomas. 2000. *The Lexus and the Olive Tree: Understanding Globalization*. New York: Farrar, Straus and Giroux.

Galen Carpenter, Ted. 2003a, "Faulty Justifications for a War Against Iraq", The Cato Institute.

Galen Carpenter, Ted. 2003b. "Time to Disagree Without Being Disagreeable", The Cato Institute, March 11th.

Ghabra, Shafeeq. 2001. "Iraq's Culture of Violence", *Middle Eastern Quarterly Vol VII: 3.*

Goldberg, Suzanne. 2003. "CIA Had Doubts On Iraq Link To Al-Qaeda", *Guardian*, June 10th.

Graham, Robert and James Harding. 2003a. "U.S. Accused Of Deserting Diplomatic Path", *Financial Times,* May 26th.

Graham, Robert, James Harding, Quentin Peel; and Judy Dempsey. 2003b. "How the U.S. Set A Course For War With Iraq", *Financial Times,* May 26th.

Grassi, Ricardo. 2003. "Thousands of Children Could Die", *Inter Press Service News Agency.* July 4th.

Grice, Andrew and David Usborn. 2003. "The Niger Connection", *Independent*, June 5th.

Halliday, Denis. 1998. "Why I Resigned My U.N. Post In Protest of Sanctions", Presented at Harvard University in Cambridge, Massachusetts, November 5th. Transcript recorded by Chris Nicholson of the Campaign for the Iraqi People.

Hussain Hindawi and John Thomson. 2003. "Dealing With Debt – Problem or Opportunity." *National Review*, May 6th.

Holley, David. 2003. "3 Nation Summit Pushing U.N. Role in Iraq", *Los Angeles Times,* April 12th.

Hutcheson, Ron, Juan Tamayo and Ken Moritsugu. 2003. "Bush gives U.N. Monday deadline; decision seen as imminent", *Knight Ridder,* March 16th.

International Center for Industrial Studies. 1977. "Unido World Input-Output Tables", Hamburg, Germany.

International Financial Statistics. 2003. The International Monetary Fund, Washington D.C., July. Volume LVI, No.7.

International Institute for Strategic Studies. 1999. *The Military Balance 1998/99*, Oxford University Press, London.

International Institute for Strategic Studies. 2000. *The Military Balance 1999/2000*, Oxford University Press, London.

International Institute for Strategic Studies. 2001. *The Military Balance 2000/2001*, Oxford University Press, London.

International Institute for Strategic Studies. 2002. *The Military Balance 2001/2002*, Oxford University Press, London.

International Institute for Strategic Studies. 2003. *The Military Balance 2002/2003* Oxford University Press, London.

International Monetary Fund. 2003. *World Economic Outlook,* May, Washington D.C.: International Monetary Fund.

ITU. 2003. "Arab States Telecommunication Indicators, 1992-2001", International Telecommunications Union. http://www.itu.int/itu-D/ict/statistics

Jabar, Faleh A. 2003. "Analysis: Conditions For Democracy In Iraq", *BBC News,* April 16th.

Johnson, Chalmers. 2002. "Rebuilding Iraq: Japan Is No Model" in *Los Angeles Times*. October 17th.

Jones, Gary and Alexandra Williams. 2003. "Real Authors of Iraq Dossier Blast Blair", *The Daily Mirror*, February 8th.

Kamfner, John. 2003. "The Truth About Jessica Lynch", *Guardian,* May 5th.

Kristof, Nicholas D. 2003a. "White House In Denial", *New York Times,* June 13th.

Kristof, Nicholas D. 2003b. "16 Words And Counting", *New York Times,* June 13th.

Kristof, Nicholas D. 2003c. "Why Truth Matter.: *New York Times,* May 6th.

Ladki, Nadim. 2003. "Saddam Defiant On TV; Iraq Downs U.S. Helicopter", *Reuters*, March 24th.

Lederer, Edith. 2003. "Blix Likely to Order Destruction of Missiles", *Associated Press*, February 2nd.

Library of Congress. n.d.. Country Studies On-Line. Washington D.C.: GPO. http://lcweb2.loc.gov/frd/cs/

Linzer, Dafna. 2003. "U.N. draft report: No link between Iraqis, al-Qaeda", *Associated Press*, June 26th.

Luhnow, David. 2003. "Among the U.S. Post-war Tasks: Overseeing a Tobacco Company", *The Wall Street Journal*, August 5th, p A1.

MacArthur. John R. 2003. "Lessons of History in Iraq" in *Providence Journal,* July 8th.

Mason, Barnaby. 2003a. "The Unpredictable War", *BBC News*, March 28th.

Mason, Barnaby. 2003b. "Behind the French-U.S. Bonhomie", *BBC News,* June 22nd.

McLeod, Scott.2003. "Searching For The Ace Of Spades", *Time,* June 22nd.

McMahon, Robert. 2003. "U.N.: Broader United Nations Role In Iraq A Looming Issue For Coalition", *Radio Free Europe*, July 16th.

Mearsheimer, John J. and Stephen M. Walt 2002. "An Unnecessary War", *Foreign Policy,* December.

NBC News. 2003. "Meet the Press", March 16th. Transcript of program available from NBC; program was hosted by Tim Russet.

Milbank, Dana. 2003. "White House Didn't Gain CIA Nod for Claim On Iraqi Strikes", *Washington Post,* July 20th.

National Public Radio. 2003. "Iraqi Government", April 23rd. Tavis Smiley talks to Phoebe Marr, former senior fellow and scholar at the National Defense University, and Samer Shehata, acting director of Arab studies at Georgetown University, about the past, present and future of government in Iraq.

National Public Radio. 2002. "Lack of Water, Sewer System Takes Toll in Iraq", November 7th. Interview on Morning Edition with Bob Edwards.

Niskanen, William. 2003. "The Case Against A War With Iraq", The Cato Institute, February 25th.

Okazaki, Hisahiko. 2003. "U.S. Must Learn Lessons from Occupation of Japan" in *Daily Yomiuri*, January 19th.

Observer. 2003. "The Iraq Bush Will Build", February.

O'Neil, Tim. 1999. "Focus on Crude Oil", Bank of Montreal, Toronto, Ontario. http://www.bmo.com/economic/regular/oil0999.pdf

OPEC. 2001. "OPEC Annual Statistical Bulletin".

Oxfam Policy Papers. 2003. "A Fresh Start for Iraq." May 3rd.

Papandreou, George Greek Foreign Minister, and Lord Robertson, NATO General Secretary. 2003. Statements made at the Joint EU-NATO meeting of foreign ministers on April 3rd. Transcript available via Greek Foreign Ministry.

Pacific Gas and Electric Company (PG&E). 2003. "2002 Annual Report", February 27th, http://www.onlineproxy.com/wilink/PGEb/ .

PBS. 2003. "The Afterwar in Iraq" on *Newshour,* July 2nd. The program included an interview between host, Jim Lehrer and guest, Edmund Andrews. Transcript available from *PBS*.

Rangwala, Glen and Raymond Whitaker. 2003. "20 Lies About the War", *Independent,* July 12th.

Rawls, John. 1995. *Political Liberalism.* New York: Columbia University Press.

Reuters. 2003a. "Table of Casualties in Iraq", July 24th.

Reuters. 2003b. "U.S. Plans Iraq Mobile Phone Network Tender", June 12th.

Reuters. 2002. "U.S. Plan For Post-Saddam Iraq Reported", November 24th.

Reynolds, Paul. 2003. "Analysis: Need For Quick Result", *BBC News,* March 20th.

Risen, James, David Sanger and Tom Shanker. 2003. "In Sketchy Data, White House Sought Clues to Gauge Threat", *The New York Time,* July 20th.

Rivlin, Paul. 2003. "Iraq's Economy: What's Left?" Moshe Dayan Center for Middle Eastern and African Studies, February 2nd.

Royce, Knut. 2003. "CIA Chief Takes Rap", *New York Newsday,* July 12th.

Rulon, Malia. 2003. "Candidate Wants Probe of Rescue of Jessica Lynch", *Associated Press*, June 4th.

Sen, Amartya. 2000. *Development as Freedom.* New York: Anchor Books; Random House.

Solomon, John. 2003. "Tenet Takes Blame on Iraq Uranium Claim", *Associated Press.* July 11th.

Steele, Jonathan. 2003. "Shi'a Cleric Challenges Bush Plan For Iraq", *Guardian,* July 2nd.

Stiglitz, Joseph E. 2002. *Globalization and Its Discontents.* New York: Norton and Company.

Stoullig, Jean Michel. 2003. "Rumsfeld Pays Homage To Garner", *Agence France-Presse,* May 13th.

Stratfor. 2003a. "War Diary", April 22nd.

Stratfor. 2003b. "War Diary", March 20th.

Tyson, Ann Scott. 2003. "Anatomy Of The Raid On Hussein's Sons", *Christian Science Monitor,* July 24th.

UNICEF. 2003. "New Study To Assist Iraq's Most Vulnerable Children", United Nations, June 26th.

United Nations Data, Office of the Iraq Oil-for-Food Programme. 2003. http://www.un.org/Depts/oip/background/scrsindex.html

United Nations. 2000. "UNICEF's State of the World's Children Report", December.

United Nations. 1999. "United Nations Report On The Current Humanitarian Situation In Iraq", March.

United Nations. 2003. "United Nations Commission on Human Rights: Resolution 2003/84".

United Nations Security Council. 2003a. "United Nations Security Council Draft Resolution of March 7, 2003". http://www.un.org/News/dh/iraq/res-iraq-07mar03-en-rev.pdf

United Nations Security Council. 2003b. "United Nations Security Council Resolution 1483".
http://ods-dds-ny.un.org/doc/UNDOC/GEN/N03/368/53/PDF/N0336853.pdf

United Nations Security Council. 2002. "United Nations Security Council Resolution 1441".
URL:http://odsddsny.un.org/doc/UNDOC/GEN/N02/682/26/PDF/N0268226.pd

United Nations Special Commission (UNSCOM) website. n.d. United Nations. URL: http://www.un.org/Depts/unscom/

United Press International. 2003. "45 Minutes Claim Had No Support", July 21st.

USA Today. 2003. "Northwest File Application to Fly to Iraq", May 8th.

U.S. Census Bureau. 2003. "IDB Summary Demographic Data", Washington, D.C.: GPO.

U.S. Central Intelligence Agency. 2003. *The World Factbook 2002: Iraq* Washington, D.C.: Printing and Photography Group. http://www.cia.gov/cia/publications/factbook/index.html

U.S. Department of Energy. 2003a. "Iraq Country Analysis Brief", February. Washington D.C.: GPO. http://www.eia.doe.gov/emeu/cabs/iraq.html

U.S. Department of Energy. 2003b. *International Petroleum Monthly,* June 2003. Washington D.C.: GPO. http://www.eia.doe.gov/emeu/ipsr/contents.html

U.S. Department of Energy. 2003c. *Energy Information Administration, Monthly Energy Review*, June. Washington D.C.: GPO. http://www.eia.doe.gov/emeu/mer/contents.html

U.S. Department of Energy. 2003d. "World Crude Oil and Natural Gas Reserves", http://www.eia.doe.gov/emeu/international/reserves.html

U.S. Department of Energy. 2003e. "Canada Country Analysis Brief". http://www.eia.doe.gov/emeu/cabs/canada.html

U.S. Department of Energy. 2003f. "U.S. EIA International Energy Annual, 2001 Edition (released March 2003)"p. 98. http://www.eia.doe.gov/emeu/iea/contents.html

U.S. Department of Energy. 2003g. "Weekly Petroleum Status Report", 11 June. Table 12 p. 22. http://www.eia.doe.gov/oil_gas/petroleum/data_publications/weekly_petroleum_status_report/wpsr.html

U.S. Department of Energy. 2003h. "OPEC Brief", July 9th, p. 2. www.eia.doe.gov/emeu/cabs/opec.html

U.S. Department of Energy, Energy Information Administration. 2003. International Electricity Information, July 7th. Washington D.C., GPO.

U.S. Department of Energy, Energy Information Administration. 1996. "Oil Production Capacity Expansion Losses for the Persian Gulf", January, Washington D.C., GPO.

U.S. Department of State. 2003. Washington D.C.

U.S. Department of State, Bureau of Political Military Affairs. 1998. "Chronology of Events Leading to U.S.-led Attack on Iraq", January 8th.

U.S. Geological Survey. 2003. "The Mineral Industry of Iraq", Washington D.C. July 9th.

Wall Street Journal. 2003a. "Iraq's Odious Debts", April 30th, p. A16.

Wall Street Journal. 2003b. "Rumsfeld Puts Monthly Cost of Troops in Iraq at $3.9 Billion", July 10th, p. A4.

Warrick, Joby. 2003. "Some Evidence on Iraq Called Fake: U.N. Nuclear Inspector Says Documents on Purchases Were Forged", *Washington Post,* March 8th.

Washington Post. 2003. "Rash Of Attacks Raise Concern Of Full-Blown Guerilla War", July 7th.

Washington State University. n.d. – a. "The Sumerians" in *World Civilizations Website.* http://www.wsu.edu/~dee/WORLD.HTM

Washington State University. n.d. – b. "The Code of Hammurabi" in *World Civilizations Website.* http://www.wsu.edu/~dee/WORLD.HTM

Washington State University. n.d. – c. "The Assyrians" in *World Civilizations Website.* http://www.wsu.edu/~dee/WORLD.HTM

Washington State University. n.d. – d. "The Chaldeans in *World Civilizations Website.* http://www.wsu.edu/~dee/WORLD.HTM

The White House. 2002a. "The National Security Strategy of the United States", U.S. Department of State. September. http://usinfo.state.gov/topical/pol/terror/secstrat.htm

The White House. 2002b. "President Bush Outlines Iraqi Threat", October 7th, Cincinnati, Ohio. Remarks made by the President on Iraq at the Cincinnati Museum Center, Office of the Press Secretary.

The White House. 2003. "Bush Announces Combat Operations in Iraq have ended", May 1st, Remarks made by the President from the USS Abraham Lincoln off the coast of San Diego. For Immediate Release, Office of the Press Secretary.

Williams, Ada and Shannon Meehan. 2003. "Iraq: A Dangerous Environment For Children", Refugees International. July 1st.

Wisner II, Frank G., Nicholas Platt, and Marshall M. Bouton with Dennis Kux and Mahnaz Isphani. 2003. "Afghanistan: Are We Losing the Peace?" Independent Task Force Report by Council of Foreign Relations and the Asia Society.

World Health Organization. 1997. "Iraqi Health System Close to Collapse", February 27th.

Wright, Jonathan. 2003. "Afghan Minister Warns U.S. Credibility at Stake" in *Reuters*, July 14th.

Index

About CountryWatch

CountryWatch, Inc. is an information provider for businesses, government organizations, schools, universities, libraries and individuals who need up-to-date information and news on the countries of the world.

Other books published by CountryWatch include *The Carbon Conundrum*, the *CountryWatch Forecast Yearbook*, and the *Country Reviews 2003* currently available for 192 countries. CountryWatch also offers on-line versions of their Country Reviews along with data and news information in the Country Wire, CountryWatch Data, CountryWatch Map Gallery, CountryWatch@School, and the CountryWatch Forecast online. All of these products are described in greater detail online at http://www.countrywatch.com.

Author Biographies

Thomas E. White - Mr. White is the former Secretary of the Army. He was nominated by President Bush, confirmed by the United States Senate, and served from May 2001 to May 2003. Mr. White holds a BS from the United States Military Academy and an MS in Operations Research from the Naval Postgraduate School.

Robert C. Kelly - Mr. Kelly is Chairman and CEO of CountryWatch, Inc. He is an expert on stabilization aid in post-war developing economies. Mr. Kelly has a BS from the United States Military Academy and an MPA and Ph.D. in Economics from Harvard University.

John M. Cape - Mr. Cape is a Senior VP of CountryWatch and Editor of the CountryWatch Forecast. The Country Watch Forecast provides a detailed macroeconomic forecast for each of the 192 countries in the world. Mr. Cape spent two years in Saudi Arabia working with the U.S. Army Corps of Engineers to build a military city near the Iraqi border. He holds a BS from the United States Military Academy and an MBA from the Stanford Graduate School of Business.

Denise Youngblood Coleman - Ms. Youngblood Coleman is a VP and Editor of the CountryWatch Country Review and the Country Wire. The Country Review provides a strategic overview of each of the 192 countries in the world and the Country Wire provides a real time news service on each of the 192 countries in the world. Ms. Youngblood-Coleman holds a B.A. from King's University (Alberta, Canada); and an M.A. from Rice University where she is also a Ph.D. Candidate in Anthropology.